IN THE NAME OF

ALLAH

THE ALL-COMPASSIONATE, ALL-MERCIFUL

Muslim-Christian
Interactions
Past, Present & Future

- Title: Muslim-Christian Interactions: Past, Present & Future
- Author: Yahya M. A. Ondigo
- English Edition 1 (2011)
- Layout Design: IIPH, Riyadh, Saudi Arabia
- Filming and Cover Design: Samo Press Group

Muslim-Christian Interactions

Past, Present & Future

تفاعلات المسلمون والنصارى

في الماضي والحاضر والمستقبل

Compiled and written by

Capt. (Rtd) Yahya M. A. Ondigo

الدار العالمية للكتاب الإسلامي

INTERNATIONAL ISLAMIC PUBLISHING HOUSE

Copyright © 2011 International Islamic Publishing House
King Fahd National Library Cataloging-in-Publication Data

Ondigo, Yahya M. A.
   Muslim-Christian Interactions, past, present & future. / Yahya
M. A. Ondigo .- Riyadh, 2011

   336 p ; 21 cm

   ISBN Hardcover: 978-603-501-085-6

   1- Islam - Relations - Christianity   I- Title

   210.95 dc   1431/8815

   Legal Deposit no. **1431/8815**
   ISBN Hardcover: **978-603-501-085-6**

International Islamic Publishing House (IIPH)
P.O. Box 55195 Riyadh 11534, Saudi Arabia
Tel: 966 1 4650818 / 4647213 — Fax: 966 1 4633489
E-mail: iiph@iiph.com.sa — iiphsa@gmail.com
www.iiph.com.sa

Contents

Arabic honorific symbols
used in this book

(ﷻ): *Subḥânahu wa ta'âlâ* — 'The Exalted'

(ﷺ): *Ṣalla-Allâhu 'alayhi wa sallam* — 'Blessings and peace
be upon him'

(ﷺ): *'Alayhis-salâm* — 'Peace be upon him'

(﵁): *Raḍiya Allâhu 'anhu* — 'May Allah be pleased with <u>him</u>'

(﵂): *Raḍiya Allâhu 'anhâ* — 'May Allah be pleased with <u>her</u>'

Pronunciation and Transliteration Chart

Arabic script	Pronunciation	Transliterated as:
أ	short 'a', as in *cat*	a
ى – آ	longer 'a', as in *cab* (not as in *cake*)	â
ب	/b/ as in *bell, rubber* and *tab*	b
ت	/t/ as in *tap, mustard* and *sit*	t
ة	takes the sound of the preceding diactrical mark sometimes ending in h (when in pausal form): ah, ih, or ooh; or atu(n), ati(n) or ata(n) when in uninterrupted speech	h or t (when followed by another Arabic word)
ث	/th/ as in *thing, maths* and *wealth*	th
ج	/j/ as in *jam, ajar* and *age*	j
ح	a 'harsher' sound than the English initial /h/, and may occur medially and in word-final position as well	ḥ
خ	as in *Bach* (in German); may occur initially and medially as well	kh
د	/d/ as in *do, muddy* and *red*	d
ذ	as in *this, father,* and *with*	dh
ر	/r/ as in *raw, art* and *war*; may also be a rolled r, as with Spanish words	r

Arabic script	Pronunciation	Transliterated as:
ز	/z/ as in *zoo*, *easy* and *gaze*	z
س	/s/ as in *so*, *messy* and *grass*	s
ش	as in *ship*, *ashes* and *rush*	sh
ص	no close equivalent in English, but may be approximated by pronouncing it as /sw/ or /s/ farther back in the mouth	ṣ
ض	no close equivalent in English, but may be approximated by pronouncing /d/ farther back in the mouth	ḍ
ط	no close equivalent in English, but may be approximated by pronouncing /t/ farther back in the mouth	ṭ
ظ	no close equivalent in English, but may be approximated by pronouncing 'the' farther back in the mouth	<u>dh</u>
ع	no close equivalent in English: a guttural sound in the back of the throat	'
غ	no close equivalent in English, but may be closely approximated by pronouncing it like the French /r/ in 'rouge'	gh
ف	/f/ as in *fill*, *effort* and *muff*	f

Arabic script	Pronunciation	Transliterated as:
ق	no close equivalent in English, but may be approximated by pronouncing /k/ farther back in the mouth	q
ك	/k/ as in *king*, *buckle* and *tack*	k
ل	/l/ as in *lap*, *halo*; in the word *Allah*, it becomes velarized as in *ball*	l
م	/m/ as in *men*, *simple* and *ram*	m
ن	/n/ as in *net*, *ant* and *can*	n
ـﻪ – ه – ـﻬ	/h/ as in hat; unlike /h/ in English, in Arabic /h/ is pronounced in medial and word-final positions as well	h
و	as in *wet* and *away*	w
و (as a vowel)	long u, as in *boot* and *too*	oo
ي	as in *yet* and *yard*	y
ي (as a vowel)	long e, as in *eat*, *beef* and *see*	ee
ء	glottal stop: may be closely approximated by pronouncing it like 't' in the Cockney English pronunciation of *butter*: *bu'er*, or the stop sound in *uh — oh!*	' (Omitted in initial position)

Diphthongs:

Arabic script	**Pronunciation**	**Transliterated as:**
أَوَ ، و	Long o, as in *owe*, *boat* and *go*	au, aw, ow
أَيَ ، يَ	Long 'a', as in *able*, *rain* and *say*	ay, ai, ei

Diacritical marks (*tashkeel*):

Name of mark	**Pronunciation**	**Transliterated as:**
ـَ fatḥah	very short 'a' or schwa (unstressed vowel)	a
ـِ kasrah	shorter version of ee or schwa (unstressed vowel)	i
ـُ Dammah	shorter version of oo	u
ـّ shaddah	a doubled consonant is stressed in the word, and the length of the sound is also doubled	Double letter
ـْ sukoon	no vowel sound between consonants or at the end of a word	Absence of vowel

About the word 'Lord'

The word *lord* in English has several related meanings. The original meaning is 'master' or 'ruler', and in this sense it is often used to refer to human beings: 'the lord of the mansion' or 'Lord So-and-So' (in the United Kingdom, for example). The word *Lord* with a capital L is used in the lexicon of Islam to refer to the One and Only God — Allah. In Islam, there is no ambiguity about the meaning of this word. While it is true that one may occasionally use the word *lord* (whether capitalized or not) to refer to a human being, in Islamic discourse the reference of this term is always clear from the context. Whereas for Christians, Hindus and other polytheists, the word *Lord* with a capital 'L' may refer to Allah, to Jesus or to some imagined deity, for Muslims, there can be no plurality of meaning. Allah alone is the Lord, and the Lord is Allah — not Jesus, not Rama, not any other being.

The Editor

Publisher's Note

All praise and thanks belong to Allah alone, the One, the Almighty, and All-Merciful. Blessings and peace be upon Prophet Muhammad, the last of His Messengers and Prophets, and upon his family, his Companions and all those who follow in his footsteps until the end of time.

Historically, Islam and Christianity have had a long, close and often uneasy relationship. In *Muslim-Christian Interactions*, Yahya Ondigo examines the past in order to make sense of the present, and looks at current discourse (scientific, religious, and social) in order to put forth seeds of hope for the future in the complex relationships between the two largest world religions and their followers.

May Allah accept the efforts of all those who contributed to the production of this book, and may it be acceptable to Him, *âmeen*.

Muhammad ibn 'Abdul Mohsin Al-Tuwaijri

Managing Director
International Islamic Publishing House
Riyadh, Saudi Arabia

Dedication

$\mathcal{T}$his work is dedicated to the late Dr. Ibrahim Ngozi and the late Professor Ali Sendaro of the Islamic University in Uganda, for their constant encouragement for me to pursue a university education, as well as their continuous guidance and care during it. May Allah (ﷻ) reward them boundlessly for the financial support that they provided for my first year at the University. May Allah (ﷻ) reward them for this work, forgive them all their sins and grant them the highest place in paradise. Our best prayers and wishes for them are in accordance to the words of The Most Merciful Allah:

(سورة المؤمنون: ١١٨)　﴿وَقُل رَّبِّ ٱغْفِرْ وَٱرْحَمْ وَأَنتَ خَيْرُ ٱلرَّٰحِمِينَ ۝﴾

﴾My Lord, forgive and have mercy, for You are the best of the merciful.﴿

(Qur'an 23: 118)

Preface

$\mathcal{A}$ll praises and thanks be to Allah (*Subḥânahu wa Taʿâlâ* — Glorified and Exalted is He), by Whose will this work has been accomplished. May the peace, blessing, and mercy of Allah (ﷻ) be upon the last Prophet and Messenger Muhammad (*Ṣalla Allâhu ʿalayhi wa sallam* — blessings and peace be upon him) and on all those prophets and messengers who came before him, together with their pure families, noble Companions, and all those who follow their righteous way until the last day. May Allah (ﷻ) shine His light of guidance into our hearts and minds and prevent our emotions from clouding our vision, thereby blinding us from seeing the truth and following the truth. *Âmeen* (Amen).

Having been born in a Christian home and having experienced a Christian way of life for 26 years, until Allah (ﷻ) by His grace and mercy guided me to Islam; and having lived as a Muslim for the last 14 years and having experienced an Islamic way of life, I felt the need to write about interactions between Muslims and Christians from the point of view, not only as an academic exercise, but as one who has had the opportunity of both experiences. I have supplicated to Allah (ﷻ) to help me in this noble endeavour so as to be as impartial as humanly possible, while at the same time being honest and truthful. If, in the process, we fall short of human expectation and inadvertently hurt the feelings of people of either faith, then the readers should rest assured that this is not the intention whatsoever, but rather, we mean well. This work looks at the relationship between Muslims and Christians at a global level, from a historical perspective, as well as at the similarities and differences between the two great faiths that have moved not only the cause of history, but also changed millions of lives.

I do hereby acknowledge and thank my wives and children for the patience they had with me while I could not avail myself in the process of preparing this work. May Allah (ﷻ) reward them abundantly and increase them in faith, and the doing of righteous deeds that can merit the grace of Allah (ﷻ) on the Day of Judgement. I do also sincerely acknowledge and thank one of my very bright students by the name of Khalid A. Mohamood. He lived in America for over twelve years, and then went on to pursue a degree in medicine at Benadir University, Mogadishu, Somalia. He read through the scripts and did a lot of editing before its publication. May Allah (ﷻ) reward him abundantly, make his task easy, and grant him success and a bright future to continue serving Islam and Muslims, especially in war-torn Somalia.

Yahya M. A. Ondigo

Introduction

With regard to Muslim-Christian interactions, one may take two different approaches: a concordant approach, or a conflicting approach. Or one may take both approaches together. A concordant approach means that one tries to harmonize or look for similarities between the two faiths and the people adhering to them. The conflicting approach means the opposite. Since the Qur'an has alluded to both approaches, we have chosen to use both approaches. There are many passages in the Qur'an where Allah (ﷻ) alluded to these approaches. For example, Allah (ﷻ) says:

﴿۞ لَتَجِدَنَّ أَشَدَّ ٱلنَّاسِ عَدَٰوَةً لِّلَّذِينَ ءَامَنُواْ ٱلۡيَهُودَ وَٱلَّذِينَ أَشۡرَكُواْ وَلَتَجِدَنَّ أَقۡرَبَهُم مَّوَدَّةً لِّلَّذِينَ ءَامَنُواْ ٱلَّذِينَ قَالُوٓاْ إِنَّا نَصَٰرَىٰ ذَٰلِكَ بِأَنَّ مِنۡهُمۡ قِسِّيسِينَ وَرُهۡبَانًا وَأَنَّهُمۡ لَا يَسۡتَكۡبِرُونَ ٨٢﴾

(سورة المَائدة: ٨٢)

﴿You will surely find the most intense of people in animosity towards the believers [Muslims] [to be] the Jews and those who associate others with Allah; and you will find the nearest of them in loving affection to the believers those who say: We are Christians. That is because among them are priests and monks and because they are not arrogant.﴾

(Qur'an 5: 82)[1]

﴿ ۞ لَيۡسُواْ سَوَآءٗۗ مِّنۡ أَهۡلِ ٱلۡكِتَٰبِ أُمَّةٞ قَآئِمَةٞ يَتۡلُونَ ءَايَٰتِ ٱللَّهِ ءَانَآءَ ٱلَّيۡلِ وَهُمۡ يَسۡجُدُونَ ۝ يُؤۡمِنُونَ بِٱللَّهِ وَٱلۡيَوۡمِ ٱلۡأٓخِرِ وَيَأۡمُرُونَ بِٱلۡمَعۡرُوفِ وَيَنۡهَوۡنَ عَنِ ٱلۡمُنكَرِ وَيُسَٰرِعُونَ فِي ٱلۡخَيۡرَٰتِ وَأُوْلَٰٓئِكَ مِنَ ٱلصَّٰلِحِينَ ۝ ﴾

(سورة آل عِمران: ١١٣–١١٤)

﴾They are not [all] the same; among the people of the scripture is a community standing [in obedience], reciting the verses of Allah during periods of the night and prostrating [in prayer]. They believe in Allah and the Last Day, and they enjoin what is right, and forbid what is wrong and hasten to good deeds. And those are among the righteous.﴿   *(Qur'an 3: 113-114)*

﴿لَّا يَنۡهَىٰكُمُ ٱللَّهُ عَنِ ٱلَّذِينَ لَمۡ يُقَٰتِلُوكُمۡ فِي ٱلدِّينِ وَلَمۡ يُخۡرِجُوكُم مِّن دِيَٰرِكُمۡ أَن تَبَرُّوهُمۡ وَتُقۡسِطُوٓاْ إِلَيۡهِمۡۚ إِنَّ ٱللَّهَ يُحِبُّ ٱلۡمُقۡسِطِينَ ۝ إِنَّمَا يَنۡهَىٰكُمُ ٱللَّهُ عَنِ ٱلَّذِينَ قَٰتَلُوكُمۡ فِي ٱلدِّينِ وَأَخۡرَجُوكُم مِّن دِيَٰرِكُمۡ وَظَٰهَرُواْ عَلَىٰٓ إِخۡرَاجِكُمۡ أَن تَوَلَّوۡهُمۡۚ وَمَن يَتَوَلَّهُمۡ فَأُوْلَٰٓئِكَ هُمُ ٱلظَّٰلِمُونَ ۝ ﴾

(سورة المُمتَحنة: ٨–٩)

﴾Allah does not forbid you from those who do not fight you because of religion and do not expel you from your homes — from being righteous towards them and acting justly towards them. Indeed Allah loves those who act justly. Allah only forbids you from those who fight you because of religion and expel you from your homes and aid in your expulsion — [forbids] that you make allies of them. And whoever makes allies with them, it is those who are wrongdoers.﴿   *(Qur'an 60: 8-9)*

﴿وَقَالُواْ لَن يَدۡخُلَ ٱلۡجَنَّةَ إِلَّا مَن كَانَ هُودًا أَوۡ نَصَٰرَىٰۗ تِلۡكَ أَمَانِيُّهُمۡۗ قُلۡ هَاتُواْ بُرۡهَٰنَكُمۡ إِن كُنتُمۡ صَٰدِقِينَ ۝ بَلَىٰ مَنۡ أَسۡلَمَ وَجۡهَهُۥ لِلَّهِ وَهُوَ

مُحۡسِنٌ فَلَهُۥٓ أَجۡرُهُۥ عِندَ رَبِّهِۦ وَلَا خَوۡفٌ عَلَيۡهِمۡ وَلَا هُمۡ يَحۡزَنُونَ ۝ ﴾

(سُورَةُ البَقَرَة: ١١١-١١٢)

❪And they say [Jews and Christians]: None shall enter paradise unless he be a Jew or a Christian. Those are their [vain] desires. Say: Produce your proof if you are truthful. Nay, whoever submits his whole self to Allah and is a doer of good he will get his reward with his Lord; on such shall be no fear, nor shall they grieve.❫

(Qur'an 2: 111-112)

﴿وَلَن تَرۡضَىٰ عَنكَ ٱلۡيَهُودُ وَلَا ٱلنَّصَٰرَىٰ حَتَّىٰ تَتَّبِعَ مِلَّتَهُمۡۗ قُلۡ إِنَّ هُدَى ٱللَّهِ هُوَ ٱلۡهُدَىٰۗ وَلَئِنِ ٱتَّبَعۡتَ أَهۡوَآءَهُم بَعۡدَ ٱلَّذِى جَآءَكَ مِنَ ٱلۡعِلۡمِ مَا لَكَ مِنَ ٱللَّهِ مِن وَلِيٍّ وَلَا نَصِيرٍ ۝ ﴾

(سُورَةُ البَقَرَة: ١٢٠)

❪Never will the Jews or the Christians be satisfied with you unless you follow their form of religion. Say: The Guidance of Allah; that is the [only true] Guidance. And if you were to follow their desires after the knowledge has reached you, then you would find neither Protector nor Helper against Allah.❫   *(Qur'an 2: 120)*

﴿ ۞ يَٰٓأَيُّهَا ٱلَّذِينَ ءَامَنُوا۟ لَا تَتَّخِذُوا۟ ٱلۡيَهُودَ وَٱلنَّصَٰرَىٰٓ أَوۡلِيَآءَۘ بَعۡضُهُمۡ أَوۡلِيَآءُ بَعۡضٖۚ وَمَن يَتَوَلَّهُم مِّنكُمۡ فَإِنَّهُۥ مِنۡهُمۡۗ إِنَّ ٱللَّهَ لَا يَهۡدِى ٱلۡقَوۡمَ ٱلظَّٰلِمِينَ ۝ ﴾ (سُورَةُ المَائدة: ٥١)

❪O you who believe! Do not take the Jews and the Christians for your protecting friends; they are protecting friends only to each other. And he amongst you that turns to them [for protection] is of them. Verily Allah guides not a people unjust.❫   *(Qur'an 5: 51)*

﴿إِنَّ ٱلدِّينَ عِندَ ٱللَّهِ ٱلۡإِسۡلَٰمُۗ وَمَا ٱخۡتَلَفَ ٱلَّذِينَ أُوتُوا۟ ٱلۡكِتَٰبَ إِلَّا مِنۢ بَعۡدِ مَا جَآءَهُمُ ٱلۡعِلۡمُ بَغۡيَۢا بَيۡنَهُمۡۗ وَمَن يَكۡفُرۡ بِـَٔايَٰتِ ٱللَّهِ فَإِنَّ ٱللَّهَ سَرِيعُ ٱلۡحِسَابِ ۝ ﴾

(سُورَةُ آل عِمۡرَان: ١٩)

❨The religion before Allah is Islam [submission to His will]: nor did the people of the Book dissent therefrom except through envy of each other, after knowledge had come to them. But if any deny the Signs of Allah, Allah is swift in calling to account.❩ *(Qur'an 3: 19)*

﴿وَمَن يَبْتَغِ غَيْرَ ٱلْإِسْلَمِ دِينًا فَلَن يُقْبَلَ مِنْهُ وَهُوَ فِى ٱلْأَخِرَةِ مِنَ ٱلْخَسِرِينَ ۝﴾ (سورة آل عِمرَان: ٨٥)

❨And anyone who desires a religion other than Islam [submission to Allah], never will it be accepted of him; and in the Hereafter he will be among the losers.❩ *(Qur'an 3: 85)*

﴿لَّقَدْ كَفَرَ ٱلَّذِينَ قَالُوٓاْ إِنَّ ٱللَّهَ هُوَ ٱلْمَسِيحُ ٱبْنُ مَرْيَمَ وَقَالَ ٱلْمَسِيحُ يَٰبَنِىٓ إِسْرَٰٓءِيلَ ٱعْبُدُواْ ٱللَّهَ رَبِّى وَرَبَّكُمْ إِنَّهُۥ مَن يُشْرِكْ بِٱللَّهِ فَقَدْ حَرَّمَ ٱللَّهُ عَلَيْهِ ٱلْجَنَّةَ وَمَأْوَىٰهُ ٱلنَّارُ وَمَا لِلظَّٰلِمِينَ مِنْ أَنصَارٍ ۝﴾ (سورة المَائدة: ٧٢)

❨They have certainly disbelieved who say: Allah is Messiah, the son of Mary. But said the Messiah: O Children of Israel! Worship Allah, my Lord and your Lord. Whoever associates other deities with Allah, Allah will forbid him the Garden, and the Fire will be his abode. There will be for the wrongdoers no helpers.❩ *(Qur'an 5: 72)*

A Muslim's attitude and approach to Christianity and other faiths is not the same as the Christian's approach to people of other faiths. A Christian is brought up believing that his or her religion is the best and the only true one, with Judaism being a preparation for Christianity, and that all other religions are false. Therefore s/he is made to believe that God chose and set apart the children of Israel for the special purpose of revealing His Messages and sending His prophets to them only. Thus a Christian believes only in the prophets and religious teachers of Israel and considers all other claimants to prophethood[2] false and impostors.

Christian missionaries have all along been employing their energies in raising the dust, especially in Africa, so as to prove that the holy men and founders of other religions are false and wicked people, thus establishing the unique claim of Jesus Christ.[3] It is enough to have a casual look at what they have written about Prophet Muhammad (ﷺ) and his religion to see how their religious attitude and prejudices have made the Christian incapable of making fair judgements and arriving at the truth about others. It is this sort of attitude that has made the ordinary Christian who, when confronted with something in another religion resembling his or her own, feels discouraged instead of feeling happy. As such s/he hastens to explain it away by asserting that it is either due to the influence of Christianity or a plagiarism on the part of the other religions.[4]

The Muslim, on the other hand, is taught to believe in the divine origin of all the great world religions before they were corrupted by the hands of men. Allah (ﷻ) clearly said in the Qur'an that He sent to every nation a prophet or messenger to guide the people to the straight path of truth and righteousness. Allah (ﷻ), being the loving Creator, Cherisher, and Sustainer of all the worlds, cannot become partial and thus choose one nation to the exclusion of all others for revealing His will and guidance. Allah (ﷻ) says:

$$﴿وَلَقَدْ بَعَثْنَا فِى كُلِّ أُمَّةٍ رَسُولًا أَنِ اعْبُدُوا اللَّهَ وَاجْتَنِبُوا الطَّاغُوتَ ...﴾$$

(سورة النحل : ٣٦)

﴿And verily We have sent among every nation, a messenger [proclaiming]: Worship Allah alone and avoid false deities...﴾

(Qur'an 16: 36)

$$﴿وَلِكُلِّ أُمَّةٍ رَسُولٌ فَإِذَا جَاءَ رَسُولُهُمْ قُضِىَ بَيْنَهُمْ بِالْقِسْطِ وَهُمْ لَا يُظْلَمُونَ﴾$$

(سورة يونس : ٤٧)

﴿And for every nation there is a messenger, so when their messenger comes, the matter will be judged between them with justice, and they will not be wronged.❥   *(Qur'an 10: 47)*

Thus a Muslim believes in all the prophets of all divine religions and can only feel sorry that the Jews and Christians have in part forsaken and altered the true teachings of Moses and Jesus (*'alayhim as-salâm* — peace be upon them) and rejected the teachings of Muhammad (ﷺ). Yet he can never belittle or speak against the prophets of those religions. For the Muslim has been commanded by Allah (ﷻ) in the Glorious Qur'an not only to believe in all the prophets but also to love and respect these true righteous prophets to the same extent as he loves and respects Prophet Muhammad (ﷺ).

According to the Qur'an, the only divine religion is Islam. It is the same as what was revealed to Moses (ﷺ), Abraham (ﷺ), and Jesus (ﷺ). Christianity and Judaism however, are distorted religions and no longer divine. The last prophet of Islam is Prophet Muhammad (ﷺ), who came to revive the message of Islam, which had been distorted through human intervention and corruption of the scriptures, resulting in such beliefs as the crucifixion of Jesus, original sin, and the death and resurrection of Jesus (ﷺ). Allah (ﷻ) subsequently sent down His final revelation through Prophet Muhammad (ﷺ), and with him the institution of prophethood has come to an end.

Chapter 1

Muslim and Christian Beliefs: An Overview

Muslim and Christian understanding of God

The belief in God Almighty is very much central to all world religions, especially in the two major world religions of Islam and Christianity. Each claims a population of over 1.2 billion followers. Muslims and Christians believe in and worship the same Creator, God Almighty, whom the Muslims call Allah (ﷻ) and the English-speaking Christians call Jehovah or Lord God. Allah (ﷻ) says:

﴿ ۞ وَلَا تُجَـٰدِلُوٓاْ أَهْلَ ٱلْكِتَـٰبِ إِلَّا بِٱلَّتِى هِىَ أَحْسَنُ إِلَّا ٱلَّذِينَ ظَلَمُواْ مِنْهُمْ وَقُولُوٓاْ ءَامَنَّا بِٱلَّذِىٓ أُنزِلَ إِلَيْنَا وَأُنزِلَ إِلَيْكُمْ وَإِلَـٰهُنَا وَإِلَـٰهُكُمْ وَٰحِدٌ وَنَحْنُ لَهُۥ مُسْلِمُونَ ﴿٤٦﴾ ﴾ (سورة العَنكبوت: ٤٦)

﴾And do not argue with the People of the Scripture [Jews and Christians] except in a way that is best, except for those who commit injustice among them, and say: We believe in that which has been revealed to us and revealed to you. And our God and your God is one; and we are Muslims [in submission] to Him.﴿ *(Qur'an 29: 46)*

﴿ قُلْ أَتُحَآجُّونَنَا فِى ٱللَّهِ وَهُوَ رَبُّنَا وَرَبُّكُمْ وَلَنَآ أَعْمَٰلُنَا وَلَكُمْ أَعْمَٰلُكُمْ وَنَحْنُ لَهُۥ مُخْلِصُونَ ﴿١٣٩﴾ ﴾ (سورة البَقَرَة: ١٣٩)

❨Say [O Muhammad]: Will you dispute with us about Allah, seeing that He is our Lord and your Lord; that we are responsible for our doings and you for yours; and that we are sincere [in our faith] in Him?❩   *(Qur'an 2: 139)*

Yet the Muslim and Christian understanding of God and conceptions of God differ very much. Christianity today is divided into two major sects: the Roman Catholics and the Protestants. Both Catholics and most Protestants believe in the Holy Trinity. They believe in God the father, who is the Creator; God the son, who is the redeemer; and God the Holy Spirit, who is the helper.

They believe in one God manifested in three distinct personalities. What is known as the Holy Trinity, and is claimed to be a mystery, has to be accepted blindly without reasoning as an act of faith. However, what is the definition of a mystery? People may not comprehensively understand the true nature of God Almighty, yet they agree that whatever little knowledge of Himself that Allah (ﷻ) has chosen to reveal to His servants about His nature and essence must be logical and simple to comprehend, not complicated and somewhat contradictory.

The Protestants are further divided into many denominations to name but a few: Seventh Day Adventists, Methodists, Lutherans, Pentecostals, Baptists, Presbyterians, Anglicans, Assemblies of God, Mennonites, Nazarene, and Jehovah's Witnesses. Catholics and most Protestant denominations believe in the doctrine of trinity, yet this doctrine was never taught by any prophet of God, not even Jesus Christ (ﷺ). Rather, it was originated by St. Paul who taught it, and the same St. Paul is considered by both Muslim and Christian scholars to be the real founder of Christianity. Jesus never taught a religion called Christianity, although he laid the ethical foundation of what has become the Christian faith today. Rather, Jesus himself is 'the Christ'. 'Christ' is a title of Jesus, not a religion.

Christianity began long after God Almighty had lifted Jesus Christ up to heaven, approximately 43 years after his departure. The word *Christianity* does not appear anywhere in any version of the Bible, but rather the word *Christian* occurs only in three places, and all are found in the books of Paul and Peter, but not the four Gospels: Matthew, Mark, Luke, and John. Rather they appear in:

Acts 11:25-26 NIV
Then Barnabas went to Tarsus to look for Saul, and when he found him, he brought him to Antioch. So for a whole year Barnabas and Saul met with the church and taught a great number of people. The disciples were first called Christians at Antioch.

Acts 26:28 NIV
Then Agrippa said to Paul, "Do you think that in such a short time you can persuade me to be a Christian?"

1 Peter 4:16 NIV
However if you suffer as a Christian do not be ashamed, but praise God that you bear that name.

So it is St. Paul who is the real founder of Christianity, who wrote more than half of the New Testament. He wrote 14 out of 27 books of the New Testament and he taught the concept of trinity as we find it in his books, or epistles.

Theirs are the patriarchs, and from them is traced the human ancestry of Christ, who is God over all, forever praised! Amen. (Romans 9: 5 NIV)

Your attitude should be the same as that of Christ Jesus who, being in very nature God, did not consider equality with God something to be grasped but made himself nothing, taking the very nature of a servant. (Philippians 2:5-7 NIV)

> While we wait for the blessed hope of the glorious appearing of
> our great God and saviour, Jesus Christ who gave himself for us
> to redeem us from all wickedness... (Titus 2:13-14 NIV)

In both the Roman Catholic and Anglican churches, Christians do
not only worship God the father, but also God the son and God the
Holy Spirit. In effect, they also worship angels, holy Mary as the
mother of God, and numerous other saints, such as St. Anthony of
Thebes, St. Jude Thaddeus, and St. Christopher.[1]

On the other hand, Muslims believe that there is only one true
God; his proper name is Allah. He is the only creator, cherisher, and
sustainer of all that exists.

﴿قُلْ هُوَ ٱللَّهُ أَحَدٌ ۝ ٱللَّهُ ٱلصَّمَدُ ۝ لَمْ يَلِدْ وَلَمْ يُولَدْ ۝
وَلَمْ يَكُن لَّهُۥ كُفُوًا أَحَدٌۢ ۝﴾   (سورة الإخلاص: ١-٤)

{Say: He is Allah, the One and Only; Allah, the Eternal Refuge. He
begets not, nor is He begotten; And there is none like unto Him.}
(Qur'an 112: 1-4)

﴿ٱللَّهُ خَٰلِقُ كُلِّ شَىْءٍ وَهُوَ عَلَىٰ كُلِّ شَىْءٍ وَكِيلٌ ۝﴾   (سورة الزُّمَر: ٦٢)

{Allah is the creator of all things, and He is over all things, disposer
of affairs.}   *(Qur'an 39: 62)*

Allah (ﷻ) is numerically One (without partners)

﴿لَوْ كَانَ فِيهِمَآ ءَالِهَةٌ إِلَّا ٱللَّهُ لَفَسَدَتَا فَسُبْحَٰنَ ٱللَّهِ رَبِّ ٱلْعَرْشِ عَمَّا يَصِفُونَ ۝﴾
(سورة الأنبِيَاء: ٢٢)

{Had there been within them [the heavens and the earth] gods besides
Allah, they both would have been ruined. So exalted is Allah, Lord of
the throne, above what they describe.}   *(Qur'an 21: 22)*

Allah (ﷻ) is the only one with perfect,
beautiful names and attributes

Muslims believe that Allah (ﷻ) is the only one that is perfect in his knowledge, wisdom, power, and all other names and attributes. No one shares with Him these names and attributes in their perfection as He (ﷻ) says:

﴿هُوَ ٱللَّهُ ٱلَّذِى لَآ إِلَٰهَ إِلَّا هُوَ عَٰلِمُ ٱلْغَيْبِ وَٱلشَّهَٰدَةِ هُوَ ٱلرَّحْمَٰنُ
ٱلرَّحِيمُ ۝ هُوَ ٱللَّهُ ٱلَّذِى لَآ إِلَٰهَ إِلَّا هُوَ ٱلْمَلِكُ ٱلْقُدُّوسُ ٱلسَّلَٰمُ
ٱلْمُؤْمِنُ ٱلْمُهَيْمِنُ ٱلْعَزِيزُ ٱلْجَبَّارُ ٱلْمُتَكَبِّرُ سُبْحَٰنَ ٱللَّهِ عَمَّا
يُشْرِكُونَ ۝ هُوَ ٱللَّهُ ٱلْخَٰلِقُ ٱلْبَارِئُ ٱلْمُصَوِّرُ لَهُ ٱلْأَسْمَآءُ ٱلْحُسْنَىٰ يُسَبِّحُ لَهُ
مَا فِى ٱلسَّمَٰوَٰتِ وَٱلْأَرْضِ وَهُوَ ٱلْعَزِيزُ ٱلْحَكِيمُ ۝﴾   (سورة الحشر: ٢٢-٢٤)

﴾He is Allah, other than whom there is no deity, Knower of the unseen and the witnessed. He is the entirely Merciful, the especially Merciful. He is Allah, other than whom there is no deity, the Sovereign, the Pure, the Perfection, the Bestower of faith, the Overseer, the Exalted in might, the Compeller, the Superior. Exalted is Allah above whatever they associate with him. He is Allah, the Creator, the Inventor, the Fashioner; to Him belong the best names. Whatever is in heavens and earth is exalting Him. And He is the Exalted in might, the wise.﴿   *(Qur'an 59: 22-24)*

Allah (ﷻ) is the only lawgiver (governor)

Muslims also believe that Allah (ﷻ) is the only lawgiver and the only one who legislates in all human affairs. As such whoever claims legislation for himself or herself is only committing the grave sin of associating partners with Allah (ﷻ). He says:

﴿مَا تَعْبُدُونَ مِن دُونِهِۦٓ إِلَّآ أَسْمَآءً سَمَّيْتُمُوهَآ أَنتُمْ وَءَابَآؤُكُم مَّآ أَنزَلَ ٱللَّهُ بِهَا

مِن سُلْطَنٍ إِنِ الْحُكْمُ إِلَّا لِلَّهِ أَمَرَ أَلَّا تَعْبُدُوٓا إِلَّآ إِيَّاهُ ذَٰلِكَ الدِّينُ الْقَيِّمُ
وَلَٰكِنَّ أَكْثَرَ النَّاسِ لَا يَعْلَمُونَ ﴿٤٠﴾ ۞ (سورة يُوسُف: ٤٠)

❨You worship not besides Him except [mere] names you have named them,[2] you and your fathers, for which Allah has sent down no authority. Legislation is not but for Allah. He has commanded that you worship not except Him. That is the correct religion, but most of the people do not know.❩ *(Qur'an 12: 40)*

Allah is the only saviour, helper, and redeemer

Muslims believe that since Allah (﷾) is the only saviour, helper, and redeemer, then it is only He Who should be worshipped and sought for help. All good and bad fortunes are by His will, and therefore whenever one wants to avoid bad fortune, get help, good luck, or any other kind of assistance he or she should only turn to Allah (﷾) and ask sincerely from Him all his needs. Allah (﷾) says:

۞ وَمَآ أُمِرُوٓا إِلَّا لِيَعْبُدُوا اللَّهَ مُخْلِصِينَ لَهُ الدِّينَ حُنَفَآءَ وَيُقِيمُوا الصَّلَوٰةَ وَيُؤْتُوا
الزَّكَوٰةَ وَذَٰلِكَ دِينُ الْقَيِّمَةِ ﴿٥﴾ ۞ (سورة البَيِّنَة: ٥)

❨And they were not commanded except to worship Allah, [being] sincere to him in religion, inclining to truth, and to establish prayer and to give obligatory charity. And that is the correct religion.❩
(Qur'an 98: 5)

۞ أَمَّن يُجِيبُ الْمُضْطَرَّ إِذَا دَعَاهُ وَيَكْشِفُ السُّوٓءَ وَيَجْعَلُكُمْ خُلَفَآءَ الْأَرْضِ
أَءِلَٰهٌ مَّعَ اللَّهِ قَلِيلًا مَّا تَذَكَّرُونَ ﴿٦٢﴾ ۞ (سورة النَّمل: ٦٢)

❨Is He [not best] Who responds to the desperate one when he calls upon Him and removes evil and makes you inheritors of the earth? Is there a deity with Allah? Little do you remember.❩ *(Qur'an 27: 62)*

﴿وَقَالَ رَبُّكُمُ ٱدْعُونِي أَسْتَجِبْ لَكُمْ إِنَّ ٱلَّذِينَ يَسْتَكْبِرُونَ عَنْ عِبَادَتِي
سَيَدْخُلُونَ جَهَنَّمَ دَاخِرِينَ ﴿٦٠﴾ ﴾   (سورة غَافِر: ٦٠)

﴿And your Lord says: Call on Me; I will answer your [Prayer]: but those who are too arrogant to serve Me will surely find themselves in Hell, in humiliation!﴾

(Qur'an 40: 60)

'Abdullah, son of 'Abbâs (*râḍiya Allâhu 'anhuma* — may Allah be pleased with them both) reported: «One day I was riding behind the Prophet (ﷺ) and he said to me: Young man, I shall teach you some words (of advice): Be mindful of Allah, and Allah will protect you. Be mindful of Allah and you will find Him in front of you. If you ask, ask Allah; if you seek help, seek help of Allah. Know that if the whole nation were to gather together to benefit you with anything they will not benefit you with anything except that which Allah had already prescribed for you, and that if they gather together to harm you with anything, they would not harm you except with that which Allah had already prescribed for you. The pens have been lifted and the pages have dried.» (a sound hadith recorded by Tirmidhi) So Allah (ﷻ) is the helper, redeemer, and saviour, He says about saving the God-fearing on the Day of Judgement:

﴿ثُمَّ نُنَجِّي ٱلَّذِينَ ٱتَّقَوا وَّنَذَرُ ٱلظَّالِمِينَ فِيهَا جِثِيًّا ﴿٧٢﴾ ﴾   (سورة مَريَم: ٧٢)

﴿Then We will save those who feared Allah and leave the wrongdoers within it [the fire], on their knees.﴾   *(Qur'an 19: 72)*

Allah (ﷻ) is the Only Unique God, without images or likeness

Muslims also believe that any picture or image that one imagines in his or her mind to be like God is not God. Therefore Muslims have no statues or images of Allah as objects of worship; they worship

Allah (ﷻ) directly without any intermediaries, whether prophet, king, saint, idols, man-made ideology, passions, philosophy, or any such objects of veneration. Allah says:

﴿ ۞ وَٱعْبُدُوا۟ ٱللَّهَ وَلَا تُشْرِكُوا۟ بِهِۦ شَيْـًٔا ... ۞ ﴾   (سورة النِّساء: ٣٦)

﴾And worship Allah and join none with Him [in worship]...﴿

(Qur'an 4: 36)

﴿ ... لَيْسَ كَمِثْلِهِۦ شَىْءٌ ۖ وَهُوَ ٱلسَّمِيعُ ٱلْبَصِيرُ ۞ ﴾   (سورة الشُّورى: ١١)

﴾...There is nothing like unto Him and He is the All-hearing the All-seeing.﴿

(Qur'an 42: 11)

﴿ٱللَّهُ لَآ إِلَٰهَ إِلَّا هُوَ ٱلْحَىُّ ٱلْقَيُّومُ ۚ لَا تَأْخُذُهُۥ سِنَةٌ وَلَا نَوْمٌ ۚ لَهُۥ مَا فِى ٱلسَّمَٰوَٰتِ وَمَا فِى ٱلْأَرْضِ ۗ مَن ذَا ٱلَّذِى يَشْفَعُ عِندَهُۥٓ إِلَّا بِإِذْنِهِۦ ۚ يَعْلَمُ مَا بَيْنَ أَيْدِيهِمْ وَمَا خَلْفَهُمْ ۖ وَلَا يُحِيطُونَ بِشَىْءٍ مِّنْ عِلْمِهِۦٓ إِلَّا بِمَا شَآءَ ۚ وَسِعَ كُرْسِيُّهُ ٱلسَّمَٰوَٰتِ وَٱلْأَرْضَ ۖ وَلَا يَـُٔودُهُۥ حِفْظُهُمَا ۚ وَهُوَ ٱلْعَلِىُّ ٱلْعَظِيمُ ۞﴾   (سورة البَقَرَة: ٢٥٥)

﴾Allah! There is no other deity but He, the Living, the Self-subsisting, Eternal [Sustainer of all existence]. No slumber can seize Him nor sleep. His are all things in the heavens and on earth. Who is there that can intercede in His presence except as He permits? He knows what [appears to His creatures as] before or after or behind them. Nor shall they encompass aught of His knowledge except as He wills. His footstool extends over the heavens and the earth, and He feels no fatigue in guarding and preserving them for He is the Most High, the Supreme [in glory].﴿   *(Qur'an 2: 255)*

Yet Muslims also believe that Allah's existence does not have the least relevance for humankind if He is not actively concerned with His creation, or if, as some people imagine, Allah (ﷻ) created the universe and humankind and then went off and forgot about them, leaving them on their own to sink or swim. Rather Muslims believe and proclaim that Allah (ﷻ) is the Reality, and that His existence has absolute relevance and meaning for every single human being, since it is solely in relation to Allah (ﷻ) that we exist and move through the journey of this life on our way back to Him.

Muslims therefore assert that Allah (ﷻ) is always active and is concerned and creatively involved in every single part of His creation, from the vastest stars down to the very atoms which comprise them, with every part of its macro and micro-systems. They assert that the universe exists, continues, and fulfils its functions by His command and will. For Allah (ﷻ) is not only concerned with merely creating, but also with sustaining, directing, guiding, and providing for His creations; maintaining, ordering, and regulating them; and in respect to human beings, in giving them the direction necessary for living their lives in this world in a manner that will ensure their everlasting good life in the life to come.

Muslims also believe however, that Allah (ﷻ) is not concerned with humans as the sole or necessarily the most important of His creation, but as the one creature on earth (among His unimaginably vast complex creation) that has been endowed with a thinking mind, a feeling heart, the ability to store and transmit knowledge, and the freedom to choose. Yet at the same time Allah (ﷻ) asks humanity to use this freedom of choice voluntarily and deliberately to choose what Allah (ﷻ) wants for him/her rather than to follow his or her own random and often chaotic desires; that is to submit his or her will to Allah's higher will, and by this means, carry out the responsibilities, both personal and collective which Allah (ﷻ) has entrusted to him/her. For not only does the Creator have the absolute right to make whatever rules or laws He sees fit for His creatures, but He also has the absolute right to their obedience. At the same time He alone possesses the all-embracing absolute knowledge and wisdom to provide His creation with such guidance as will lead to their assured well-being, both in this world and in the hereafter.

Such a belief however, to a careful and committed Muslim, is no mere intellectual exercise. Rather he or she believes that Allah (ﷻ) alone is the Master of the universe, the Lord of humankind, the sole Authority and Legislator; and that humankind is nothing but a humble slave before Him. Consequently, there must not be any other lords or authorities in his or her life besides Allah (ﷻ). Therefore, the Muslim rejects all other elements that claim humanity's obedience and devotion which attempt to rule or dominate life. The Muslim further insists that anyone who truly and wholeheartedly believes that Allah (ﷻ) alone is the sole and rightful Sovereign and Lawgiver, must not and will not obey or give his devotion or allegiance to other claimants to authority and sovereignty. Rather, s/he must reject them all, submit himself or herself to Allah (ﷻ) alone, and strive with all his or her energies against the domination of deities other than Allah.[3]

This, in brief, is the way Muslims perceive God in Islam, as taught by all the prophets of Allah throughout history, including Jesus (ﷺ) and Mohammad (ﷺ). Allah is the loving compassionate Creator, Cherisher, and Sustainer of all that exists. Allah (ﷻ) is alive, real and close to humanity, yet no vision can grasp Him, whereas He grasps all vision. As He (ﷻ) says:

﴿لَّا تُدْرِكُهُ ٱلْأَبْصَٰرُ وَهُوَ يُدْرِكُ ٱلْأَبْصَٰرَ وَهُوَ ٱللَّطِيفُ ٱلْخَبِيرُ ﴿١٠٣﴾﴾

(سورة الأنعام: ١٠٣)

﴾Vision cannot perceive Him, but He perceives [all] vision, and He is the Subtle, the Acquainted.﴿   *(Qur'an 6: 103)*

Muslim and Christian belief in prophethood

Belief in prophets as messengers of God sent to human societies is another central doctrine in many religions, just as it is in Islam and

Christianity. Muslims believe in all the prophets and messengers sent by God to guide people to the straight path leading to paradise: a place of eternal life filled with peace, joy, and happiness. Jews and Christians however, do not believe in all the prophets sent by God; they believe in some and reject others. For example, most Jews do not believe in Jesus (﷽), nor in Muhammad (﷽), and some even go further and abuse a great and righteous prophet of God, Jesus Christ (﷽), calling him a bastard.

Christians have fallen into the same error as Jews in that they believe in all other prophets, but reject Muhammad (﷽), and many even claim that Muhammad (﷽) was an impostor, a false prophet who copied 'his' Qur'an from the Bible.

Some prophecies about Muhammad in the Bible

Yet Muhammad (﷽) has been prophesied in many places in the Bible.[4] For example, in the Old Testament, the following prophecy made by Prophet Moses may refer to the coming of three prophets: himself, Jesus (﷽), and Muhammad (﷽).

> And this is the blessing, wherewith Moses the man of God blessed the children of Israel before his death (his last will and testament). And he said, "The Lord came from Sinai, and rose up from Seir unto them, he shone forth from Mount Paran and he came with ten thousand saints; from his right hand went a fiery law for them." (Deuteronomy 33:1-3 KJV)

There are three distinct prophecies here:

❖ The Ten Commandments (the Torah) given to Prophet Moses (﷽) at Mount Sinai.
❖ The Gospel given to Prophet Jesus (﷽) at Mount Seir in Jerusalem.
❖ The Qur'an given to Prophet Muhammad (﷽) at Mount Paran in Makkah.

Mount Paran is the place where Ishmael (in Arabic, Ismâ'eel) dwelt with his mother Hagar (Hâjar), according to the following verses of the holy Bible:

> "I will make the son of the maidservant into a nation also, because he is your offspring." Early the next morning Abraham took some food and a skin of water and gave them to Hagar. He set them on her shoulders and then sent her off with the boy. She went on her way and wandered in the desert of Beersheba. When the water in the skin was gone, she put the boy under one of the bushes. Then she went off and sat down nearby, about a bowshot away, for she thought, "I cannot watch the boy die." And as she sat there nearby, she began to sob. God heard the boy crying, and the angel of God called to Hagar from heaven and said to her, "What is the matter, Hagar? Do not be afraid; God has heard the boy crying as he lies there. Lift the boy up and take him by the hand, for I will make him into a great nation." Then God opened her eyes and she saw a well of water.[5] So she went and filled the skin with water and gave the boy a drink. God was with the boy as he grew up. He lived in the desert and became an archer. While he was living in the Desert of Paran, his mother got a wife for him from Egypt. (Genesis 21:13-21 NIV)

Furthermore Makkah has been mentioned by its old name (Baca) both in the Bible and the Qur'an, clarifying that Mount Paran is in Makkah.

> ...O Lord Almighty, my King and my God. Blessed are those who dwell in your house;[6] they are ever praising you. *Selah.* Blessed are those whose strength is in you, who have set their hearts on pilgrimage.[7] As they pass through the Valley of **Baca**, they make it a place of springs;[8] the autumn rains also cover it with pools. They go from strength to strength, till each appears before God in Zion. Hear my prayer, O Lord God Almighty; listen to me, O God of Jacob. Selah. Look upon our shield, O

God; look with favour on your anointed one. Better is one day in your courts than a thousand elsewhere;[9] I would rather be a doorkeeper in the house of my God than dwell in the tents of the wicked. For the LORD God is a sun and shield; the LORD bestows favour and honour; no good thing does he withhold from those whose walk is blameless. O LORD Almighty, blessed is the man who trusts in you. (Psalms 84:3-12 NIV)

The verses above from the Bible are a vivid description of the fifth pillar of Islam known as the hajj, which is normally performed in the twelfth month of the lunar calendar in Makkah.

﴿قُلْ صَدَقَ ٱللَّهُ فَٱتَّبِعُوا۟ مِلَّةَ إِبْرَٰهِيمَ حَنِيفًا وَمَا كَانَ مِنَ ٱلْمُشْرِكِينَ ﴿٩٥﴾ إِنَّ أَوَّلَ بَيْتٍ وُضِعَ لِلنَّاسِ لَلَّذِى بِبَكَّةَ مُبَارَكًا وَهُدًى لِّلْعَٰلَمِينَ ﴿٩٦﴾ فِيهِ ءَايَٰتٌۢ بَيِّنَٰتٌ مَّقَامُ إِبْرَٰهِيمَ وَمَن دَخَلَهُۥ كَانَ ءَامِنًا وَلِلَّهِ عَلَى ٱلنَّاسِ حِجُّ ٱلْبَيْتِ مَنِ ٱسْتَطَاعَ إِلَيْهِ سَبِيلًا وَمَن كَفَرَ فَإِنَّ ٱللَّهَ غَنِىٌّ عَنِ ٱلْعَٰلَمِينَ ﴿٩٧﴾ قُلْ يَٰٓأَهْلَ ٱلْكِتَٰبِ لِمَ تَكْفُرُونَ بِـَٔايَٰتِ ٱللَّهِ وَٱللَّهُ شَهِيدٌ عَلَىٰ مَا تَعْمَلُونَ ﴿٩٨﴾﴾ (سورة آل عِمرَان: ٩٥-٩٨)

﴿Say [O Muhammad]: Allah has spoken the truth; follow the religion of Abraham, inclining toward truth, and he was not of the polytheists. Verily, the first House [of worship] appointed for humankind was that at Baccah [Makkah], full of blessing, and guidance for the worlds. In it are manifest signs [such as], the standing place of Abraham; whosoever enters it, he attains security. And a pilgrimage to the House [Ka'bah] is a duty that humankind owes to Allah, those who can find thereto a way; and whoever disbelieves [refuses], then indeed, Allah is free from need of the worlds. Say: O people of the Scripture [Jews and Christians]! Why do you disbelieve in the verses of Allah, while Allah is Witness over what you do?﴾ *(Qur'an 3: 95-98)*

﴿قُلْ يَٰٓأَهْلَ ٱلْكِتَٰبِ لِمَ تَصُدُّونَ عَن سَبِيلِ ٱللَّهِ مَنْ ءَامَنَ تَبْغُونَهَا عِوَجًا وَأَنتُمْ شُهَدَآءُ وَمَا ٱللَّهُ بِغَٰفِلٍ عَمَّا تَعْمَلُونَ ﴿٩٩﴾﴾ (سورة آل عِمرَان: ٩٩)

❨Say: O people of the Scripture [Jews and Christians]! Why do you stop those who have believed, from the Path of Allah, seeking to make it seem crooked, while you [yourselves] are witnesses [to the truth]? And Allah is not unaware of what you do.❩ *(Qur'an 3: 99)*

Another prophecy concerning the coming of Prophet Muhammad (ﷺ) prophesied by Jesus (ﷺ) as found in the New Testament is as follows:

> Jesus said to them, "Have you never read in the Scriptures: 'the stone the builders rejected has become the capstone; the Lord has done this, and it is marvellous in our eyes?' Therefore I tell you that the kingdom of God will be taken away from you and given to a people who will produce its fruit." (Matthew 21:42-43 NIV)

In these verses it is obvious that Jesus (ﷺ) was referring to Deuteronomy 32:21, which clearly points out that the nation to be given prophethood after the Jews failed to obey God by fulfilling His covenant, was the Arab nation.

> They made me jealous by what is no god and angered me with their worthless idols. I will make them envious by those who are not a people; I will make them angry by a nation that has no understanding. (Deuteronomy 32:21 NIV)

The 'stone that was rejected' was Hagar and her son, as is found in the Old Testament:

> She (Sarah) said to Abraham, "Get rid of that slave woman and her son, for that slave woman's son will never share in the inheritance with my son Isaac." (Genesis 21:10 NIV)

But God made Ishmael into a great nation, which was given the kingdom of God (prophethood) as is found in the Old Testament:

> "I will make the son of the maidservant into a nation also, because he is your offspring." Early the next morning Abraham

took some food and a skin of water and gave them to Hagar. He set them on her shoulders and then sent her off with the boy. She went on her way and wandered in the desert of Beersheba. When the water in the skin was gone, she put the boy under one of the bushes. Then she went off and sat down nearby, about a bowshot away, for she thought, "I cannot watch the boy die." And as she sat there nearby, she began to sob. God heard the boy crying, and the angel of God called to Hagar from heaven and said to her, "What is the matter, Hagar? Do not be afraid; God has heard the boy crying as he lies there. Lift the boy up and take him by the hand, for I will make him into a great nation." (Genesis 21:13-18 NIV)

And as for Ishmael, I have heard you: I will surely bless him; I will make him fruitful and will greatly increase his numbers. He will be the father of twelve rulers, and I will make him into a great nation. (Genesis 17:20 NIV)

Prophet John, the contemporary of Jesus (ﷺ), also prophesied about the coming of Prophet Muhammad (ﷺ) as is found in the New Testament:

Now this was John's testimony when the Jews of Jerusalem sent priests and Levites to ask him who he was. He did not fail to confess, but confessed freely, "I am not the Christ." They asked him, "Then who are you? Are you Elijah?" He said, "I am not." "Are you the Prophet?" He answered, "No." Finally they said, "Who are you? Give us an answer to take back to those who sent us. What do you say about yourself?" John replied in the words of Isaiah the prophet, "I am the voice of one calling in the desert, 'Make straight the way for the Lord.' Now some Pharisees who had been sent questioned him, 'Why then do you baptize if you are not the Christ, nor Elijah, nor the Prophet?'" (John 1:19-25 NIV)

In this prophecy, the learned men of the Jews were waiting for the

fulfilment of a prophesied coming of three prophets in succession.
That is why they asked John the Baptist three pertinent questions:

> Are you Elijah? He replied, "No."
> Are you the Christ? He again said, "No."
> Are you the Prophet? He denied again, "No."

Yet look at the words of Jesus (ﷺ) when his disciples prodded
him to understand the fulfilment of the above three prophets that
were expected to come; he said:

> Jesus replied, "To be sure, Elijah comes and will restore all
> things. But I tell you, Elijah has already come, and they did not
> recognize him, but have done to him everything they wished. In
> the same way the Son of Man is going to suffer at their hands."
> Then the disciples understood that he was talking to them about
> John the Baptist. (Matthew 17:11-13 NIV)

It is found that Elijah was to come first in his second coming, then
the Christ (Jesus), then another great prophet; in fact, the greatest
prophet after Jesus (ﷺ), whom Jesus (ﷺ) never denied would
come, was Muhammad (ﷺ). There is in fact nowhere in the Bible
where Jesus (ﷺ) claimed to be the last prophet; on the contrary, he
talked of one who was to come after him greater than all and even
gave the criteria for verifying a true prophet from a false one.[10]

Another prophecy by Prophet John about the coming of Prophet
Muhammad (ﷺ) is as follows:

> "I baptize you with water for repentance. But after me will come
> one who is more powerful than I, whose sandals I am not fit to
> carry. He will baptize you with the Holy Spirit and with fire."
> (Matthew 3:11 NIV)

A number of points are to be noted from this prophecy that prove
conclusively that this prophecy applies to none other than Prophet
Muhammad (ﷺ), instead of Jesus (ﷺ), as some Christians contend.

Here Prophet John the Baptist prophesizes about a prophet greater than he was, who would come after him. This prophet cannot be Jesus as supposed or assumed by some Christians because:

✓ John (﷽) and Jesus (﷽) were contemporary prophets (Matthew 11:1-3 NIV). They were prophets at the same time, yet John in his words of prophecy talks about a powerful prophet who is to come after him.

✓ Jesus was not the prophet to come after John because the prophet expected to come after John is greater than John and therefore cannot be baptized by John. Instead, if anything, he should baptize John, yet Jesus was baptized by John in the river Jordan, meaning Jesus (﷽) is not the candidate for this prophecy (Matthew 3:13-16 NIV).

✓ Jesus also confirmed that the prophet who was expected to come after him is greater than all prophets including John and himself, and that this prophet will be the last prophet in the kingdom of God (Matthew 11:11 & Luke 13:22-30 NIV).

Thus, Islam is more tolerant than either Judaism or Christianity in that Muslims believe in all the prophets, including those known as the 'Jewish' prophets, and all the true prophets in the Bible including Jesus Christ (﷽).

In particular, twenty-five prophets have been mentioned by name in the Qur'an, including Jesus (﷽), who has been mentioned in the Qur'an twenty-five times by name, more frequently than Muhammad (﷽). There is also a whole chapter in the glorious Qur'an which is named after the mother of Jesus, in honour of her: Chapter 19, called *Soorah* (Chapter) Maryam. Furthermore, Mary, the mother of Jesus, is highly honoured as a virtuous woman in Islam, as is found in the following words of the glorious Qur'an:

﴿وَإِذْ قَالَتِ ٱلْمَلَـٰٓئِكَةُ يَـٰمَرْيَمُ إِنَّ ٱللَّهَ ٱصْطَفَىٰكِ وَطَهَّرَكِ وَٱصْطَفَىٰكِ عَلَىٰ نِسَآءِ ٱلْعَـٰلَمِينَ ۝ يَـٰمَرْيَمُ ٱقْنُتِى لِرَبِّكِ وَٱسْجُدِى وَٱرْكَعِى مَعَ ٱلرَّٰكِعِينَ ۝﴾

(سورة آل عِمرَان: ٤٢-٤٣)

﴿And [mention] when the angels said: O Mary, indeed Allah has chosen you, purified you, and chosen you above the women of the worlds. O Mary, be devoutly obedient to your Lord and prostate and bow with those who bow [in prayers].﴾   *(Qur'an 3: 42-43)*

﴿إِذْ قَالَتِ ٱلْمَلَـٰٓئِكَةُ يَـٰمَرْيَمُ إِنَّ ٱللَّهَ يُبَشِّرُكِ بِكَلِمَةٍ مِّنْهُ ٱسْمُهُ ٱلْمَسِيحُ عِيسَى ٱبْنُ مَرْيَمَ وَجِيهًا فِى ٱلدُّنْيَا وَٱلْأَخِرَةِ وَمِنَ ٱلْمُقَرَّبِينَ ۝﴾   (سورة آل عمرَان: ٤٥)

﴿[And mention] when the angels said: O Mary, indeed Allah gives you good tidings of a word from Him, whose name will be the Messiah, Jesus, the son of Mary — distinguished in this world and the hereafter, and among those brought near [to Allah].﴾ *(Qur'an 3: 45)*

﴿وَمَرْيَمَ ٱبْنَتَ عِمْرَٰنَ ٱلَّتِى أَحْصَنَتْ فَرْجَهَا فَنَفَخْنَا فِيهِ مِن رُّوحِنَا وَصَدَّقَتْ بِكَلِمَـٰتِ رَبِّهَا وَكُتُبِهِ وَكَانَتْ مِنَ ٱلْقَـٰنِتِينَ ۝﴾   (سورة التَّحْرِيم: ١٢)

﴿And [the example of] Mary, the daughter of 'Imran, who guarded her chastity, so We blew into [her garment] through Our angel [Gabriel], and she believed in the words of her Lord and His scriptures and was of the devoutly obedient.﴾   *(Qur'an 66: 12)*

So in Islam, Allah (ﷻ) has commanded Muslims to believe in all prophets, without discriminating between them.

﴿قُولُوٓا۟ ءَامَنَّا بِٱللَّهِ وَمَآ أُنزِلَ إِلَيْنَا وَمَآ أُنزِلَ إِلَىٰٓ إِبْرَٰهِـۧمَ وَإِسْمَـٰعِيلَ وَإِسْحَـٰقَ وَيَعْقُوبَ وَٱلْأَسْبَاطِ وَمَآ أُوتِىَ مُوسَىٰ وَعِيسَىٰ وَمَآ أُوتِىَ ٱلنَّبِيُّونَ مِن رَّبِّهِمْ لَا نُفَرِّقُ بَيْنَ أَحَدٍ مِّنْهُمْ وَنَحْنُ لَهُ مُسْلِمُونَ ۝﴾   (سورة البَقَرَة: ١٣٦)

❨Say, [O believers]: We have believed in Allah and what has been revealed to us and what has been revealed to Abraham and Ishmael and Isaac and Jacob and the descendants, and what was given to Moses and Jesus and what was given to the prophets from their Lord. We make no distinction between any of them, and we are Muslims [in submission] to Him.❩

(Qur'an 2: 136)

ءَامَنَ ٱلرَّسُولُ بِمَا أُنزِلَ إِلَيْهِ مِن رَّبِّهِ وَٱلْمُؤْمِنُونَ كُلٌّ ءَامَنَ بِٱللَّهِ وَمَلَٰٓئِكَتِهِ وَكُتُبِهِ وَرُسُلِهِ لَا نُفَرِّقُ بَيْنَ أَحَدٍ مِّن رُّسُلِهِ وَقَالُوا سَمِعْنَا وَأَطَعْنَا غُفْرَانَكَ رَبَّنَا وَإِلَيْكَ ٱلْمَصِيرُ ۝

(سورة البَقَرَة: ٢٨٥)

❨The Messenger has believed in what was revealed to him from his Lord, and [so have] the believers. All of them have believed in Allah and His angels and His Books and His messengers, [saying]: We make no distinction between any of His messengers. And they say: We hear and we obey. [We seek] Your forgiveness, our Lord, and to You is the [final] destination.❩

(Qur'an 2: 285)

قُلْ ءَامَنَّا بِٱللَّهِ وَمَا أُنزِلَ عَلَيْنَا وَمَا أُنزِلَ عَلَىٰ إِبْرَٰهِيمَ وَإِسْمَٰعِيلَ وَإِسْحَٰقَ وَيَعْقُوبَ وَٱلْأَسْبَاطِ وَمَا أُوتِيَ مُوسَىٰ وَعِيسَىٰ وَٱلنَّبِيُّونَ مِن رَّبِّهِمْ لَا نُفَرِّقُ بَيْنَ أَحَدٍ مِّنْهُمْ وَنَحْنُ لَهُ مُسْلِمُونَ ۝

(سورة آل عِمرَان: ٨٤)

❨Say [O believers]: We have believed in Allah and what has been revealed to us and what has been revealed to Abraham and Ishmael and Isaac and Jacob and the descendants; and in what was given to Moses and Jesus and what was given to the prophets from their Lord. We make no distinction between any of them, and we are Muslims [in submission] to Him.❩

(Qur'an 3: 84)

Muslims believe that all those prophets who came before Muhammad (ﷺ) were only sent to their specific communities. For example, Prophet Moosâ (Moses) (ﷺ) was sent to the children of

Israel to release them from bondage, Prophet Jonah (ﷺ) was sent to the people of Nineveh, and Prophet Noah (ﷺ) was sent to preach to his community.

Prophet Jesus (ﷺ) was also sent to his own community, the children of Israel. Allah (ﷺ) says about Jesus (ﷺ), the son of Mary:

﴿وَإِذْ قَالَ عِيسَى ٱبْنُ مَرْيَمَ يَٰبَنِيٓ إِسْرَٰٓءِيلَ إِنِّي رَسُولُ ٱللَّهِ إِلَيْكُم مُّصَدِّقًا لِّمَا بَيْنَ يَدَيَّ مِنَ ٱلتَّوْرَىٰةِ وَمُبَشِّرًا بِرَسُولٍ يَأْتِي مِنۢ بَعْدِي ٱسْمُهُۥٓ أَحْمَدُ ... ﴿٦﴾﴾   (سورة الصَّف: ٦)

❰And [mention] when Jesus, the son of Mary, said: O Children of Israel, indeed I am the messenger of Allah to you confirming what came before me of the Torah and bringing good tidings of a messenger to come after me, whose name is *Ahmad*.[11]❱ *(Qur'an 61: 6)*

Even the Gospel according to John, Matthew, and Acts of the Apostles, confirm that Jesus (ﷺ), son of Mary, was only sent to the Children of Israel, as follows:

> He came to that, which was his own, but his own did not receive him. (John 1:11 NIV)

> He called his twelve disciples to him and gave them authority to drive out evil spirits and to heal every disease and sickness. These are the names of the twelve apostles: first, Simon (who is called Peter) and his brother Andrew; James son of Zebedee, and his brother John; Philip and Bartholomew; Thomas and Matthew the tax collector; James son of Alphaeus, and Thaddeus; Simon the Zealot and Judas Iscariot, who betrayed him. These twelve Jesus sent out with the following instructions: "Do not go among the Gentiles or enter any town of the Samaritans. Go rather to the lost sheep of Israel." (Matthew 10:1-6 NIV)

> A Canaanite woman from that vicinity came to him, crying out, "Lord, son of David, have mercy on me! My daughter is

suffering terribly from demon-possession." Jesus did not answer a word. So his disciples came to him and urged him, "Send her away, for she keeps crying out after us." He answered, "I was sent only to the lost sheep of Israel." The woman came and knelt before him. "Lord, help me!" she said. He replied, "It is not right to take the children's bread and toss it to the dogs." "Yes, Lord," she said, "but even the dogs eat the crumbs that fall from their masters' table." Then Jesus answered, "Woman, you have great faith! Your request is granted." And her daughter was healed from that very hour. (Matthew 15:22-28 NIV)

The crowds answered, "This is Jesus, the prophet from Nazareth in Galilee." (Matthew 21:11 NIV)

Men of Israel, listen to this: Jesus of Nazareth was a man accredited by God to you by miracles, wonders and signs, which God did among you through him, as you yourselves know. (Acts 2:22 NIV)

Muslims believe that it was only Prophet Muhammad (ﷺ) who was sent as a universal prophet and the final messenger to the whole of humanity with a universal message. Allah (ﷻ) says:

(سورة الأنبياء: ١٠٧)   ﴿وَمَآ أَرْسَلْنَٰكَ إِلَّا رَحْمَةً لِّلْعَٰلَمِينَ ۝﴾

﴿And We have sent you [O Muhammad] only as a mercy to the worlds.﴾

(Qur'an 21: 107)

﴿وَمَآ أَرْسَلْنَٰكَ إِلَّا كَآفَّةً لِّلنَّاسِ بَشِيرًا وَنَذِيرًا وَلَٰكِنَّ أَكْثَرَ ٱلنَّاسِ لَا يَعْلَمُونَ ۝﴾

(سورة سبإ: ٢٨)

﴿And We have not sent you except to all people as a bringer of good tidings and a warner. But most of the people do not know.﴾

(Qur'an 34: 28)

قُلْ يَأَيُّهَا ٱلنَّاسُ إِنِّي رَسُولُ ٱللَّهِ إِلَيْكُمْ جَمِيعًا ٱلَّذِى لَهُ مُلْكُ
ٱلسَّمَٰوَٰتِ وَٱلْأَرْضِ لَآ إِلَٰهَ إِلَّا هُوَ يُحْىِۦ وَيُمِيتُ فَـَٔامِنُوا۟ بِٱللَّهِ وَرَسُولِهِ ٱلنَّبِىِّ
ٱلْأُمِّىِّ ٱلَّذِى يُؤْمِنُ بِٱللَّهِ وَكَلِمَٰتِهِۦ وَٱتَّبِعُوهُ لَعَلَّكُمْ تَهْتَدُونَ ﴿١٥٨﴾

(سورة الأعراف: ١٥٨)

⟪Say, [O Muhammad]: O people, indeed I am the Messenger of Allah
to you all, [from Him] to Whom belongs the dominion of the heavens
and the earth. There is no deity except Him; He gives life and causes
death. So believe in Allah and His Messenger, the unlettered Prophet,
who believes in Allah and His words, and follow him that you may
be guided.⟫   *(Qur'an 7: 158)*

وَمَا كَانَ مُحَمَّدٌ أَبَآ أَحَدٍ مِّن رِّجَالِكُمْ وَلَٰكِن رَّسُولَ ٱللَّهِ وَخَاتَمَ ٱلنَّبِيِّـۧنَ وَكَانَ
ٱللَّهُ بِكُلِّ شَىْءٍ عَلِيمًا ﴿٤٠﴾

(سورة الأحزاب: ٤٠)

⟪Muhammad is not the father of [any] one of your men, but [he is] the
Messenger of Allah and the seal [last] of the prophets. And ever is
Allah, of all things, knowing.⟫   *(Qur'an 33: 40)*

Thus the Qur'an is emphatic in proclaiming that Muhammad (ﷺ)
is the last messenger of Allah (ﷻ) and the Seal of the Prophets. This
means that he is the last prophet and that anyone who claims
prophethood after him is a false one. Yet one may ask, if Allah (ﷻ)
had sent messengers to earlier people as the need arose, and
humankind's course on this planet has not run out yet and the need
for guidance is so evident today, why should there be no further
prophets sent after him?

This is so because the Qur'an is Allah's final statement, or rather
His final and complete guidance for all of humanity, and as such it
does not require any amendment, abrogation, or restatement.
Moreover, it was revealed at a time when human intellect,
consciousness, and the ability to preserve and transmit knowledge

through writing had reached full maturity. The Qur'an has been preserved word for word, letter for letter, exactly as it was revealed in the original language of revelation. Allah promised to safeguard it from any corruption until the last Day, such that there is no need for any further revelation for guidance.

Therefore the Qur'an is complete and perfect, with its principles and teachings valid, binding and applicable for all time. Although the style and mode of human life may have changed, the ultimate realities and nature of good and evil and humankind's own nature do not change and are in no way affected by the passage of time or change in the human technological and scientific condition. Besides this, there is another reason why no further messengers are needed.

Supplementing the guidance set forth in the Qur'an is the living example of the recipient of the Qur'an, the Messenger Muhammad (ﷺ). A divinely revealed book may be wonderful and excellent, containing all the guidance that people need, but words alone cannot be enough, however powerful they may be. Therefore someone was needed to translate that guidance into reality, to be a living embodiment of the message. And that someone was not to be a super-human being or an angel, but an ordinary man like any other men, a man from among the community to which the guidance was immediately addressed, who would serve as a living example to others and give concrete form to the laws which Allah (ﷻ) had revealed amidst the conditions of the ordinary human existence. That man was Muhammad (ﷺ), the final Prophet and Messenger to the entire human race, thus no other prophet or revelation is required after him.[12]

It is an Islamic belief that prophets and messengers of Allah (ﷻ) are protected from committing major sins, since they are the role models for humanity to emulate. Allah (ﷻ) says:

﴿وَتِلْكَ حُجَّتُنَآ ءَاتَيْنَٰهَآ إِبْرَٰهِيمَ عَلَىٰ قَوْمِهِۦ نَرْفَعُ دَرَجَٰتٍ مَّن نَّشَآءُ إِنَّ رَبَّكَ

حَكِيمٌ عَلِيمٌ ۝ وَوَهَبْنَا لَهُ إِسْحَقَ وَيَعْقُوبَ كُلًّا هَدَيْنَا وَنُوحًا
هَدَيْنَا مِن قَبْلُ وَمِن ذُرِّيَّتِهِ دَاوُدَ وَسُلَيْمَنَ وَأَيُّوبَ وَيُوسُفَ وَمُوسَىٰ
وَهَرُونَ وَكَذَلِكَ نَجْزِى ٱلْمُحْسِنِينَ ۝ وَزَكَرِيَّا وَيَحْيَىٰ وَعِيسَىٰ وَإِلْيَاسَ كُلٌّ مِّنَ
ٱلصَّلِحِينَ ۝ وَإِسْمَعِيلَ وَٱلْيَسَعَ وَيُونُسَ وَلُوطًا وَكُلًّا فَضَّلْنَا عَلَى
ٱلْعَلَمِينَ ۝ وَمِنْ ءَابَآئِهِمْ وَذُرِّيَّتِهِمْ وَإِخْوَنِهِمْ وَٱجْتَبَيْنَهُمْ وَهَدَيْنَهُمْ إِلَىٰ صِرَطٍ
مُّسْتَقِيمٍ ۝ ذَلِكَ هُدَى ٱللَّهِ يَهْدِى بِهِ مَن يَشَآءُ مِنْ عِبَادِهِ وَلَوْ أَشْرَكُوا لَحَبِطَ
عَنْهُم مَّا كَانُوا يَعْمَلُونَ ۝ أُوْلَئِكَ ٱلَّذِينَ ءَاتَيْنَهُمُ ٱلْكِتَبَ وَٱلْحُكْمَ وَٱلنُّبُوَّةَ فَإِن
يَكْفُرْ بِهَا هَؤُلَآءِ فَقَدْ وَكَّلْنَا بِهَا قَوْمًا لَّيْسُوا بِهَا بِكَفِرِينَ ۝ أُوْلَئِكَ ٱلَّذِينَ هَدَى
ٱللَّهُ فَبِهُدَىٰهُمُ ٱقْتَدِهْ ... ۝   (سورة الأنعام: ۸۳–۹۰)

❨And that was Our [conclusive] argument which We gave Abraham against his people. We raise by degrees whom We will. Indeed, your Lord is Wise and Knowing. And We gave to him [Abraham] Isaac and Jacob — all [of them] We guided. And Noah, We guided before; and among his descendants: David and Solomon and Job and Joseph and Moses and Aaron. Thus do We reward the doers of good. And Zachariah and John and Jesus and Elias — and all were of the righteous. And Ishmael and Elisha and Jonah and Lot — and all [of them] We preferred over the rest of creation. And [some] among their fathers and their descendants and their brothers — and We chose them and We guided them to a straight path. That is the guidance of Allah by which He guides whomever He wills of His servants. But if they had associated others with Allah, then worthless for them would be whatever they were doing. Those are the ones to whom We gave the Scripture, authority and prophethood. But if they [the disbelievers] deny it, then We have entrusted it to a people who are not therein disbelievers. Those are the ones whom Allah has guided, so from their guidance take an example.❩   *(Qur'an 6: 83-90)*

﴿قَدْ كَانَتْ لَكُمْ أُسْوَةٌ حَسَنَةٌ فِي إِبْرَاهِيمَ وَالَّذِينَ مَعَهُۥ ...﴾

(سورة المُمْتَحَنَة : ٤)

﴿There has already been for you an excellent pattern in Abraham and those with him...﴾

(Qur'an 60: 4)

﴿وَلَقَدْ كَانَ لَكُمْ فِيهِمْ أُسْوَةٌ حَسَنَةٌ لِّمَن كَانَ يَرْجُوا۟ اللَّهَ وَالْيَوْمَ الْآخِرَ وَمَن يَتَوَلَّ فَإِنَّ اللَّهَ هُوَ الْغَنِيُّ الْحَمِيدُ ٦﴾

(سورة المُمْتَحَنَة : ٦)

﴿There has certainly been for you in them an excellent pattern for anyone whose hope is in Allah and the last day. And whoever turns away — then indeed, Allah is the Free of need, the Praiseworthy.﴾

(Qur'an 60: 6)

﴿لَّقَدْ كَانَ لَكُمْ فِي رَسُولِ اللَّهِ أُسْوَةٌ حَسَنَةٌ لِّمَن كَانَ يَرْجُوا۟ اللَّهَ وَالْيَوْمَ الْآخِرَ وَذَكَرَ اللَّهَ كَثِيرًا ٢١﴾

(سورة الأحزاب : ٢١)

﴿There has certainly been for you in the Messenger of Allah [Muhammad] an excellent pattern for anyone whose hope is in Allah and the last day and [who] remembers Allah often.﴾ *(Qur'an 33: 21)*

These prophets and messengers sent by God were being supported by the power of God. Yet in Christianity many prophets have been accused falsely of many major sins. For example:

❖ Prophet Lot (ﷺ) was accused of incest with his daughters. (Genesis 19:33-35)

❖ Prophet Abraham (ﷺ) was accused of marrying his own sister. (Genesis 20:1-12)

❖ Prophet Noah (ﷺ) was accused of getting drunk with wine and lying naked in front of his sons. (Genesis 9:20-25)

❖ Prophet David (ﷺ) was accused of adultery with Uriah's wife and impregnating her and also accused falsely of murdering Uriah. (2 Samuel 11:1-17)

❖ Prophet Solomon (﷽), who built the temple in Jerusalem, was accused of worshipping idols and having 700 wives and 300 concubines. (I King 11:1-6)

Muslim and Christian belief in divine revelation

Both Muslims and Christians believe in divine books of revelation from God given to the messengers for the guidance of human beings. In particular, Muslims believe that God did not create humankind and leave them without proper guidance; rather, the Most Merciful Creator sent down revelation for humanity's guidance. Allah (ﷻ) said to Adam and his wife, as well as *Iblees* (Satan):

﴿قُلْنَا ٱهْبِطُوا۟ مِنْهَا جَمِيعًا فَإِمَّا يَأْتِيَنَّكُم مِّنِّى هُدًى فَمَن تَبِعَ هُدَاىَ فَلَا خَوْفٌ عَلَيْهِمْ وَلَا هُمْ يَحْزَنُونَ ۝ وَٱلَّذِينَ كَفَرُوا۟ وَكَذَّبُوا۟ بِـَٔايَٰتِنَآ أُو۟لَٰٓئِكَ أَصْحَٰبُ ٱلنَّارِ هُمْ فِيهَا خَٰلِدُونَ ۝﴾   (سورة البَقَرَة: ٣٨-٣٩)

❨We said: Go down from it, all of you. And when guidance comes to you from Me, whoever follows My guidance, there will be no fear concerning them, nor will they grieve. And those who disbelieve and deny our signs — those will be the companions of the fire; they will abide therein eternally.❩   *(Qur'an 2: 38-39)*

﴿يَٰٓأَيُّهَا ٱلَّذِينَ ءَامَنُوٓا۟ ءَامِنُوا۟ بِٱللَّهِ وَرَسُولِهِۦ وَٱلْكِتَٰبِ ٱلَّذِى نَزَّلَ عَلَىٰ رَسُولِهِۦ وَٱلْكِتَٰبِ ٱلَّذِىٓ أَنزَلَ مِن قَبْلُ ... ۝﴾   (سورة النِّسَاء: ١٣٦)

❨O you who believe! Believe in Allah and His Messenger, and the Book, which He has sent down to His Messenger and the Scripture, which He sent down to those before [him].❩   *(Qur'an 4: 136)*

Muslims believe in all the divine books revealed by God to his beloved servants, particularly:

1. The scrolls given to Abraham
2. The scrolls given to Moses and Aaron
3. The law given to Moses (the Torah)
4. The psalms given to David
5. The Gospel given to Jesus, son of Mary
6. The Qur'an given to Muhammad ibn 'Abdullah

However, Christians do not believe that there was another book that was sent after the Bible; they are taught to believe that the Bible is the only book of revelation sent down for the guidance of humankind. So again it can be seen that Islam is more tolerant than Christianity in accepting in principle the revelations that preceded the Glorious Qur'an. Allah (ﷻ) says:

﴿ٱللَّهُ لَآ إِلَٰهَ إِلَّا هُوَ ٱلْحَيُّ ٱلْقَيُّومُ ۝ نَزَّلَ عَلَيْكَ ٱلْكِتَٰبَ بِٱلْحَقِّ مُصَدِّقًا لِّمَا بَيْنَ يَدَيْهِ وَأَنزَلَ ٱلتَّوْرَىٰةَ وَٱلْإِنجِيلَ ۝ مِن قَبْلُ هُدًى لِّلنَّاسِ وَأَنزَلَ ٱلْفُرْقَانَ إِنَّ ٱلَّذِينَ كَفَرُوا۟ بِـَٔايَٰتِ ٱللَّهِ لَهُمْ عَذَابٌ شَدِيدٌ ... ۝ ﴾　　(سورة آل عِمرَان: ٢-٤)

﴾Allah! There is no deity except Him, the Ever-living, the Sustainer of existence. He has sent down upon you, [O Muhammad], the book in truth, confirming what was before it. And He revealed the Torah and the Gospel before, as guidance for people. And He revealed the criterion [the Qur'an]. Indeed, those who disbelieve in the verses of Allah will have a severe punishment...﴿　　*(Qur'an 3: 2-4)*

﴿بَلْ تُؤْثِرُونَ ٱلْحَيَوٰةَ ٱلدُّنْيَا ۝ وَٱلْءَاخِرَةُ خَيْرٌ وَأَبْقَىٰ ۝ إِنَّ هَٰذَا لَفِى ٱلصُّحُفِ ٱلْأُولَىٰ ۝ صُحُفِ إِبْرَٰهِيمَ وَمُوسَىٰ ۝ ﴾　　(سورة الأعلى: ١٦-١٩)

﴾But you prefer the worldly life, while the hereafter is better and more lasting. Indeed, this is in the former Scriptures, the Scriptures of Abraham and Moses.﴿　　*(Qur'an 87: 16-19)*

﴿وَلَقَدْ ءَاتَيْنَا مُوسَىٰ وَهَـٰرُونَ ٱلْفُرْقَانَ وَضِيَآءً وَذِكْرًا لِّلْمُتَّقِينَ ۝﴾

(سورة الأنبياء: ٤٨)

❨And we had already given Moses and Aaron the criterion, a light, and a reminder for the righteous.❩   *(Qur'an 21: 48)*

﴿وَءَاتَيْنَا مُوسَى ٱلْكِتَـٰبَ وَجَعَلْنَـٰهُ هُدًى لِّبَنِىٓ إِسْرَٰٓءِيلَ أَلَّا تَتَّخِذُواْ مِن دُونِى وَكِيلًا ۝﴾

(سورة الإسرَاء: ٢)

❨And we gave Moses the scripture and made it guidance for the children of Israel that you may not take other than Me as a disposer of affairs.❩   *(Qur'an 17: 2)*

﴿وَلَقَدْ ءَاتَيْنَا مُوسَى ٱلْكِتَـٰبَ فَٱخْتُلِفَ فِيهِ وَلَوْلَا كَلِمَةٌ سَبَقَتْ مِن رَّبِّكَ لَقُضِىَ بَيْنَهُمْ وَإِنَّهُمْ لَفِى شَكٍّ مِّنْهُ مُرِيبٍ ۝﴾   (سورة هُود: ١١٠)

❨And we had certainly given Moses the scripture, but it came under disagreement. And if not for a word that preceded it from your Lord, it would have been judged between them. And indeed they are, concerning it [the Qur'an], in disquieting doubt.❩ *(Qur'an 11: 110)*

﴿۞ إِنَّآ أَوْحَيْنَآ إِلَيْكَ كَمَآ أَوْحَيْنَآ إِلَىٰ نُوحٍ وَٱلنَّبِيِّـۧنَ مِنۢ بَعْدِهِۦ وَأَوْحَيْنَآ إِلَىٰٓ إِبْرَٰهِيمَ وَإِسْمَـٰعِيلَ وَإِسْحَـٰقَ وَيَعْقُوبَ وَٱلْأَسْبَاطِ وَعِيسَىٰ وَأَيُّوبَ وَيُونُسَ وَهَـٰرُونَ وَسُلَيْمَـٰنَ وَءَاتَيْنَا دَاوُۥدَ زَبُورًا ۝﴾   (سورة النِّساء: ١٦٣)

❨Indeed, we have revealed to you, [O Muhammad], as we revealed to Noah and the prophets after him. And we revealed to Abraham, Ishmael, Isaac, Jacob, the descendants, Jesus, Job, Jonah, Aaron, and Solomon, and to David we gave the book [of Psalms].❩

(Qur'an 4: 163)

﴿إِنَّآ أَنزَلْنَا ٱلتَّوْرَىٰةَ فِيهَا هُدًى وَنُورٌ يَحْكُمُ بِهَا ٱلنَّبِيُّونَ ٱلَّذِينَ أَسْلَمُواْ

لِلَّذِينَ هَادُواْ وَٱلرَّبَّـٰنِيُّونَ وَٱلْأَحْبَارُ بِمَا ٱسْتُحْفِظُواْ مِن كِتَٰبِ ٱللَّهِ وَكَانُواْ
عَلَيْهِ شُهَدَآءَ فَلَا تَخْشَوُاْ ٱلنَّاسَ وَٱخْشَوْنِ وَلَا تَشْتَرُواْ بِـَٔايَٰتِي ثَمَنًا قَلِيلًا
وَمَن لَّمْ يَحْكُم بِمَآ أَنزَلَ ٱللَّهُ فَأُوْلَٰٓئِكَ هُمُ ٱلْكَٰفِرُونَ ﴿٤٤﴾﴿سورة المائدة: ٤٤)

❨Indeed, we sent down the Torah, in which was guidance and light.
The prophets who submitted [to Allah] judged by it for the Jews, as
did the rabbis and scholars, by that with which they were entrusted of
the scripture of Allah, and they were witnesses thereto. So do not fear
people but fear Me, and do not exchange My verses for a small price
[worldly gain]. And whoever does not judge by what Allah has
revealed, then it is those who are the disbelievers.❩ *(Qur'an 5: 44)*

﴿وَقَفَّيْنَا عَلَىٰٓ ءَاثَٰرِهِم بِعِيسَى ٱبْنِ مَرْيَمَ مُصَدِّقًا لِّمَا بَيْنَ يَدَيْهِ مِنَ ٱلتَّوْرَىٰةِ
وَءَاتَيْنَٰهُ ٱلْإِنجِيلَ فِيهِ هُدًى وَنُورٌ وَمُصَدِّقًا لِّمَا بَيْنَ يَدَيْهِ مِنَ ٱلتَّوْرَىٰةِ وَهُدًى
وَمَوْعِظَةً لِّلْمُتَّقِينَ ﴿٤٦﴾﴾   (سورة المائدة: ٤٦)

❨And We sent, following in their footsteps, Jesus the son of Mary,
confirming that which came before him in the Torah; and We gave
him the Gospel, in which was guidance and light and confirming that
which preceded it of the Torah as guidance and instruction for the
righteous.❩
                                         (Qur'an 5: 46)

﴿وَرَبُّكَ أَعْلَمُ بِمَن فِي ٱلسَّمَٰوَٰتِ وَٱلْأَرْضِ وَلَقَدْ فَضَّلْنَا بَعْضَ ٱلنَّبِيِّـۧنَ عَلَىٰ بَعْضٍ وَءَاتَيْنَا
دَاوُۥدَ زَبُورًا ﴿٥٥﴾﴾   (سورة الإسراء: ٥٥)

❨And your Lord is most knowing of whoever is in the heavens and
the earth. And We have made some of the prophets exceed others [in
various ways], and to David We gave the book [of Psalms].❩
                                         (Qur'an 17: 55)

Yet Muslims do not believe that the versions of the Bible that are
available today are the true original Torah, Psalms, Gospel, or scrolls

of Abraham, because the various versions of the Bible have not been preserved from corruption by additions, deletions, or interpolations. Rather the multiple versions of the Bible that are in use currently are actually a product of corrupted oral traditions, mixed with the philosophical interpretations of the original divine Torah, Psalms, Gospel, and of course blended with ideas from Greco-Roman culture. As the Bible itself bears witness, so does the Qur'an say likewise.

> How can you say, "We are wise, for we have the law of the LORD," when actually the lying pen of the scribes has handled it falsely? (Jeremiah 8:8 NIV)

> And it came to pass, that when Jehudi had read three or four leaves, he cut it with the penknife, and cast it into the fire that was on the hearth, until all the scroll was consumed in the fire that was on the hearth. (Jeremiah 36:23 NIV)

> Since many have taken in hand to set forth in order a declaration of those things which are most surely believed among us, even as they delivered them unto us, who from the beginning were eyewitnesses, and ministers of the word; it seemed good to me also, having had perfect understanding of all things from the very first, to write unto you in order, most excellent Theophilus. (Luke 1:1-3 KJV)

The Qur'an also bears witness like the Bible that the hands of men have corrupted the Bible for their own miserable gains. Allah (ﷻ) says:

﴿فَوَيْلٌ لِّلَّذِينَ يَكْتُبُونَ ٱلْكِتَٰبَ بِأَيْدِيهِمْ ثُمَّ يَقُولُونَ هَٰذَا مِنْ عِندِ ٱللَّهِ لِيَشْتَرُواْ بِهِۦ ثَمَنًا قَلِيلًا فَوَيْلٌ لَّهُم مِّمَّا كَتَبَتْ أَيْدِيهِمْ وَوَيْلٌ لَّهُم مِّمَّا يَكْسِبُونَ ٧٩﴾ (سورة البَقَرَة: ٧٩)

So woe to those who write the 'scripture' with their own hands, then say: This is from Allah — in order to exchange it for a small price. Woe to them for what their hands have written and woe to them for what they earn.》

(Qur'an 2: 79)

From these verses it follows that the Bible has four grades of evidence.

1. The word of God or what sounds like the word of God

> I will raise them up a prophet from among their brethren, like unto you, and will put my words in his mouth; and he shall speak unto them all that I shall command him. (Deuteronomy. 18:18 KJV)

> Let the wilderness and its cities lift up their voice, the villages that Kedar does inhabit: let the inhabitants of the rock sing; let them shout from the top of the mountains. (Isaiah 42:11 KJV)

> To whom will you liken Me and make Me equal, and compare Me, that We may be alike? (Isaiah 46:5 KJV)

2. What sounds like the word of a prophet of God

> And about the ninth hour Jesus cried with a loud voice, saying, Eli, Eli, lama sabachthani? That is to say, My God, My God, why have you forsaken me? (Matthew 27:46 KJV)

> And Jesus answered him, "The first of all the commandments is, Hear, O Israel; The Lord our God is one Lord." (Mark 12:29 KJV)

> And Jesus said unto him, "Why call me good? There is none good but one, that is God." (Mark 10:18 KJV)

3. What sounds like a historian's word

> And seeing a fig tree afar off having leaves, he came, if haply he might find anything thereon: and when he came to it, he found nothing but leaves; for the time of figs was not yet. (Mark 11:13 KJV)

And as Jesus passed forth from there, he saw a man, named Matthew, sitting at the receipt of custom: and he said unto him, follow me. And he arose, and followed him. (Matthew 9:9 KJV)

Since many have taken in hand to set forth in order a declaration of those things which are most surely believed among us, even as they delivered them unto us, who from the beginning were eyewitnesses, and ministers of the word; it seemed good to me also, having had perfect understanding of all things from the very first, to write unto you in order, most excellent Theophilus. (Luke 1:1-3 KJV)

4. What sounds like pornography

And when she brought them unto him to eat, he took hold of her, and said unto her, come lie with me, my sister... Howbeit he would not hearken unto her voice: but, being stronger than she, forced her, and lay with her. (2 Samuel 13:11, 14 KJV)

Then went Samson to Gaza and saw there a harlot, and went in unto her... (Judges 16:1 KJV)

And the Babylonians came to her into the bed of love, and they defiled her with their whoredom, and she was polluted with them... (Ezekiel 23:17 KJV)

Therefore, Muslims believe that the many multiple versions of the Holy Bible that are circulating in the world today do not represent the true word of God, not with all the grades of evidence seen above. Among the most widely circulated versions are:
1. The Roman Catholic version with 73 books
2. The King James Version with 66 books
3. The RSV (Revised Standard Version) of 1952
4. The Revised Standard Version of 1971
5. The Good News version

6. The American Standard Version
7. The Living Bible
8. The New World Translation (Latter-day Saints)
9. The NIV (New International Version) of 1978

Consequently, Muslims believe that Allah (ﷻ) chose to reveal the last revelation, which is the glorious Qur'an, to Prophet Muhammad (ﷺ) and promised to guard it from the corruption that had occurred to the previous revelations. All that which was meant to remain intact in the Torah, Psalms, Gospel, and scrolls of Abraham, for the benefit of humanity has been preserved in the Qur'an for the guidance of humankind. Allah (ﷻ) says:

﴿إِنَّا نَحْنُ نَزَّلْنَا ٱلذِّكْرَ وَإِنَّا لَهُۥ لَحَٰفِظُونَ ۝﴾ (سورة الحجر : ٩)

❨Indeed, it is We Who sent down the message [the Qur'an] and indeed, We will be its guardian.❩   *(Qur'an 15: 9)*

﴿إِنَّ ٱلَّذِينَ كَفَرُواْ بِٱلذِّكْرِ لَمَّا جَآءَهُمْ وَإِنَّهُۥ لَكِتَٰبٌ عَزِيزٌ ۝ لَّا يَأْتِيهِ ٱلْبَٰطِلُ مِنۢ بَيْنِ يَدَيْهِ وَلَا مِنْ خَلْفِهِۦ تَنزِيلٌ مِّنْ حَكِيمٍ حَمِيدٍ ۝﴾ (سورة فُصِّلَت : ٤١-٤٢)

❨Indeed, those who disbelieve in the message [the Qur'an] after it has come to them. And indeed, it is a mighty Book. Falsehood cannot approach it from before it or from behind it; [it is] a revelation from a [Lord Who is] Wise and Praiseworthy.❩   *(Qur'an 41: 41-42)*

Muslims therefore firmly believe that the glorious Qur'an is the only divine authentic book left on earth, whose laws and regulations abrogate the rules and regulations of the previous divine books. The Qur'an is also the only divine authentic book on earth that has withstood the test of time as a living miracle for the last 1400 years without any change as it was revealed in Arabic and memorized by millions of Muslims around the globe in Arabic. Both Muslim and non-Muslim orientalist scholars bear witness to this fact. Muslim

Qur'anic scholars further affirm that the Qur'an is a linguistic, historical, and scientific miracle unparalleled by any human writings, ever.

The concept of belief in angels

Muslims, like Christians, believe that Allah created angels who are the unseen messengers of Allah. They were created from light, and were created for various duties as designated by Allah (ﷻ). Angels are not like human beings in their nature, and as such they do not have human necessities like eating, drinking, sleeping, or getting married. It is also wrong to assume that they are either male or female. Allah alone knows the exact number and nature of these angels. They fall into different categories according to the duties assigned by Allah (ﷻ). There are, amongst others, those who bear the throne of Allah, those who guard paradise and hell, those who record deeds of human beings, the bringer of revelation, the blower of the trumpet, those who guard human beings from devils and other evil people and those in charge of taking human souls at the time of death.

Prophet Muhammad (ﷺ) had informed the Muslims about the names of these angels in some of his night supplications. For example, he used to supplicate in the following words: «O Allah, Lord of Jibreel, Mikâ'eel, and Isrâfeel! Originator of the heavens and the earth! Knower of the unseen and the seen! You who judge between your servants in what they used to dispute over! Guide me by Your permission when the truth is opposed; You guide whom you will to the Straight Path.» (Muslim)

1. There are angels who record the good and bad deeds of human beings; they are called 'noble recording angels'.

﴿وَإِنَّ عَلَيْكُمْ لَحَافِظِينَ ۞ كِرَامًا كَاتِبِينَ ۞ يَعْلَمُونَ مَا تَفْعَلُونَ ۞﴾

(سورة الانفطار: ١٠-١٢)

﴿And indeed, [appointed] over you are keepers, noble and recording. They know whatever you do.﴾ *(Qur'an 82: 10-12)*

2. Gabriel is the angel who brings down revelation.

﴿قُلْ مَن كَانَ عَدُوًّا لِّجِبْرِيلَ فَإِنَّهُ نَزَّلَهُ عَلَىٰ قَلْبِكَ بِإِذْنِ اللَّهِ مُصَدِّقًا لِّمَا بَيْنَ يَدَيْهِ وَهُدًى وَبُشْرَىٰ لِلْمُؤْمِنِينَ ۞ مَن كَانَ عَدُوًّا لِّلَّهِ وَمَلَائِكَتِهِ وَرُسُلِهِ وَجِبْرِيلَ وَمِيكَالَ فَإِنَّ اللَّهَ عَدُوٌّ لِّلْكَافِرِينَ ۞﴾

(سورة البَقَرَة: ٩٧-٩٨)

﴿Say: Whoever is an enemy to Gabriel, it is [none but] he who has brought it [the Qur'an] down upon your heart [O Muhammad], by permission of Allah, confirming that which was before it and as guidance and good tidings for the believers. Whoever is an enemy to Allah, His angels, and His messengers, and to Gabriel [Jibreel] and Michael [Mikâ'eel], then indeed, Allah is an enemy to the disbelievers.﴾ *(Qur'an 2: 97-98)*

3. Isrâfeel is the angel who will blow the trumpet for the Last Hour.[13]

﴿وَنُفِخَ فِي الصُّورِ ذَٰلِكَ يَوْمُ الْوَعِيدِ ۞ وَجَاءَتْ كُلُّ نَفْسٍ مَّعَهَا سَائِقٌ وَشَهِيدٌ ۞ لَّقَدْ كُنتَ فِي غَفْلَةٍ مِّنْ هَٰذَا فَكَشَفْنَا عَنكَ غِطَاءَكَ فَبَصَرُكَ الْيَوْمَ حَدِيدٌ ۞ وَقَالَ قَرِينُهُ هَٰذَا مَا لَدَيَّ عَتِيدٌ ۞ أَلْقِيَا فِي جَهَنَّمَ كُلَّ كَفَّارٍ عَنِيدٍ ۞ مَّنَّاعٍ لِّلْخَيْرِ مُعْتَدٍ مُّرِيبٍ ۞ الَّذِي جَعَلَ مَعَ اللَّهِ إِلَٰهًا آخَرَ فَأَلْقِيَاهُ فِي الْعَذَابِ الشَّدِيدِ ۞﴾

(سورة قَ: ٢٠-٢٦)

﴿And the horn will be blown. That is the day of [carrying out] the threat. And every soul will come, with it a driver and a witness. [It will be said]: You were certainly heedless of this, and we have removed from you your blindfold, so your sight this day is sharp. And his companion, [the angel], will say: This [record] is what is with me, prepared. [Allah will say]: Throw into hell every obstinate disbeliever, preventer of good, aggressor, and doubter, who made [as equal] with Allah another deity; then throw him in the severe punishment.❭   *(Qur'an 50: 20-26)*

4. *Malak ul-Mawt* (Angel of Death) is the angel who takes the soul of each human at the time of death, by the command of Allah (ﷻ).

﴿۞ قُلْ يَتَوَفَّىٰكُم مَّلَكُ ٱلْمَوْتِ ٱلَّذِى وُكِّلَ بِكُمْ ثُمَّ إِلَىٰ رَبِّكُمْ تُرْجَعُونَ ١١ ﴾

(سورة السَّجدَة : ١١)

❬Say: The Angel of Death, put in charge of you, will [duly] take your souls, then shall you be brought back to your Lord.❭ *(Qur'an 32: 11)*

﴿لَهُۥ مُعَقِّبَٰتٌ مِّنۢ بَيْنِ يَدَيْهِ وَمِنْ خَلْفِهِۦ يَحْفَظُونَهُۥ مِنْ أَمْرِ ٱللَّهِ ... ١١ ﴾

(سورة الرَّعد : ١١)

❬For him [each person] there are angels in succession before and after him. They guard him by the command of Allah...❭ *(Qur'an 13: 11)*

5. Mâlik is the guardian of the Hellfire.

﴿وَمَا جَعَلْنَآ أَصْحَٰبَ ٱلنَّارِ إِلَّا مَلَٰٓئِكَةً وَمَا جَعَلْنَا عِدَّتَهُمْ إِلَّا فِتْنَةً لِّلَّذِينَ كَفَرُواْ لِيَسْتَيْقِنَ ٱلَّذِينَ أُوتُواْ ٱلْكِتَٰبَ وَيَزْدَادَ ٱلَّذِينَ ءَامَنُوٓاْ إِيمَٰنًا وَلَا يَرْتَابَ ٱلَّذِينَ أُوتُواْ ٱلْكِتَٰبَ وَٱلْمُؤْمِنُونَ وَلِيَقُولَ ٱلَّذِينَ فِى قُلُوبِهِم مَّرَضٌ وَٱلْكَٰفِرُونَ مَاذَآ أَرَادَ ٱللَّهُ بِهَٰذَا مَثَلًا كَذَٰلِكَ يُضِلُّ ٱللَّهُ مَن يَشَآءُ وَيَهْدِى مَن يَشَآءُ وَمَا يَعْلَمُ جُنُودَ رَبِّكَ إِلَّا هُوَ وَمَا هِىَ إِلَّا ذِكْرَىٰ لِلْبَشَرِ ٣١ ﴾

(سورة المدَّثِّر : ٣١)

❴And We have set none but angels as guardians of the Fire; and We have fixed their number only as a trial for unbelievers, in order that the People of the Book may arrive at certainty, and the believers may increase in faith, and that no doubts may be left for the People of the Book and the believers, and that those in whose hearts is a disease and the unbelievers may say: What does Allah intend by this as an example? Thus does Allah leave astray whom He pleases; and guides whom He pleases; and none can know the forces of you Lord, except He. And this is no other than a warning to humankind.❵

(Qur'an 74: 31)

6. Angels guard and protect the human being from harm wherever he or she goes, and also record all deeds.

﴿وَلَقَدۡ خَلَقۡنَا ٱلۡإِنسَٰنَ وَنَعۡلَمُ مَا تُوَسۡوِسُ بِهِۦ نَفۡسُهُۥ وَنَحۡنُ أَقۡرَبُ إِلَيۡهِ مِنۡ حَبۡلِ ٱلۡوَرِيدِ ۝ إِذۡ يَتَلَقَّى ٱلۡمُتَلَقِّيَانِ عَنِ ٱلۡيَمِينِ وَعَنِ ٱلشِّمَالِ قَعِيدٌ ۝ مَّا يَلۡفِظُ مِن قَوۡلٍ إِلَّا لَدَيۡهِ رَقِيبٌ عَتِيدٌ ۝ وَجَآءَتۡ سَكۡرَةُ ٱلۡمَوۡتِ بِٱلۡحَقِّ ذَٰلِكَ مَا كُنتَ مِنۡهُ تَحِيدُ ۝﴾

(سورة قٓ: ١٦-١٩)

❴And We have already created the human and know what his soul whispers to him, and We are closer to him than [his] jugular vein. When the two receivers [recording angels] receive, seated on the right and on the left, he [the human] does not utter any word except that with him is an observer prepared [to record]. And the intoxication of death will bring the truth; that is what you were trying to avoid.❵ *(Qur'an 50: 16-19)*

﴿وَهُوَ ٱلۡقَاهِرُ فَوۡقَ عِبَادِهِۦ وَيُرۡسِلُ عَلَيۡكُمۡ حَفَظَةً حَتَّىٰٓ إِذَا جَآءَ أَحَدَكُمُ ٱلۡمَوۡتُ تَوَفَّتۡهُ رُسُلُنَا وَهُمۡ لَا يُفَرِّطُونَ ۝﴾

(سورة الأنعام: ٦١)

❴And He is the subjugator over His servants, and He sends over you guardian angels until, when death comes to one of you, our messengers [angels of death] take him, and they do not fail [in their duties].❯   *(Qur'an 6: 61)*

7. Michael is the head of the angels concerned with the climate, vegetation and provision. Al-Ashqar quoted the well-known scholar of the Qur'an, Ibn Katheer, as stating:

> Mikâ'eel is appointed over the rain and vegetation from which is created provision of this world. He has helpers who do whatever he commands them to do by the command of his Lord. They control the winds and clouds as the Lord wills.[14]

Though Christians also believe in the angels, their concept of angels is slightly different from that in Islam. In Christianity, Satan is considered a fallen angel who disobeyed Allah (ﷻ) and wanted to be equal with Allah.

> Satan, the chief of the fallen angels, is mentioned in a number of places in the Old Testament. It is clear that from the very moment of the creation of this world that Satan and fallen angels were on the scene, rebels against God.[15]

In Islamic belief, angels are created without a free will; they obey Allah (ﷻ) without choice, and hence cannot disobey Him. Satan/ Iblees was not a fallen angel, but was one of the *jinn*, who are non-human beings with free will that were created by Allah (ﷻ) from smokeless flames of fire. Satan disobeyed Allah, because he had the choice — free will. Allah (ﷻ) says about him:

$$﴿وَإِذْ قُلْنَا لِلْمَلَـٰٓئِكَةِ ٱسْجُدُواْ لِأَدَمَ فَسَجَدُوٓاْ إِلَّآ إِبْلِيسَ كَانَ مِنَ ٱلْجِنِّ فَفَسَقَ عَنْ أَمْرِ رَبِّهِۦٓ أَفَتَتَّخِذُونَهُۥ وَذُرِّيَّتَهُۥٓ أَوْلِيَآءَ مِن دُونِي وَهُمْ لَكُمْ عَدُوٌّۢ بِئْسَ لِلظَّـٰلِمِينَ بَدَلًا ۝﴾$$

(سورة الكهف: ٥٠)

❮And [mention] when We said to the angels: Prostrate to Adam, and they prostrated except for Iblees. He was of the jinn and transgressed against [disobeyed] the command of his Lord. Then will you take him and his descendants as allies other than Me, while they are enemies to you? Wretched it is for the wrongdoers as an exchange.❳

(Qur'an 18: 50)

﷽قَالَ مَا مَنَعَكَ أَلَّا تَسْجُدَ إِذْ أَمَرْتُكَ قَالَ أَنَا۠ خَيْرٌ مِّنْهُ خَلَقْتَنِي مِن نَّارٍ وَخَلَقْتَهُۥ مِن طِينٍ ۝ قَالَ فَٱهْبِطْ مِنْهَا فَمَا يَكُونُ لَكَ أَن تَتَكَبَّرَ فِيهَا فَٱخْرُجْ إِنَّكَ مِنَ ٱلصَّٰغِرِينَ ۝ قَالَ أَنظِرْنِى إِلَىٰ يَوْمِ يُبْعَثُونَ ۝ قَالَ إِنَّكَ مِنَ ٱلْمُنظَرِينَ ۝ قَالَ فَبِمَآ أَغْوَيْتَنِى لَأَقْعُدَنَّ لَهُمْ صِرَٰطَكَ ٱلْمُسْتَقِيمَ ۝ ثُمَّ لَءَاتِيَنَّهُم مِّنۢ بَيْنِ أَيْدِيهِمْ وَمِنْ خَلْفِهِمْ وَعَنْ أَيْمَٰنِهِمْ وَعَن شَمَآئِلِهِمْ وَلَا تَجِدُ أَكْثَرَهُمْ شَٰكِرِينَ ۝﷽

(سورة الأعراف: ١٢–١٧)

❴[Allah] said: What prevented you from prostrating when I commanded you? [Satan] said: I am better than he. You created me from fire and created him from clay [earth]. [Allah] said: Descend from it [paradise], for it is not for you to be arrogant therein. So get out; indeed, you are debased. [Satan] said: Reprieve me until the day they are resurrected. [Allah] said: You are of those reprieved. [Satan] said: Because You have put me in error, I will surely sit in wait for them [humankind] on Your straight path. Then I will come to them from before them and from behind them and on their right and on their left, and You will not find most of them grateful [to You].❵

(Qur'an 7: 12-17)

﷽يَٰٓأَيُّهَا ٱلَّذِينَ ءَامَنُوا۟ قُوٓا۟ أَنفُسَكُمْ وَأَهْلِيكُمْ نَارًا وَقُودُهَا ٱلنَّاسُ وَٱلْحِجَارَةُ عَلَيْهَا مَلَٰٓئِكَةٌ غِلَاظٌ شِدَادٌ لَّا يَعْصُونَ ٱللَّهَ مَآ أَمَرَهُمْ وَيَفْعَلُونَ مَا يُؤْمَرُونَ ۝﷽

(سورة التحريم: ٦)

❴O you who have believed, protect yourselves and your families from a fire whose fuel is people and stones, over which are [appointed] angels, harsh and severe; they do not disobey Allah in what He commands them but do what they are commanded.❩ *(Qur'an 66: 6)*

'Â'ishah (Raḍiya Allâhu 'anhâ — may Allah be pleased with her — ﷺ) reported that the Prophet (ﷺ) said: «The angels were created from light, the jinn were created from smokeless flame of fire, and Adam was created from what has been described to you.» (Muslim)

The concept of belief in the Day of Judgement

In Islam and Christianity the concept of life after death is very important. This concept pertains to the Day of Judgement, bodily resurrection, and heaven and hell, and is a fundamental article of belief in Islam. According to Islam, the life of this world is not the end of everything, and this is the whole reason why human beings believe in God and worship Him, otherwise believing in God Almighty would be meaningless. If people did not believe that they would be responsible for all that they do in this world and will be rewarded or punished accordingly, then human society would have been much more corrupted than it is today.

Islam asserts that the present life is but a minute part of the totality of all existence. The Qur'an informs humanity of the reality of another life of a higher and different nature from the life of this world, of an infinite duration. Human beings may try to disprove such existence but the Qur'an again and again speaks of familiar and obvious examples and situations of such transformations. For example, the coming to life again of the earth after it lies dead and barren in the grip of winter or drought; and the development of a sperm and an ovum into an embryo in the environment of the mother's womb, and its further development from that state into a thinking, feeling, acting human being living in the world. Allah (ﷻ) says:

وَمِنْ ءَايَٰتِهِۦٓ أَنَّكَ تَرَى ٱلْأَرْضَ خَٰشِعَةً فَإِذَآ أَنزَلْنَا عَلَيْهَا ٱلْمَآءَ ٱهْتَزَّتْ وَرَبَتْ إِنَّ ٱلَّذِىٓ أَحْيَاهَا لَمُحْىِ ٱلْمَوْتَىٰٓ إِنَّهُۥ عَلَىٰ كُلِّ شَىْءٍ قَدِيرٌ ﴿٣٩﴾   (سورة فُصِّلَت: ٣٩)

◆And of His signs is that you see the earth barren and desolate [stilled], but when We send down upon it rain, it quivers and grows. Indeed, He Who has given it life is the Giver of Life to the dead. Indeed, He is competent over all things.◆   *(Qur'an 41: 39)*

كَيْفَ تَكْفُرُونَ بِٱللَّهِ وَكُنتُمْ أَمْوَٰتًا فَأَحْيَٰكُمْ ثُمَّ يُمِيتُكُمْ ثُمَّ يُحْيِيكُمْ ثُمَّ إِلَيْهِ تُرْجَعُونَ ﴿٢٨﴾   (سورة ٱلْبَقَرَة: ٢٨)

◆How can you reject faith in Allah, seeing that you were without life, and He gave you life; then will He cause you to die, and will again bring you to life; and again to Him you will return.◆   *(Qur'an 2: 28)*

يَٰٓأَيُّهَا ٱلنَّاسُ إِن كُنتُمْ فِى رَيْبٍ مِّنَ ٱلْبَعْثِ فَإِنَّا خَلَقْنَٰكُم مِّن تُرَابٍ ثُمَّ مِن نُّطْفَةٍ ثُمَّ مِنْ عَلَقَةٍ ثُمَّ مِن مُّضْغَةٍ مُّخَلَّقَةٍ وَغَيْرِ مُخَلَّقَةٍ لِّنُبَيِّنَ لَكُمْ وَنُقِرُّ فِى ٱلْأَرْحَامِ مَا نَشَآءُ إِلَىٰٓ أَجَلٍ مُّسَمًّى ثُمَّ نُخْرِجُكُمْ طِفْلًا ثُمَّ لِتَبْلُغُوٓا۟ أَشُدَّكُمْ وَمِنكُم مَّن يُتَوَفَّىٰ وَمِنكُم مَّن يُرَدُّ إِلَىٰٓ أَرْذَلِ ٱلْعُمُرِ لِكَيْلَا يَعْلَمَ مِنۢ بَعْدِ عِلْمٍ شَيْـًٔا وَتَرَى ٱلْأَرْضَ هَامِدَةً فَإِذَآ أَنزَلْنَا عَلَيْهَا ٱلْمَآءَ ٱهْتَزَّتْ وَرَبَتْ وَأَنۢبَتَتْ مِن كُلِّ زَوْجٍۭ بَهِيجٍ ﴿٥﴾ ذَٰلِكَ بِأَنَّ ٱللَّهَ هُوَ ٱلْحَقُّ وَأَنَّهُۥ يُحْىِ ٱلْمَوْتَىٰ وَأَنَّهُۥ عَلَىٰ كُلِّ شَىْءٍ قَدِيرٌ ﴿٦﴾ وَأَنَّ ٱلسَّاعَةَ ءَاتِيَةٌ لَّا رَيْبَ فِيهَا وَأَنَّ ٱللَّهَ يَبْعَثُ مَن فِى ٱلْقُبُورِ ﴿٧﴾   (سورة ٱلْحَجّ: ٥-٧)

◆O people, if you should be in doubt about the Resurrection, then [consider that] indeed, We created you from dust, then from a sperm-drop, then from a clinging clot, and then from a lump of flesh, formed and unformed — that We may show you. And We settle in the wombs whom We will for a specified term, then We bring you out as a child, and then [We develop you] that you may reach your [time of] maturity. And among you is he who is taken in [early] death, and among you is he who is returned to the most decrepit [old] age so that he knows, after [once having] knowledge, nothing. And you see the earth barren, but when We send down upon it rain, it quivers and swells and grows [something] of every beautiful kind. That is because Allah is the Truth and because He gives life to the dead and because He is over all things competent. And [that they may know] that the Hour is coming — no doubt about it — and that Allah will resurrect those in the graves.❩   *(Qur'an 22: 5-7)*

Muslims believe that their first life in this world constitutes a trial and an examination period during which they prepare themselves either for good or for ill in the next life of infinite duration. The Day of Judgement may be compared to the ending of an examination, during which the teacher will ask each individual student, "What were you doing during the examination?" and will then evaluate the work s/he hands in. For although a person's body dies, the soul and personality have an existence extending beyond the present life. It is a continuous entity whose inner state will accompany it into the hereafter. It is this state with one's deeds, which will determine one's ultimate destiny.[16]

The essence of such an examination is so that Allah (ﷻ) may test people as to whether they will control their vain desires and obey Him, by choosing with their own free will to submit to Him alone, love Him, obey Him and worship Him alone even though they have their our own freedom to do otherwise. When people use their God-given intellect to choose the path of Allah (ﷻ) shown them by His prophets and messengers, then they will surely have passed the test of this life. Otherwise they fail, as Allah (ﷻ) says:

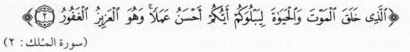

﴿ٱلَّذِى خَلَقَ ٱلْمَوْتَ وَٱلْحَيَوٰةَ لِيَبْلُوَكُمْ أَيُّكُمْ أَحْسَنُ عَمَلًا وَهُوَ ٱلْعَزِيزُ ٱلْغَفُورُ ۝﴾

(سورة المُلك : ٢)

‹[He] Who created death and life to test you [as to] which of you is best in deeds — and He is the Exalted in might, the Forgiving.›

(Qur'an 67: 2)

﴿أَحَسِبَ ٱلنَّاسُ أَن يُتْرَكُوٓاْ أَن يَقُولُوٓاْ ءَامَنَّا وَهُمْ لَا يُفْتَنُونَ ۝ وَلَقَدْ فَتَنَّا ٱلَّذِينَ مِن قَبْلِهِمْ فَلَيَعْلَمَنَّ ٱللَّهُ ٱلَّذِينَ صَدَقُواْ وَلَيَعْلَمَنَّ ٱلْكَٰذِبِينَ ۝﴾

(سورة العنكبوت: ٢-٣)

‹Do people think that they will be left to say: We believe, and they will not be tried? But We have certainly tried those before them and Allah will surely make evident those who are truthful, and He will surely make evident the liars.›

(Qur'an 29: 2-3)

﴿وَلَنَبْلُوَنَّكُم بِشَىْءٍ مِّنَ ٱلْخَوْفِ وَٱلْجُوعِ وَنَقْصٍ مِّنَ ٱلْأَمْوَٰلِ وَٱلْأَنفُسِ وَٱلثَّمَرَٰتِ وَبَشِّرِ ٱلصَّٰبِرِينَ ۝ ٱلَّذِينَ إِذَآ أَصَٰبَتْهُم مُّصِيبَةٌ قَالُوٓاْ إِنَّا لِلَّهِ وَإِنَّآ إِلَيْهِ رَٰجِعُونَ ۝ أُوْلَٰٓئِكَ عَلَيْهِمْ صَلَوَٰتٌ مِّن رَّبِّهِمْ وَرَحْمَةٌ وَأُوْلَٰٓئِكَ هُمُ ٱلْمُهْتَدُونَ ۝﴾

(سورة البَقَرَة: ١٥٥-١٥٧)

‹And We will surely test you with something of fear, and hunger and a loss of wealth and lives and fruits, but give good tidings to the patient, who, when disaster strikes them say: Indeed we belong to Allah, and indeed to Him we will return. Those are the ones upon whom are blessings from their Lord and mercy. And it is those who are the [rightly] guided.›

(Qur'an 2: 155-157)

﴿أَمْ حَسِبْتُمْ أَن تَدْخُلُواْ ٱلْجَنَّةَ وَلَمَّا يَأْتِكُم مَّثَلُ ٱلَّذِينَ خَلَوْاْ مِن قَبْلِكُم مَّسَّتْهُمُ ٱلْبَأْسَاءُ وَٱلضَّرَّاءُ وَزُلْزِلُواْ حَتَّىٰ يَقُولَ ٱلرَّسُولُ وَٱلَّذِينَ ءَامَنُواْ مَعَهُ مَتَىٰ نَصْرُ ٱللَّهِ أَلَآ إِنَّ نَصْرَ ٱللَّهِ قَرِيبٌ ۝﴾

(سورة البَقَرَة: ٢١٤)

‹Or do you think that you will enter paradise while such [trial] has not yet come to you as came to those who passed on before you?

They were touched by poverty and hardship and were shaken until [even their] messenger and those who believed with him said: When is the help of Allah? Unquestionably, the help of Allah is near.⟩

(Qur'an 2: 214)

This is also the path of continuous struggle in this life that Jesus Christ the son of Mary (ﷺ) talked about in one of his sermons, as recorded in the Holy Bible:

> And he went through the cities and villages, teaching, and journeying toward Jerusalem. Then said one unto him, Lord, are there few that will be saved? And he said unto them, strive to enter in at the strait gate: for many, I say unto you, will seek to enter in, and shall not be able. When once the master of the house is risen up, and hath shut the door, and ye begin to stand without, and to knock at the door, saying, Lord, Lord, open unto us; and he shall answer and say unto you, I know you not whence ye are: Then shall ye begin to say, We have eaten and drunk in thy presence, and thou hast taught in our streets. But he shall say, I tell you, I know you not whence ye are; depart from me, all ye workers of iniquity. There shall be weeping and gnashing of teeth, when ye shall see Abraham, and Isaac, and Jacob, and all the prophets, in the kingdom of God, and you yourselves thrust out. And they shall come from the east, and from the west, and from the north, and from the south, and shall sit down in the kingdom of God. And, behold, there are last which shall be first, and there are first which shall be last. (Luke 13: 22-30 KJV)

The same scenario is vividly portrayed in the awe-inspiring language of the Glorious Qur'an in several places. These events of the Last Day will come when Allah (ﷻ) sees fit, at a moment known only to Him. This world will be brought to an end in a terrifying cosmic cataclysmic event, frightful beyond imagination. On the awesome Day of Judgement, the bodies of the dead will be raised up from their graves and rejoined with their souls, while at the same time those who are still alive on earth at that time will die and be joined to the assembly. All people, past and present, will then stand in front of Allah (ﷻ), as totally alone and helpless as they were when they first came into the world, to render their reckoning in the following words:

﴿ إِذَا ٱلسَّمَآءُ ٱنشَقَّتۡ ۝ وَأَذِنَتۡ لِرَبِّهَا وَحُقَّتۡ ۝ وَإِذَا ٱلۡأَرۡضُ مُدَّتۡ ۝ وَأَلۡقَتۡ مَا فِيهَا وَتَخَلَّتۡ ۝ وَأَذِنَتۡ لِرَبِّهَا وَحُقَّتۡ ۝ يَٰٓأَيُّهَا ٱلۡإِنسَٰنُ إِنَّكَ كَادِحٌ إِلَىٰ رَبِّكَ كَدۡحٗا فَمُلَٰقِيهِ ۝ فَأَمَّا مَنۡ أُوتِيَ كِتَٰبَهُۥ بِيَمِينِهِۦ ۝ فَسَوۡفَ يُحَاسَبُ حِسَابٗا يَسِيرٗا ۝ وَيَنقَلِبُ إِلَىٰٓ أَهۡلِهِۦ مَسۡرُورٗا ۝ وَأَمَّا مَنۡ أُوتِيَ كِتَٰبَهُۥ وَرَآءَ ظَهۡرِهِۦ ۝ فَسَوۡفَ يَدۡعُواْ ثُبُورٗا ۝ وَيَصۡلَىٰ سَعِيرًا ۝ إِنَّهُۥ كَانَ فِيٓ أَهۡلِهِۦ مَسۡرُورًا ۝ إِنَّهُۥ ظَنَّ أَن لَّن يَحُورَ ۝ بَلَىٰٓ إِنَّ رَبَّهُۥ كَانَ بِهِۦ بَصِيرٗا ۝ فَلَآ أُقۡسِمُ بِٱلشَّفَقِ ۝ وَٱلَّيۡلِ وَمَا وَسَقَ ۝ وَٱلۡقَمَرِ إِذَا ٱتَّسَقَ ۝ لَتَرۡكَبُنَّ طَبَقًا عَن طَبَقٖ ۝ ﴾

(سورة الانشقاق: ١-١٩)

﴿When the sky has split [open]. And has listened [responded] to its Lord and was obligated [to do so]. And when the earth has been extended. And has cast out that within it and relinquished [it]. And has listened [responded] to its Lord and was obligated [to do so]. O humankind, indeed you are labouring toward your Lord with [great] exertion and will meet it. Then as for he who is given his record in his right hand, he will be judged with an easy account. And return to his people in happiness. But as for he who is given his record behind his back, he will cry out for destruction. And [enter to] burn in a blaze. Indeed, he had [once] been among his people in happiness; indeed, he had thought he would never return [to Allah]. But yes! Indeed, his Lord was ever, of him, Watching. So I swear by the twilight glow. And [by] the night and what it envelops and [by] the moon when it becomes full [that] you will surely embark upon [experience] state after state.﴾

(Qur'an 84: 1-19)

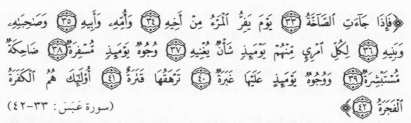

(سورة عَبَس : ٣٣-٤٢)

❨But when there comes the Deafening Blast. On that Day a man will flee from his brother, his mother, his father, his wife and his children. For every person, that Day, will be a matter adequate for him. [Some] faces that Day, will be bright: laughing, rejoicing at good news. And [other] faces, that Day, will have dust upon them. Humiliation will cover them. Those are the disbelievers, the wicked ones.❩

(Qur'an 80: 33-42)

Muslims believe that it is by struggling continuously to remain on this straight path and going through the tests and trials from Allah (ﷻ) that a believer grows in faith and endures the temptations of Satan; that it is by living a righteous life on this earth that one may qualify on the Day of Judgement to earn the grace of Allah (ﷻ) so as to be admitted to paradise. As for those who deny Allah and reject His guidance, who devote themselves to the worship of other deities other than Allah (ﷻ), and persist in doing evil deeds, they will be consigned to a fearsome and terrible abode in which their companions will be others who, like themselves are completely alienated from Allah (ﷻ). There, they will be in a state of enduring torment and agony from which there will be no respite. They will long to return to the world in order to live their lives differently in the light of their present knowledge of reality, but alas, the examination will have been over and all books closed, and they will have no choice but to acknowledge the absolute justice of their destiny, which is due to what they had done wrong and not done right, in spite of all the clear warnings which were sent to guide them. Allah (ﷻ) says about this dreadful day:

﴿وَنُفِخَ فِي ٱلصُّورِ فَصَعِقَ مَن فِي ٱلسَّمَٰوَٰتِ وَمَن فِي ٱلْأَرْضِ إِلَّا مَن شَآءَ ٱللَّهُ ثُمَّ نُفِخَ فِيهِ أُخْرَىٰ فَإِذَا هُمْ قِيَامٌ يَنظُرُونَ ۝ وَأَشْرَقَتِ ٱلْأَرْضُ بِنُورِ رَبِّهَا وَوُضِعَ ٱلْكِتَٰبُ وَجِا۟ىٓءَ بِٱلنَّبِيِّۦنَ وَٱلشُّهَدَآءِ وَقُضِيَ بَيْنَهُم بِٱلْحَقِّ وَهُمْ لَا يُظْلَمُونَ ۝ وَوُفِّيَتْ كُلُّ نَفْسٍ مَّا عَمِلَتْ وَهُوَ أَعْلَمُ بِمَا يَفْعَلُونَ ۝ وَسِيقَ ٱلَّذِينَ كَفَرُوٓا۟ إِلَىٰ جَهَنَّمَ زُمَرًا حَتَّىٰٓ إِذَا جَآءُوهَا فُتِحَتْ أَبْوَٰبُهَا وَقَالَ لَهُمْ خَزَنَتُهَآ أَلَمْ يَأْتِكُمْ رُسُلٌ مِّنكُمْ يَتْلُونَ عَلَيْكُمْ ءَايَٰتِ رَبِّكُمْ وَيُنذِرُونَكُمْ لِقَآءَ يَوْمِكُمْ هَٰذَا قَالُوا۟ بَلَىٰ وَلَٰكِنْ حَقَّتْ كَلِمَةُ ٱلْعَذَابِ عَلَى ٱلْكَٰفِرِينَ ۝ قِيلَ ٱدْخُلُوٓا۟ أَبْوَٰبَ جَهَنَّمَ خَٰلِدِينَ فِيهَا فَبِئْسَ مَثْوَى ٱلْمُتَكَبِّرِينَ ۝ وَسِيقَ ٱلَّذِينَ ٱتَّقَوْا۟ رَبَّهُمْ إِلَى ٱلْجَنَّةِ زُمَرًا حَتَّىٰٓ إِذَا جَآءُوهَا وَفُتِحَتْ أَبْوَٰبُهَا وَقَالَ لَهُمْ خَزَنَتُهَا سَلَٰمٌ عَلَيْكُمْ طِبْتُمْ فَٱدْخُلُوهَا خَٰلِدِينَ ۝ وَقَالُوا۟ ٱلْحَمْدُ لِلَّهِ ٱلَّذِى صَدَقَنَا وَعْدَهُ وَأَوْرَثَنَا ٱلْأَرْضَ نَتَبَوَّأُ مِنَ ٱلْجَنَّةِ حَيْثُ نَشَآءُ فَنِعْمَ أَجْرُ ٱلْعَٰمِلِينَ ۝ وَتَرَى ٱلْمَلَٰٓئِكَةَ حَآفِّينَ مِنْ حَوْلِ ٱلْعَرْشِ يُسَبِّحُونَ بِحَمْدِ رَبِّهِمْ وَقُضِيَ بَيْنَهُم بِٱلْحَقِّ وَقِيلَ ٱلْحَمْدُ لِلَّهِ رَبِّ ٱلْعَٰلَمِينَ ۝﴾ (سورة الزُّمَر: ٦٨–٧٥)

{And the horn will be blown, and whoever is in the heavens and whoever is on the earth will fall dead except whom Allah wills. Then it will be blown again, and at once they will be standing, looking on. And the earth will shine with the light of its Lord and the record [of deeds] will be placed, and the prophets and the witnesses will be brought, and it will be judged between them in truth, and they will not be wronged. And every soul will be compensated fully for what it did; and He is most knowing of what they do. And those who disbelieved will be driven to hell in groups until, when they reach it, its gates are opened and its keepers will say: Did there not come to you messengers from among you, reciting to you the verses of your Lord and warning you of the meeting of this Day of yours? They will say: Yes. But the word [decree] of punishment has come into effect upon the disbelievers. [To them] it will be said: Enter the gates of hell to abide eternally therein — and wretched is the residence of the arrogant. But those who feared their Lord will be driven to paradise in groups until, when they reach it while its gates have been opened and its keepers say: Peace be upon you; you have become pure; so enter it to abide eternally therein. [They will enter] and they will say: All praise to Allah, Who has fulfilled for us His promise and made us inherit the earth, [so] we may settle in paradise wherever we will. Excellent is the reward of [righteous] workers. And you will see the angels surrounding the Throne, exalting [Allah] with praise of their Lord. And it will be judged between them in truth, and it will be said: [All] praise to Allah, Lord of the worlds.   *(Qur'an 39: 68-75)*

Muslims believe that these two states of heaven and hell will be experienced in the physical form by the new bodies with which Allah (ﷻ) will resurrect humanity; these bodies will not merely be spiritual ones or psychic states. Although their exact nature may not fully be known or understood by us, the Qur'an is very clear about some of the experiences that the inhabitants of heaven and hell will go through. This will remind them of their life on earth: that the beauty and happiness in heaven will far exceed anything imaginable, and the ultimate triumph and bliss in paradise will be nearness to Allah (ﷻ) and seeing Him with the naked eye.

As for those who deserve hell, theirs will be a temporary or permanent state of torture depending on their inner condition and the nature and extent of their sins. Thus the Qur'an describes hell as a state of intense, fearful burning and agony without respite, among the most horrifyingly loathsome surroundings and companions, but the most excruciating and awful part of the suffering in hell will be the terrible inescapable awareness that hellfire is their final eternal destiny, which they deserved and brought upon themselves by rejecting Allah (ﷻ) and ignoring the guidance conveyed to them through His messengers. Allah (ﷻ) says:

وَأُزْلِفَتِ ٱلْجَنَّةُ لِلْمُتَّقِينَ غَيْرَ بَعِيدٍ ﴿٣١﴾ هَٰذَا مَا تُوعَدُونَ لِكُلِّ أَوَّابٍ حَفِيظٍ ﴿٣٢﴾ مَّنْ خَشِيَ ٱلرَّحْمَٰنَ بِٱلْغَيْبِ وَجَاءَ بِقَلْبٍ مُّنِيبٍ ﴿٣٣﴾ ٱدْخُلُوهَا بِسَلَٰمٍ ذَٰلِكَ يَوْمُ ٱلْخُلُودِ ﴿٣٤﴾ لَهُم مَّا يَشَاءُونَ فِيهَا وَلَدَيْنَا مَزِيدٌ ﴿٣٥﴾ (سورة ق: ٣١-٣٥)

﴾And paradise will be brought near to the righteous, not far. [It will be said]: This is what you were promised — for every returner [to Allah in sincere repentance] and keeper [of His covenant] who feared the Most Merciful unseen, and came with a repentant heart. Enter it in peace. This is the Day of Eternity. They will have whatever they wish therein, and with Us is more.﴿
(Qur'an 50: 31-35)

وَيَوْمَ يُعْرَضُ ٱلَّذِينَ كَفَرُوا عَلَى ٱلنَّارِ أَلَيْسَ هَٰذَا بِٱلْحَقِّ قَالُوا بَلَىٰ وَرَبِّنَا قَالَ فَذُوقُوا ٱلْعَذَابَ بِمَا كُنتُمْ تَكْفُرُونَ ﴿٣٤﴾ (سورة الأحقاف: ٣٤)

﴾And the Day those who disbelieved are exposed to the Fire [it will be said]: Is this not the truth? They will say: Yes by our Lord. He will say: Then taste the punishment because you used to disbelieve.﴿
(Qur'an 46: 34)

إِنَّ ٱلْمُجْرِمِينَ فِي عَذَابِ جَهَنَّمَ خَالِدُونَ ﴿٧٤﴾ لَا يُفَتَّرُ عَنْهُمْ وَهُمْ فِيهِ مُبْلِسُونَ ﴿٧٥﴾ وَمَا ظَلَمْنَاهُمْ وَلَٰكِن كَانُوا هُمُ ٱلظَّالِمِينَ ﴿٧٦﴾ (سورة الزخرف: ٧٤-٧٦)

﴾Indeed, the criminals will be in the punishment of hell, abiding eternally. It will not be allowed to subside for them, and they, therein, are in despair. And We did not wrong them, but it was they who were the wrongdoers.﴿
(Qur'an 43: 74-76)

So in Islamic theology, Allah (ﷻ) will be the Master of the Day of Judgement and will judge humankind with absolute justice, for He is the wisest of Judges. Allah (ﷻ) says:

لَقَدْ خَلَقْنَا ٱلْإِنسَٰنَ فِي أَحْسَنِ تَقْوِيمٍ ﴿٤﴾ ثُمَّ رَدَدْنَٰهُ أَسْفَلَ سَٰفِلِينَ ﴿٥﴾ إِلَّا ٱلَّذِينَ

ءَامَنُوا وَعَمِلُوا الصَّٰلِحَٰتِ فَلَهُمْ أَجْرٌ غَيْرُ مَمْنُونٍ ۝ فَمَا يُكَذِّبُكَ بَعْدُ بِالدِّينِ ۝ أَلَيْسَ

اللَّهُ بِأَحْكَمِ الْحَٰكِمِينَ ۝ ﴾   (سورة التين: ٤-٨)

❨We have certainly created the human in the best of stature; then we return him to the lowest of the low, except for those who believe and do righteous deeds, for they will have a reward uninterrupted. So what yet causes you to deny the recompense? Is not Allah the Most Just of Judges?❩

(Qur'an 95: 4-8)

According to the Qur'an, all the prophets and their people to whom they were sent will stand in front of the justice of Allah (ﷻ), including Jesus (ﷺ) and his people, the children of Israel. Allah says:

﴿فَلَنَسْـَٔلَنَّ الَّذِينَ أُرْسِلَ إِلَيْهِمْ وَلَنَسْـَٔلَنَّ الْمُرْسَلِينَ ۝ فَلَنَقُصَّنَّ عَلَيْهِم بِعِلْمٍ

وَمَا كُنَّا غَآئِبِينَ ۝ وَالْوَزْنُ يَوْمَئِذٍ الْحَقُّ فَمَن ثَقُلَتْ مَوَٰزِينُهُۥ فَأُولَٰٓئِكَ هُمُ

الْمُفْلِحُونَ ۝ وَمَنْ خَفَّتْ مَوَٰزِينُهُۥ فَأُولَٰٓئِكَ الَّذِينَ خَسِرُوٓا أَنفُسَهُم بِمَا كَانُوا

بِـَٔايَٰتِنَا يَظْلِمُونَ ۝ ﴾   (سورة الأعراف: ٦-٩)

❨Then We will surely question those to whom [a message] was sent, and We will surely question the messengers. Then We will surely relate [their deeds] to them with knowledge, and We were not [at all] absent. And the weighing [of deeds] that day will be the truth. So those whose scales are heavy, it is they who will be the successful. And those whose scales are light, they are the ones who have ruined themselves for what injustice they were doing to Our verses.❩

(Qur'an 7: 6-9)

﴿وَإِذْ قَالَ اللَّهُ يَٰعِيسَى ابْنَ مَرْيَمَ ءَأَنتَ قُلْتَ لِلنَّاسِ اتَّخِذُونِي وَأُمِّيَ إِلَٰهَيْنِ مِن

دُونِ اللَّهِ قَالَ سُبْحَٰنَكَ مَا يَكُونُ لِيٓ أَنْ أَقُولَ مَا لَيْسَ لِي بِحَقٍّ إِن كُنتُ قُلْتُهُۥ فَقَدْ

عَلِمْتَهُۥ تَعْلَمُ مَا فِي نَفْسِي وَلَآ أَعْلَمُ مَا فِي نَفْسِكَ إِنَّكَ أَنتَ عَلَّٰمُ الْغُيُوبِ ۝ مَا

قُلْتُ لَهُمْ إِلَّا مَآ أَمَرْتَنِي بِهِۦٓ أَنِ اعْبُدُوا اللَّهَ رَبِّي وَرَبَّكُمْ وَكُنتُ عَلَيْهِمْ شَهِيدًا مَّا دُمْتُ

فِيهِمْ فَلَمَّا تَوَفَّيْتَنِي كُنتَ أَنتَ ٱلرَّقِيبَ عَلَيْهِمْ وَأَنتَ عَلَىٰ كُلِّ شَىْءٍ شَهِيدٌ ۝ إِن
تُعَذِّبْهُمْ فَإِنَّهُمْ عِبَادُكَ وَإِن تَغْفِرْ لَهُمْ فَإِنَّكَ أَنتَ ٱلْعَزِيزُ ٱلْحَكِيمُ ۝ قَالَ ٱللَّهُ هَٰذَا يَوْمُ
يَنفَعُ ٱلصَّٰدِقِينَ صِدْقُهُمْ لَهُمْ جَنَّٰتٌ تَجْرِى مِن تَحْتِهَا ٱلْأَنْهَٰرُ خَٰلِدِينَ فِيهَا أَبَدًا رَّضِىَ
ٱللَّهُ عَنْهُمْ وَرَضُوا۟ عَنْهُ ذَٰلِكَ ٱلْفَوْزُ ٱلْعَظِيمُ ۝ لِلَّهِ مُلْكُ ٱلسَّمَٰوَٰتِ وَٱلْأَرْضِ وَمَا فِيهِنَّ
وَهُوَ عَلَىٰ كُلِّ شَىْءٍ قَدِيرٌ ۝   ﴾ (سورة المائدة: ١١٦–١٢٠)

❨And [beware the day] when Allah will say: O Jesus, son of Mary, did you say to people: Take me and my mother as deities besides Allah? He will say: Exalted are You! It was not for me to say that to which I have no right; if I had said it, You would have known it. You know what is within me, and I do not know what is within You. Indeed, it is You Who is Knower of the unseen. I said nothing to them except what You commanded me: to worship Allah, my Lord and your Lord. And I was a witness over them as long as I was among them; but when You took me up, You were the Observer over them, and You are, over all things, Witness. If you should punish them, indeed they are your servants; but if you forgive them, indeed it is You Who are the Exalted in might, the Wise. Allah will say: This is the day when the truthful will benefit from their truthfulness. For them are gardens [in paradise] beneath which rivers flow, wherein they will abide forever, Allah being pleased with them, and they with Him. That is the great attainment. To Allah belongs the dominion of the heavens and the earth and whatever is within them. And He is over all things Competent.❩   *(Qur'an 5: 116-120)*

These are some of the many vivid accounts of the Day of Resurrection and subsequent judgement that Muslims believe in as revelation from God. In fact, belief in the Last Day includes all that will happen after death, such as the trial in the grave with its torment or bliss therein, the bridge set over hellfire, the balance or scales of

God's justice, reckoning, reward and punishment, the giving of records, and paradise and hellfire.

To a conscious and devout Muslim this clear reality of the future life is always in his or her mind, because it is this awareness that keeps the present life, which at times is full of intense happiness while at other times the deepest of pain, in true perspective — the perspective that the present life is a temporary passing station where one is tested in order to qualify and prepare oneself for the long journey back to one's true future home. This understanding is essential for the maintenance of mental balance and stability amidst the unpleasant difficulties of this worldly life. At the same time no Muslim, even the best among them, prides him/herself on guaranteed entry into paradise; on the contrary, the more conscious and God-fearing s/he is, the more s/he becomes aware of his or her shortcomings and weaknesses. Therefore, Muslims, knowing that Allah (ﷻ) alone is the controller of life and death, and that death may come to them at any moment, know they must hasten to carry out such good deeds as will benefit their future existence and merit the pleasure of their Lord, so as to look forward, hoping for His mercy and grace.

Contrary to this, in Christianity the hereafter (life after death) is not very clear. People are not told exactly how the judgement will be, what rewards they will get in paradise, and what kinds of punishments are awaiting the wrongdoers. The whole picture of life after death in Christianity is spiritualized and mystified. Christians believe that those who will deserve paradise will be walking with God in the gardens, but that everything in paradise is spiritual, not physical.

Furthermore, it is claimed in Christianity that Jesus (ﷺ) will be the judge and will come and reward people accordingly, yet Jesus (ﷺ) himself claims that he has no knowledge of the hour of judgement.

But of that day and that hour knows no man, no, not the Angels
who are in heaven, neither the son, but the Father. (Mark 13:32
KJV)

This is the same understanding according to Islam: that only Allah
(عَزَّوَجَلَّ) knows the hour of Judgement and He is the one to judge all
people with absolute justice based on their true faith in Him and their
righteous deeds done solely for His sake. Allah, the Exalted, the
Almighty says:

$$﴿إِنَّ ٱللَّهَ عِندَهُۥ عِلْمُ ٱلسَّاعَةِ وَيُنَزِّلُ ٱلْغَيْثَ وَيَعْلَمُ مَا فِى ٱلْأَرْحَامِ ۖ وَمَا تَدْرِى نَفْسٌ مَّاذَا تَكْسِبُ غَدًا ۖ وَمَا تَدْرِى نَفْسٌ بِأَيِّ أَرْضٍ تَمُوتُ ۚ إِنَّ ٱللَّهَ عَلِيمٌ خَبِيرٌ ۝٣٤﴾$$

(سورة لقمَان : ٣٤)

﴾Indeed Allah [alone] has the knowledge of the hour and sends down
the rain and knows what is in the wombs. And no soul perceives what
it will earn tomorrow, and no soul perceives in what land it will die.
Indeed, Allah is Knowing and Acquainted with all things.﴿

(Qur'an 31: 34)

The concept of belief in divine destiny

Muslims and Christians believe in divine destiny. This represents
the belief in Allah's measure and plans, His limitless power to do as
He wills, yet it includes the fact that it is against the majesty of Allah
(عَزَّوَجَلَّ) to do things that are against His perfection, majesty and essence.
For example, Allah (عَزَّوَجَلَّ), who is the Creator, cannot create another
Creator nor can He change His form to take the form of His creation,
like becoming a man or giving birth, or having a wife or son. Both the
Qur'an and the Bible bear witness about this understanding.

بَدِيعُ ٱلسَّمَوَتِ وَٱلْأَرْضِ أَنَّىٰ يَكُونُ لَهُۥ وَلَدٌ وَلَمْ تَكُن لَّهُۥ صَـٰحِبَةٌ وَخَلَقَ كُلَّ
شَىْءٍ وَهُوَ بِكُلِّ شَىْءٍ عَلِيمٌ ۞ ذَٰلِكُمُ ٱللَّهُ رَبُّكُمْ لَا إِلَـٰهَ إِلَّا هُوَ خَـٰلِقُ
كُلِّ شَىْءٍ فَٱعْبُدُوهُ وَهُوَ عَلَىٰ كُلِّ شَىْءٍ وَكِيلٌ ۞ لَّا تُدْرِكُهُ
ٱلْأَبْصَـٰرُ وَهُوَ يُدْرِكُ ٱلْأَبْصَـٰرَ وَهُوَ ٱللَّطِيفُ ٱلْخَبِيرُ ۞ قَدْ جَآءَكُم بَصَآئِرُ مِن
رَّبِّكُمْ فَمَنْ أَبْصَرَ فَلِنَفْسِهِۦ وَمَنْ عَمِيَ فَعَلَيْهَا وَمَآ أَنَا۠ عَلَيْكُم بِحَفِيظٍ ۞

(سورة الأنعَام: ١٠١–١٠٤)

◆He is the Originator of the heavens and the earth. How could He
have a son when He does not have a companion [wife] and He
created all things? And He is, of all things, Knowing. That is Allah,
your Lord; there is none worthy of worship other than Him, the
Creator of all things, so worship Him. And He is Disposer of all
things. Vision cannot perceive Him, but He perceives [all] vision, and
He is the Subtle, the Acquainted. There has come to you
enlightenment from your Lord. So whoever will see does so for [the
benefit of] his soul, and whoever is blind [does harm] against it. And
[say]: I am not a guardian over you.◆   *(Qur'an 6: 101-104)*

> God is not a man, that he should lie; neither the son of man, that
> he should repent: hath he said, and shall he not do it? or hath he
> spoken, and shall he not make it good? (Numbers 23:19 KJV)

> How then can man be justified with God? or how can he be
> clean that is born of a woman? Behold even to the moon, and it
> shineth not; yea, the stars are not pure in his sight. How much
> less man, that is a worm? and the son of man, which is a worm?
> (Job 25:4-6 KJV)

In Islam, the belief in divine destiny comprises four major issues,
namely:

That Allah's Knowledge encompasses all things

Allah (🙶) knows what has been and what will be. He is aware of everything concerning all human beings, those that have been born and will be born, their provisions and sustenance, their appointed terms on earth, their deeds, and everything else relating to them. Nothing is hidden from Him; His knowledge encompasses all things, as He says:

﴿۞ وَعِندَهُۥ مَفَاتِحُ ٱلْغَيْبِ لَا يَعْلَمُهَآ إِلَّا هُوَ وَيَعْلَمُ مَا فِي ٱلْبَرِّ وَٱلْبَحْرِ وَمَا تَسْقُطُ مِن وَرَقَةٍ إِلَّا يَعْلَمُهَا وَلَا حَبَّةٍ فِي ظُلُمَٰتِ ٱلْأَرْضِ وَلَا رَطْبٍ وَلَا يَابِسٍ إِلَّا فِي كِتَٰبٍ مُّبِينٍ ﴿٥٩﴾﴾   (سورة الأنعام: ٥٩)

❨And with Him are the keys of the unseen; none knows them except Him. And He knows what is on the land and in the sea. Not a leaf falls but that He knows it. And no grain is there within the darkness of the earth and no moist or dry [thing] but that it is [written] in a clear record.❩   *(Qur'an 6: 59)*

﴿أَلَمْ تَرَ أَنَّ ٱللَّهَ يَعْلَمُ مَا فِي ٱلسَّمَٰوَٰتِ وَمَا فِي ٱلْأَرْضِ مَا يَكُونُ مِن نَّجْوَىٰ ثَلَٰثَةٍ إِلَّا هُوَ رَابِعُهُمْ وَلَا خَمْسَةٍ إِلَّا هُوَ سَادِسُهُمْ وَلَا أَدْنَىٰ مِن ذَٰلِكَ وَلَا أَكْثَرَ إِلَّا هُوَ مَعَهُمْ أَيْنَ مَا كَانُوا۟ ثُمَّ يُنَبِّئُهُم بِمَا عَمِلُوا۟ يَوْمَ ٱلْقِيَٰمَةِ إِنَّ ٱللَّهَ بِكُلِّ شَيْءٍ عَلِيمٌ ﴿٧﴾﴾

(سورة المجَادلة: ٧)

❨Have you not considered that Allah knows what is in the heavens and what is on the earth? There is no private conversation among three but that He is the fourth of them, nor among five but He is the sixth of them — and no less than that and no more, except that He is with them [by His knowledge] wherever they are. Then He will inform them of what they did, on the Day of Resurrection. Indeed Allah is the All-Knower of everything.❩   *(Qur'an 58: 7)*

﴿ ... لِتَعْلَمُوٓاْ أَنَّ ٱللَّهَ عَلَىٰ كُلِّ شَىْءٍ قَدِيرٌ وَأَنَّ ٱللَّهَ قَدْ أَحَاطَ بِكُلِّ شَىْءٍ عِلْمَۢا ۝ ﴾

(سورة الطَّلَاق : ١٢)

﴿...So that you may know that Allah Has power over all things and that Allah has encompassed all things in [His] knowledge.﴾

(Qur'an 65: 12)

That Allah (ﷻ) keeps all that He decrees in a detailed Book: the Preserved Tablet

﴿مَآ أَصَابَ مِن مُّصِيبَةٍ فِى ٱلْأَرْضِ وَلَا فِىٓ أَنفُسِكُمْ إِلَّا فِى كِتَٰبٍ مِّن قَبْلِ أَن نَّبْرَأَهَآ إِنَّ ذَٰلِكَ عَلَى ٱللَّهِ يَسِيرٌ ۝ ﴾

(سورة الحديد : ٢٢)

﴿No disaster strikes upon the earth or among yourselves except that it is in a register before We bring it into being — indeed that, for Allah, is easy.﴾

(Qur'an 57: 22)

﴿أَلَمْ تَعْلَمْ أَنَّ ٱللَّهَ يَعْلَمُ مَا فِى ٱلسَّمَآءِ وَٱلْأَرْضِ إِنَّ ذَٰلِكَ فِى كِتَٰبٍ إِنَّ ذَٰلِكَ عَلَى ٱللَّهِ يَسِيرٌ ۝ ﴾

(سورة الحَجّ : ٧٠)

﴿Do you not know that Allah knows what is in the heaven and on earth? Indeed, that is in a record. Indeed that, for Allah, is easy.﴾

(Qur'an 22: 70)

The belief that the Will of Allah (ﷻ) is absolute and powerful

Allah's Will is absolute and powerful, such that whatever He decrees must happen and whatever He has not decreed does not happen and will never come to pass. There is no power nor might except from Allah. Allah (ﷻ) says:

﴾ ...إِنَّ اللَّهَ يَفْعَلُ مَا يَشَاءُ ۞ ﴿ (سورة الحَجّ : ١٨)

﴾...Verily, Allah does what He wills.﴿ *(Qur'an 22: 18)*

﴾إِنَّمَا أَمْرُهُ إِذَا أَرَادَ شَيْئًا أَن يَقُولَ لَهُ كُن فَيَكُونُ ۞ ﴿ (سورة يَس : ٨٢)

﴾Verily, when He intends a thing, His Command is: Be! — and it is.﴿
(Qur'an 36: 82)

﴾وَمَا تَشَاؤُونَ إِلَّا أَن يَشَاءَ اللَّهُ رَبُّ الْعَلَمِينَ ۞ ﴿ (سورة التَّكوير : ٢٩)

﴾And you cannot will except as Allah Wills, the Lord of the worlds.﴿
(Qur'an 81: 29)

﴾قُل لَّن يُصِيبَنَا إِلَّا مَا كَتَبَ اللَّهُ لَنَا هُوَ مَوْلَىٰنَا وَعَلَى اللَّهِ فَلْيَتَوَكَّلِ الْمُؤْمِنُونَ ۞ ﴿ (سورة التَّوبَة : ٥١)

﴾Say: Never will we be struck except by what Allah has decreed for us; He is our protector. And upon Allah let the believers rely.﴿
(Qur'an 9: 51)

The belief that Allah (ﷻ) is the Creator of both good and bad

Allah (ﷻ) is the sole Creator of all things, both the good and the bad. Furthermore, whatever good or bad that He creates is done in His wisdom, for the benefit of his creatures.

﴾وَاللَّهُ خَلَقَكُمْ وَمَا تَعْمَلُونَ ۞ ﴿ (سورة الصَّافات : ٩٦)

﴾And Allah created you and whatever you do.﴿ *(Qur'an 37: 96)*

﴾قُلِ اللَّهُمَّ مَلِكَ الْمُلْكِ تُؤْتِي الْمُلْكَ مَن تَشَاءُ وَتَنزِعُ الْمُلْكَ مِمَّن تَشَاءُ وَتُعِزُّ مَن تَشَاءُ وَتُذِلُّ مَن تَشَاءُ بِيَدِكَ الْخَيْرُ إِنَّكَ عَلَى كُلِّ شَىْءٍ قَدِيرٌ ۞ ﴿
(سورة آل عِمرَان : ٢٦)

❨Say: O Allah! Lord of Sovereignty, You give sovereignty to whom You please, and You take sovereignty away from whom You will. You honour whom You will, and You humble whom You will. In Your hand is all Good. Verily, You have power over all things.❩

(Qur'an 3: 26)

In fact the absolute understanding of good and bad is only truly known by Allah (ﷻ) because human perception of good or bad is very limited due to being too weak, feeble, and narrow-minded to understand the subtleness and complexity of good and bad events. As such, what may seem bad may turn out to be good for our own benefit, and similarly what we may consider as good, may turn out to be bad and to our detriment. Allah (ﷻ) made this point very clear in the glorious Qur'an:

﴿ ... وَعَسَىٰٓ أَن تَكْرَهُواْ شَيْـًٔا وَهُوَ خَيْرٌ لَّكُمْ وَعَسَىٰٓ أَن تُحِبُّواْ شَيْـًٔا وَهُوَ شَرٌّ لَّكُمْ وَٱللَّهُ يَعْلَمُ وَأَنتُمْ لَا تَعْلَمُونَ ﴿٢١٦﴾ ﴾ (سورة البَقَرَة: ٢١٦)

❨...But perhaps you may hate a thing and it is good for you; and perhaps you may love a thing and it is bad for you. And Allah knows, while you know not.❩

(Qur'an 2: 216)

The most common misunderstanding about the concept of divine destiny is this: if all has been destined then why should one believe in Allah and struggle to do righteous deeds if one is already destined for hell? Prophet Muhammad (ﷺ) cautioned people about the subject of predestination, saying that when one is talking about this unseen and unknown premise, he should behave as if he is walking on thorns. First, no human being knows his or her place of destiny until s/he dies. Second, Allah (ﷻ) has given people intellect, divine guidance through the prophets, free will to choose between the straight path and the wrong path, as well as enough time in this life to make a wise choice among the many choices.

Consequently, when one chooses the wrong path that was already destined for one, Allah (ﷻ) makes that path easy for that person, and s/he eventually ends in his or her rightful place of destiny — hell. Similarly, when one chooses the right path that was written for one, Allah (ﷻ) makes that path easy for him or her, so that paradise eventually becomes his or her rightful place of destiny. Therefore Allah (ﷻ) does not force anyone to do anything; the power to choose between belief and disbelief, righteousness and sin, and good deeds and evil deeds is in the hands of humanity; therefore, one is punished for the wrong choice and rewarded for the right choice. This understanding can be derived from many verses of the Qur'an, as follows:

1. No human being knows what he is going to earn tomorrow, therefore no one can rightfully claim to know whether he or she is destined for hellfire or paradise. Allah says:

﴿إِنَّ ٱللَّهَ عِندَهُۥ عِلْمُ ٱلسَّاعَةِ وَيُنَزِّلُ ٱلْغَيْثَ وَيَعْلَمُ مَا فِى ٱلْأَرْحَامِ وَمَا تَدْرِى نَفْسٌ مَّاذَا تَكْسِبُ غَدًا وَمَا تَدْرِى نَفْسٌ بِأَىِّ أَرْضٍ تَمُوتُ إِنَّ ٱللَّهَ عَلِيمٌ خَبِيرٌ ﴿٣٤﴾﴾ (سورة لقمان: ٣٤)

❨Verily the knowledge of the Hour is with Allah [alone]. It is He Who sends down rain [wherever He wills] and He Who knows what is in the wombs. Nor does anyone know what it is that he will earn on the morrow; nor does anyone know in what land he is to die. Verily with Allah is full knowledge and He is acquainted [with all things].❩

(Qur'an 31: 34)

2. Allah (ﷻ) created humans and gave them all five senses as well as intellect and guidance through revelation, so that He (ﷻ) might help people in making the right choice, and that they might be grateful. Allah says:

﴿وَٱللَّهُ أَخْرَجَكُم مِّنۢ بُطُونِ أُمَّهَٰتِكُمْ لَا تَعْلَمُونَ شَيْئًا وَجَعَلَ لَكُمُ ٱلسَّمْعَ

وَٱلْأَبْصَٰرَ وَٱلْأَفْـِٔدَةَ لَعَلَّكُمْ تَشْكُرُونَ ۝٧٨   (سورة النحل : ٧٨)

❮And Allah brought you forth from the wombs of your mothers not knowing a thing, and He appointed for you hearing and vision and hearts [intellect] that perhaps you would be grateful.❯ *(Qur'an 16: 78)*

❮إِنَّا هَدَيْنَٰهُ ٱلسَّبِيلَ إِمَّا شَاكِرًا وَإِمَّا كَفُورًا ۝٣ إِنَّا أَعْتَدْنَا لِلْكَٰفِرِينَ سَلَٰسِلَا۟ وَأَغْلَٰلًا وَسَعِيرًا ۝٤ إِنَّ ٱلْأَبْرَارَ يَشْرَبُونَ مِن كَأْسٍ كَانَ مِزَاجُهَا كَافُورًا ۝٥❯

(سورة الإنسان : ٣-٥)

❮Indeed, We guided him to the way, be he grateful or be he ungrateful. Indeed, We have prepared for the disbelievers chains and shackles and a blaze. Indeed, the righteous will drink from a cup [of wine], whose mixture is of a sweet-smelling spring in paradise.❯

(Qur'an 76: 3-5)

❮أَيَحْسَبُ أَن لَّمْ يَرَهُۥٓ أَحَدٌ ۝٧ أَلَمْ نَجْعَل لَّهُۥ عَيْنَيْنِ ۝٨ وَلِسَانًا وَشَفَتَيْنِ ۝٩ وَهَدَيْنَٰهُ ٱلنَّجْدَيْنِ ۝١٠❯   (سورة البلد : ٧-١٠)

❮Does he think that none sees him? Have We not made for him two eyes? And a tongue and two lips? And have shown him the two ways [good and evil; truth and falsehood; wrong and right].❯

(Qur'an 90: 7-10)

❮وَقُلِ ٱلْحَقُّ مِن رَّبِّكُمْ فَمَن شَاءَ فَلْيُؤْمِن وَمَن شَاءَ فَلْيَكْفُرْ إِنَّا أَعْتَدْنَا لِلظَّٰلِمِينَ نَارًا أَحَاطَ بِهِمْ سُرَادِقُهَا وَإِن يَسْتَغِيثُوا۟ يُغَاثُوا۟ بِمَاءٍ كَٱلْمُهْلِ يَشْوِى ٱلْوُجُوهَ بِئْسَ ٱلشَّرَابُ وَسَاءَتْ مُرْتَفَقًا ۝٢٩ إِنَّ ٱلَّذِينَ ءَامَنُوا۟ وَعَمِلُوا۟ ٱلصَّٰلِحَٰتِ إِنَّا لَا نُضِيعُ أَجْرَ مَنْ أَحْسَنَ عَمَلًا ۝٣٠ أُو۟لَٰٓئِكَ لَهُمْ جَنَّٰتُ عَدْنٍ تَجْرِى مِن تَحْتِهِمُ ٱلْأَنْهَٰرُ يُحَلَّوْنَ فِيهَا مِنْ أَسَاوِرَ مِن ذَهَبٍ وَيَلْبَسُونَ ثِيَابًا خُضْرًا مِّن سُندُسٍ وَإِسْتَبْرَقٍ مُّتَّكِئِينَ فِيهَا عَلَى ٱلْأَرَائِكِ ... ۝٣١❯   (سورة الكهف : ٢٩-٣١)

❨And say: The truth is from your Lord, so whoever wills — let him believe; and whoever wills — let him disbelieve. Indeed, We have prepared for the wrongdoers a fire whose walls will surround them. And if they call for relief, they will be relieved with water like murky oil, which scalds [their] faces. Wretched is the drink, and evil is the resting place. Indeed, those who have believed and done righteous deeds — indeed, We will not allow to be lost the reward of any who did well in deeds. Those will have gardens of perpetual residence; beneath them rivers will flow. They will be adorned therein with bracelets of gold and will wear green garments of fine silk and brocade, reclining therein on adorned couches.❩ *(Qur'an 18: 29-31)*

3. Whosoever therefore, chooses the path of belief (which was destined for that person without their knowledge of their own destiny) then Allah (ﷻ) will make easy for that person that path until s/he enters paradise. Similarly, whoever chooses the path of disbelief, Allah (ﷻ) will leave them on that path, making it easy for them until they enter hellfire. Allah (ﷻ) said about this:

﴾وَمَن يُشَاقِقِ ٱلرَّسُولَ مِنۢ بَعْدِ مَا تَبَيَّنَ لَهُ ٱلْهُدَىٰ وَيَتَّبِعْ غَيْرَ سَبِيلِ ٱلْمُؤْمِنِينَ نُوَلِّهِۦ مَا تَوَلَّىٰ وَنُصْلِهِۦ جَهَنَّمَ وَسَآءَتْ مَصِيرًا ١١٥﴿   (سورة النِّسَاء: ١١٥)

❨And whoever opposes the Messenger after guidance has become clear to him and follows other than the way of the believers — We will give him what he has taken and drive him into hell, and evil it is as a destination.❩ ·
(Qur'an 4: 115)

﴾مَآ أَصَابَ مِن مُّصِيبَةٍ إِلَّا بِإِذْنِ ٱللَّهِ وَمَن يُؤْمِنۢ بِٱللَّهِ يَهْدِ قَلْبَهُۥ وَٱللَّهُ بِكُلِّ شَىْءٍ عَلِيمٌ ١١﴿   (سورة التَّغَابُن: ١١)

❨No disaster strikes except by permission of Allah. And whoever believes in Allah — He will guide his heart. And Allah is Knowing of all things.❩
(Qur'an 64: 11)

﴿وَأَنَّهُ هُوَ أَضْحَكَ وَأَبْكَى ﴾ ﴿٤٣﴾   (سورة النَّجْم: ٤٣)

﴾And that it is He [Allah] who makes [whomever He wills] laugh and [whomever He wills] weep.﴿   *(Qur'an 53: 43)*

Also on the authority of Abu 'Abdur-Raḥmân 'Abdullah ibn Mas'ood (رضي الله عنه), who said: «The Messenger of Allah (ﷺ), and he is the truthful, the trustworthy one, narrated to us: Verily the creation of each of you is brought together in his mother's womb for forty days in the form of a seed, then he is a clot of blood for a like period, then a morsel of flesh for a like period, then there is sent to him an angel who blows the breath of life (his spirit or soul) into him and who is commanded about four matters: to write down his (the human's) means of livelihood, his lifespan, his actions, and whether he will be happy or unhappy. By Allah, other than whom there is none worthy of worship, verily one of you behaves like the people of paradise until there is but an arm's length between him and it, and that which has been written overtakes him and so he behaves like the people of hellfire, and thus he enters it; and one of you behaves like the people of hellfire until there is but an arm's length between him and it, and that which has been written overtakes him and so he behaves like the people of paradise and thus he enters it.» (Bukhari)

This narration in many instances has been misunderstood by many Muslims and Christians alike and has resulted in many people making fatalistic statements which motivate people to reject faith in God and religion altogether. However, this narration should be understood in the light of the aforementioned discussion. If the narration is taken out of context of the above discussion, then people will be led to reject anything to do with faith and righteousness.

In a broad sense, the Christians also have the same principles dealing with · belief in divine destiny, with a few differences. According to *Easton's Bible Dictionary*:

The decrees of God are his eternal, unchangeable, holy, wise, and sovereign purpose, comprehending at once all things that ever were or will be in their causes, conditions, successions, and relations, and determining their certain fruition.[17]

The *Bible Dictionary* states that humans cannot comprehend fully the purpose or the full effects of God's plan, but we can observe aspects of it that we understand to be His decrees. The decrees of God are not limited in duration, and they are of two sorts: 'efficacious', which means that God brings it about directly, or 'permissive', which means that He achieves it via the work of His creatures.[18]

In yet another place, *Easton's Bible Dictionary* explains that the Christian understanding of predestination 'is beset with many difficulties', for it leaves the believer with unanswered questions, and no choice but to accept it, even without comprehending it.[19]

Chapter 2

Different Theological Understanding in Islam and Christianity

Contrast between Christianity and Islam

*I*slam and Christianity appear to be so similar in many respects, including the facts that they originate from the same location in the Middle East, being the Arabian Peninsula, and each claims a majority of followers. However, they are not actually or in reality the same. They are religions which are quite opposed to one another in their:

1. Doctrinal theology and understanding of God
2. Cultural foundations and practices
3. Moral and economic bases
4. Socio-political views of the life of this world
5. Concepts of religion as either an individual or communal affair

As Professor Huntington says in one of the most important books that has emerged since the end of the Cold War, the cause of the continued conflict between Muslims and Christians does not lie in 12th century Christian passion or 20th century Muslim fundamentalism but rather in the nature of the two religions and their civilizations. The conflict is clearly seen from the Muslims' concept of Islam as a way of life transcending all spheres of life, thus uniting religion and politics, versus narrow perceptions of

Christianity that separate the church from the state. Huntington
further contends that the continued conflicts also stem from the fact
that both Islam and Christianity claim monotheism in the sense that
both reject additional deities, and that as missionary religions, both
claim to be universal, thus wanting all non-believing human beings to
adhere to their respective beliefs. According to Huntington, Islam
from its origins spread by conquest, and when Christianity had the
opportunity it did the same, thus the parallels of the terms 'jihad' and
'crusade'. Although they are different ideologically, Huntington
asserts that they are the same and that makes the twin religions distinct
from other major world faiths.[1] At any rate, the two religions are not by
any means the same even though they may have many commonalities.

The meaning of Islam in brief

The word *Islam* literally means peace — peace between the
creatures and the Lord of all creation. This peace is gained by
submission and obedience to the will of Allah. Therefore, whenever
any creature submits and obeys the will of its Creator, Allah (ﷻ),
then it is described as *Muslim*. Allah (ﷻ) says:

$$﴿أَفَغَيْرَ دِينِ ٱللَّهِ يَبْغُونَ وَلَهُۥ أَسْلَمَ مَن فِي ٱلسَّمَٰوَٰتِ وَٱلْأَرْضِ طَوْعًا$$
$$وَكَرْهًا وَإِلَيْهِ يُرْجَعُونَ ۝﴾$$

(سورة آل عِمرَان: ٨٣)

❨Do they seek other than the religion of Allah? While all creatures in
the heavens and on earth have, willing or unwilling, submitted unto
His will, and to Him shall they all be returned.❩   *(Qur'an 3: 83)*

As such, when a human being submits to the one true Almighty
God, he or she becomes Muslim and forthwith Islam profoundly
transforms his or her thinking and behavior. In fact, there is no aspect
of a person's life, nor of the life of the society that is made up of such

people who have submitted to the will of Allah, that is not touched and transformed in keeping with the basic concepts of Islam, that of the Lordship and Sovereignty of Almighty God and humanity's responsibility to Him.

Islam's first requirement is belief and its second is that of action. The Islamic concepts and beliefs require certain attitudes toward life, toward one's own self, toward other human beings and the universe; a particular mode of worship, of family relations, manners, living habits and so on and to all aspects of life. This makes Islam not merely a religion, a hotchpotch of rites and rituals, or a utopian moral philosophy, but a total way of life, a complete system governing all aspects of humanity's existence, both individual and collective.[2]

Islam is an ideology that provides guidance in every facet of life or field of human activity. It is an all-embracing system, a social order, a polity, an economic ideology. In short, it is a perfect divine code of life. Thus it does not consist of a few moral teachings, presented by utopian philosophers, however extremely admirable, but of no avail in the practical walk of life. Its moral teachings are backed by sanctions, which make them living realities.

Islam has power with virtue, and justice with strength, so that the moral values may become enshrined in daily life of the individual and the society. The Islamic state is established for one purpose — of bidding virtue and forbidding evil, thus transforming the whole society into an ideal virtuous one, where every citizen is well taken care of. Allah (ﷻ) says:

﴿ٱلَّذِينَ إِن مَّكَّنَّٰهُمْ فِى ٱلْأَرْضِ أَقَامُوا۟ ٱلصَّلَوٰةَ وَءَاتَوُا۟ ٱلزَّكَوٰةَ وَأَمَرُوا۟ بِٱلْمَعْرُوفِ وَنَهَوْا۟ عَنِ ٱلْمُنكَرِ ۗ وَلِلَّهِ عَٰقِبَةُ ٱلْأُمُورِ ﴾ (سورة الحجّ: ٤١)

﴾Those who, when We establish them in the land, they establish regular prayers and give regular charity, enjoin right and forbid wrong and with Allah rests the end of all affairs.﴿ *(Qur'an 22: 41)*

The Islamic approach to moral problems does not resemble the approach of the philosophers; it aims at changing the system of life and reconstructing it in light of the moral teachings of Allah (ﷻ). It wants to establish the moral values and as such, is, on the one hand, a philosophy of life and, on the other, a scheme of action. Islam is not a lifeless moral philosophy; rather it is a living, dynamic, revolutionary way of life, a social system, and a state. Therefore, it uses the powers of the state for the establishment of justice and virtue.[3] There are many quotations from the Qur'an and sayings of Prophet Muhammad (ﷺ) that could sum up the meaning and practice of Islam in a nutshell. Below are just two from the Qur'an and narrations of Prophet Muhammad (ﷺ), which are self-explanatory.

﴿۞ لَّيْسَ ٱلْبِرَّ أَن تُوَلُّوا۟ وُجُوهَكُمْ قِبَلَ ٱلْمَشْرِقِ وَٱلْمَغْرِبِ وَلَٰكِنَّ ٱلْبِرَّ مَنْ ءَامَنَ بِٱللَّهِ وَٱلْيَوْمِ ٱلْأَخِرِ وَٱلْمَلَٰٓئِكَةِ وَٱلْكِتَٰبِ وَٱلنَّبِيِّۦنَ وَءَاتَى ٱلْمَالَ عَلَىٰ حُبِّهِۦ ذَوِى ٱلْقُرْبَىٰ وَٱلْيَتَٰمَىٰ وَٱلْمَسَٰكِينَ وَٱبْنَ ٱلسَّبِيلِ وَٱلسَّآئِلِينَ وَفِى ٱلرِّقَابِ وَأَقَامَ ٱلصَّلَوٰةَ وَءَاتَى ٱلزَّكَوٰةَ وَٱلْمُوفُونَ بِعَهْدِهِمْ إِذَا عَٰهَدُوا۟ وَٱلصَّٰبِرِينَ فِى ٱلْبَأْسَآءِ وَٱلضَّرَّآءِ وَحِينَ ٱلْبَأْسِ أُو۟لَٰٓئِكَ ٱلَّذِينَ صَدَقُوا۟ وَأُو۟لَٰٓئِكَ هُمُ ٱلْمُتَّقُونَ ۝ ﴾

(سورة البَقَرَة: ١٧٧)

◖It is not righteousness that you turn your faces towards east or west; but it is righteousness to believe in Allah and the Last Day, and the angels, and the Book, and the prophets; and gives wealth in spite of love for it, for your kin, for orphans, for the needy, for the wayfarer, for those who ask, and for the ransom of slaves; and establishes prayer, and gives regular charity, who fulfill their promise when they promise; and who are patient, in poverty and adversity, and during battle. Such are the people of truth, such are the God-fearing.◗

(Qur'an 2: 177)

«On the authority of 'Umar ibn Khattâb (ﷺ) who said: One day while we were sitting with the Messenger of Allah (ﷺ) there appeared before us a man whose clothes were exceedingly white and whose hair was exceedingly black; no signs of journeying were to be seen on him and none of us knew him. He walked up and sat down by the Prophet (ﷺ). Resting his knees against his and placing the palms of his hands on his thighs, he said: O Muhammad, tell me about Islam. The Messenger of Allah (ﷺ) said: Islam is to testify that there is no god but Allah and Muhammad is the Messenger of Allah, to perform the prayers, to pay compulsory charity, to fast in Ramadan, and to make the pilgrimage to the House if you are able to do so. He said: You have spoken rightly. He said: Then tell me about faith. He said: It is to believe in Allah, His angels, His books, His messengers, and the Last Day, and to believe in the divine destiny, both good and evil thereof. He said: You have spoken rightly. He said: Tell me about *ihsân* (goodness, sincerity, right action). He said: It is to worship Allah as if you are seeing Him, and while you see Him not yet truly He sees you. He said: Then tell me about the hour (of the Day of Judgement). He said: The one questioned about it knows no better than the questioner. He said: Then tell me about its signs. He said: That the slave-girl will give birth to her mistress and that you will see the barefooted, naked, destitute herdsmen competing in constructing lofty buildings. Then he took himself off and I stayed for a time. Then he said: O 'Umar, do you know who the questioner was? I said: Allah and his Messenger know best. He said: It was Gabriel, who came to teach you your religion.» (Muslim)

The meaning of Christianity in brief

On the other hand, the Christian faith is directly descended from the religion of the Jews. At the time of Jesus (ﷺ) this had the following characteristics, as taught in the sacred books of the Jews, the Old Testament:

❖ Belief in the existence of one God, the Creator and Lord of the universe who is sovereign over all.
❖ Belief in the fact that man is made in the image of God, but has rebelled against his Creator and stands in danger of judgement.
❖ Belief that God, who is the righteous judge, is also gracious and merciful, that He also provided a way for man to be set free from judgement by the penitent offering of sacrifice.
❖ Belief that God revealed himself to the nation of Israel and called them to be his people.
❖ Belief that God would someday establish his rule in a sinful world, setting his people free from their enemies, and appointing his chosen agent, the Messiah, to rule over them forever.
❖ The practice of a moral life under the guidance of the law given in the Old Testament; the maintenance of a religious ritual based on the temple and involving the offering of sacrifice.

However, these beliefs were decisively affected by the coming of Jesus (ﷺ), his 'resurrection from the dead' and the gift of the 'spirit of God' received by his followers. There remained a basic similarity with the Jewish religion, but there were some fundamental changes, the most important being due to the Christian understanding of Jesus (ﷺ) as a God incarnate, meaning God became a man in the form of Jesus (ﷺ). Thus, God's action in Jesus was seen as including sacrifice. The 'death of Jesus' was understood as a means of canceling sins; the effect of this understanding was to bring to an end the system of animal sacrifices. At the same time the coming of Jesus (ﷺ) was seen as bringing an end to the ritual law of the Jews, which regulated the temple worship and a host of other matters. The ethical principles that lay behind the law, seen especially in the Ten Commandments, were no longer observed.[4]

Thus, Christianity, as is known today, could be termed as a corrupted and secularized form of true religion. It has become far from the teachings of Jesus (﷼), son of Mary, the beloved prophet of Islam. Alija Ali Izetbegovic, the former president of Bosnia, says in his book:

> To explain Christianity and to understand its historical development, we have to distinguish the life of Jesus (﷼) from the history of Christianity. From the very beginning, Jesus (﷼) was on one side, while Christianity was on the other. As time has passed, this difference has been transformed into the difference between the divine and human. This fact could also explain the emergence of the dogma of Jesus as the Son of God. In the Christian myth about the god-man lies the silent admission that pure Christianity is not possible in real life.[5]

Another prolific writer, formerly a Jew by the name of Margaret Marcus, now Maryam Jameelah, writes to explain the degeneration and deviation of Christianity from its acclaimed founder Jesus Christ (﷼), the son of Mary. She says:

> Almost from the out set Christianity has proved itself unfaithful to its founder. Christian theology has no relevance or relation to the teachings of Jesus Christ (﷼) even as recorded in the present day versions of the New Testament. Even before I embraced Islam having been reared as a Jew, I could not but regard the Christian religion as hopelessly corrupted by Greek, Roman and Persian Paganism from the very beginning. These pagan influences were never regarded by Christian leaders as extraneous innovations to be condemned resisted and combated but were all incorporated into the religion as essential dogma and practice. Christian history is devoid of any counter parts to our great Mujaddids (Muslim reformists) to resist innovation and preserve the purity of the faith in tact.[6]

Maryam Jameelah goes on to say:

> The acceptance of the Greek Pagan philosophy has resulted in the incomprehensible and meaningless theology of Christianity. The Christian dogma of the Triune, God as father, son and Holy Ghost, the incarnation of God into man, the doctrine of original sin which can only be erased by implicit faith in Christ as Redeemer and the entire ecclesiastical organization of the church, both protestant and catholic were as unpalatable to the Jewish mentality of my childhood as they are to the Muslim. In fact very few Jews have been converted to Christianity because of sincere conviction as hardly any Jew could possibly reconcile himself to these dogmas.
>
> Most Jewish conversions to Christianity in the past have been motivated by eagerness to escape discrimination and persecution or for a hunger for social acceptance among the "gentiles". In the Jewish and Muslims eyes the most irredeemable defect in Christianity is its lack of divine authority. The Gospels were merely four of the many apocryphical biographies written about Jesus (ﷺ) in a language utterly foreign to him (Greek), which were not canonized until centuries after his alleged crucifixion. As for the Epistles, I could never understand why St. Paul's letters (14 out of 27 books of the New Testament) which were merely his own instructions to the various churches in the Roman Empires, should be canonized as "divinely inspired". The Muslim and the Jew cannot but frown upon Christianity's astonishing readiness to accept fallible human authority as infallible even on those questions which concern fundamental doctrine. Hence the priestly hierarchy of the Roman Catholic Church, and the prevailing view among liberal Protestants that since every man is his own priest, we are absolutely free to believe and to do as we please! Even the most casual study of the history of Christianity reveals this religion to have evolved through the

dictates of popes, saints, worldly kings and synods thus a purely man-made religion.[7]

Maryam Jameelah goes on to tell us what Christianity truly is:

Because of St. Paul's rejection of the "Law" to be replaced by faith in Christ as a redeemer of the sins of all mankind to make the religion acceptable to the Greek and Roman world, Christianity is devoid of any complete code of guidance as determining factor in social and political affairs. Above all, what most repelled me emotionally was the complete historical identification of Christianity with Europe and Western civilization. As a child, at the mere mention of the word "Christianity" I could only conjure upon in my mind the horrors of the Spanish inquisition, the crusades, the "pogroms" in Russia and Poland and the genocide of the Jews under Nazism which the Christian authorities did not attempt to resist or even protest. During my adolescence I found Christendom actively cooperating with Zionism, supposedly as a reaction to belated guilt-feelings on account of its past sins against the Jews. At this Juncture I learned that Christendom in alliance with European imperialism, was the greatest enemy of the Arabs and the Muslims from the days of the crusades onwards. Christian missionaries always preceded European conquest and domination in America, Asia, and Africa, and with their educational and philanthropic organizations, did their best to sever the ties of the rising generation from their indigenous culture and wean them over to Western ways:

I soon learned that Christian missionary activity was an integral part of the conspiracy for westernization of the non-western world. However obedient the "pagans" and "heathens" may westernize themselves in Christian missionary institutions, even if they accepted Christianity, the White Christians of European origin would never accept them as equals![8]

Completing her picture of Christianity in the past and present history, Maryam Jameelah says:

> How far historical Christianity has strayed from the original teachings of the claimed founder Jesus Christ (ﷺ) may be gauged by the fact that the pure teachings of Jesus: "Think not that I have come to destroy the law, or the prophets, I am not come to destroy but to fulfill for verily I say unto you till heaven and earth shall pass away, one jot or one tittle shall in no way pass away from the law till all be fulfilled. Whosoever therefore shall break one of these least commandments and shall teach men so, he shall be called the least in the kingdom of heaven but whosoever shall do and teach them, the same shall be called great in the kingdom of heaven."[9] These pure Islamic teachings from Jesus (ﷺ) the beloved prophet of Islam were changed and corrupted in order to make Christianity compatible with the teachings of the Greek and Roman world, St. Paul on his authority alone took the fatal steps of rendering almost the entire body of the law of Moses nullified on the sophistry that "The law killeth but the spirit giveth life."[10]
>
> St. Paul thus preached that men are not saved by their works but by their faith in Jesus Christ as having shed on the cross his redeeming blood for the sins of Mankind. Thus he argued, whoever believes in Jesus, as his saviour shall attain eternal salvation. Henceforth the prescriptions of the Law of Moses are annulled except of course for the basic moral commandment. St. Paul never realized that although laws in themselves without faith cannot compel men to be virtuous, just as roads to the end by encouraging the right way of life combined with social backing are certainly indispensable for reducing the evils to a minimum.
>
> It is this teaching of Islam that Paul and his successors in the Christian Church rejected, leaving the religion a matter of complicated theology, sacramental rituals. Combined like in

Buddhism, with a strong streak of asceticism and monasticism, which left Christianity stripped of the divine law and so restricted, fragmented and empty, the vacuum could only be filled by opening the floodgates to paganism. Thus what is most known as Christian theology, dogma, ritual, feasts and even the so-called "Christian Calendar" is almost entirely of pagan origin.[11]

In a nutshell, this is Christianity in the past history — a religion devoid of:

1. The pure teachings of divine authentic authority
2. A firm moral foundation
3. A profound political system
4. A social-economic system

As has been seen, it is not a way of life. Rather, Christianity is a religion marred by Greek and Roman pagan culture; it failed many people of Europe, who abandoned it and chose to follow the atheism of scholars like Karl Marx, Friedrich Nietzsche, Charles Darwin, and Sigmund Freud. This was not any better, as Maryam Jameelah says:

> It is no historical coincidence that as a reaction against the injustice perpetuated by the church, the atheism of Karl Marx, was born in Christian Germany and first took root in Christian Russia for in Christianity monasticism, secularism, materialism and paganism all joined hands.[12]

The similarity and difference between Islam and Christianity can also be summarized in the words of the last Prophet and Messenger Muhammad (ﷺ), when he said, as narrated by Abu Musa (ﵟ):
«The example of Muslims, Jews and Christians is like the example of a man who employed laborers to work for him from morning until night for specific wages. They worked until midday and then said, 'We do not need your money which you have set for us, so let

whatever we have done be annulled.' The man said to them, 'Don't quit the work. Complete the rest of it and take your full wages.' But they refused and went away. The man employed another batch after them and said to them, 'Complete the rest of the day, and yours will be the wages I had set for the first batch.' So they worked until the time of mid-afternoon prayer. Then they said, 'Let what we have done be annulled, and keep for yourself the wages you promised us.' The man said to them, 'Complete the rest of the work, since only a little of the day remains,' but they refused. Thereafter he employed another batch to work for the rest of the day. They worked for the rest of the day until sunset, and they received the wages of the two former batches. So that was the example of those people (Muslims) and the example of this light (guidance), which they have accepted willingly.» (Bukhari)

Chapter 3

Islam and Christianity: A Scriptural Inquiry

There is obviously today, as in the past, an ignorance among most Muslims and Christians of each other's scriptural teachings, and this is one of the factors that have promoted intolerance between Muslims and Christians both in the past and even in the present time. Former Senator in the US Congress for twenty-two years Paul Findley asserts that the impulse towards religious intolerance is especially strong in America, where Christianity has been the dominant religion since the birth of America as a nation. Findley rightly asks whether religious intolerance is a natural phenomenon, an inevitable byproduct of intense but misdirected conviction. He concludes that most people establish religious affiliation without first studying other religions, which makes them exhibit all sorts of religious intolerance, some mild while others are quite overbearing.[1]

Findley then gives a practical example from Attorney Allen Yow, his young neighbor and a recent convert to Islam, who while reflecting on his own experience says:

> Maybe it is partly human nature to slip into religious intolerance. In my case, a commitment to Islam was a very personal soul-searching decision. In accepting Islam, I chose it over Christianity, the faith of my parents. Most people don't face a choice like that. Most Christians simply follow the religious

path of their forebears. The same is true of most Muslims and Jews. For them, it really isn't a choice, a conscious selection of one faith over others. Unfortunately, most Christians are misinformed about Islam, and that misunderstanding, I find, breeds intolerance. It is easy to be intolerant about a religion you don't understand.[2]

Findley then goes on to say that religion is usually a way of finding a moral direction and is a quest that oftentimes should be intense and personal. Hence, it should not be a surprise for one to find himself or herself falling prey to the temptation of being self-righteous about one's faith and thus shoving all others aside and thereby being intolerant towards people of other faiths. Not caring even for curiosity purposes to have a little understanding of their religion and what it stands for, all of which stems from the false human ego.[3]

Unquestionably, this religious intolerance stems from, among other reasons, ignorance of each other's religion, and of course the stereotype of religious inheritance, the consequence of which is hostility towards one another. Because of this, many wars have been fought between Muslims and Christians in the past and may be fought in the future if this trend is not checked. Classical cases in point are the eight crusade wars waged against Muslims by Christian knights under the order of the Pope. These seemingly innocent Christian soldiers sincerely believed that Muslims were pagans and heathens who were actually defiling the holy land in Palestine, the birthplace of Jesus (ﷺ).[4]

Yet a casual inquiry into what the Qur'an says about Christianity will reveal to anybody that Islam is very tolerant and respectful of other religions to the extent that the glorious Qur'an rebukes and condemns any person claiming to be a Muslim, yet abusing and insulting people of other religions, even idol worshipers. Allah (ﷻ) says:

﴿وَلَا تَسُبُّوا۟ ٱلَّذِينَ يَدْعُونَ مِن دُونِ ٱللَّهِ فَيَسُبُّوا۟ ٱللَّهَ عَدْوًۢا بِغَيْرِ عِلْمٍ ۗ كَذَٰلِكَ زَيَّنَّا لِكُلِّ أُمَّةٍ عَمَلَهُمْ ثُمَّ إِلَىٰ رَبِّهِم مَّرْجِعُهُمْ فَيُنَبِّئُهُم بِمَا كَانُوا۟ يَعْمَلُونَ ۝﴾

(سورة الأنعَام: ١٠٨)

﴾And do not insult those they invoke other than Allah, lest they insult Allah in enmity without knowledge. Thus We have made pleasing to every community their deeds. Then to their Lord is their return, and He will inform them about what they used to do.﴿ *(Qur'an 6: 108)*

Therefore, for an atmosphere of tolerance and understanding between Muslims and Christians to exist, both ought to properly study their respective religions first, then embark on studying each other's faith, not with an intention of finding fault with each other's religion, but with an aim of knowing and understanding each other's points of view and clarifying the issues that bring conflict and differences between them. This requires going back to the sources of these two great faiths and studying them with a view of understanding what their learned scholars have to say about their authenticity, history, and preservation.

Authenticity of the Bible and the Qur'an

Both Muslims and Christians claim to possess authentic divine scriptures. In fact the Christians claim that the Holy Bible was the last word of God for the guidance of mankind and as such any other book after the Holy Bible claiming to be coming from God must be false and unauthentic. Consequently, the prophet who claims any divine revelation after the Bible must be an impostor and false prophet who is cursed eternally. In support of this the Christians often quote their scriptures as follows:

All scripture (the Bible) is given by inspiration of God, and is profitable for doctrine, for reproof, for correction, for instruction in righteousness: That the man of God may be perfect, thoroughly furnished unto all good works. (2 Timothy 3:16-17 KJV)

For I testify unto every man that heareth the words of the prophecy of this book, If any man shall add unto these things, God shall add unto him the plagues that are written in this book: And if any man shall take away from the words of the book of this prophecy, God shall take away his part out of the book of life, and out of the holy city, and from the things which are written in this book. (Revelation 22:18-19 KJV)

Muslims, on the other hand, believe that the Qur'an is the final word of God revealed to Prophet Muhammad (ﷺ) as guidance to the whole of mankind. They believe that the Qur'an came to confirm the previous divine scriptures: the scrolls given to Prophet Abraham (ﷺ), the Torah given to Prophet Moses (ﷺ), the Psalms given to King and Prophet David (ﷺ), as well as the Gospel given to Prophet Jesus (ﷺ).

﴿وَمَا كَانَ هَٰذَا ٱلْقُرْءَانُ أَن يُفْتَرَىٰ مِن دُونِ ٱللَّهِ وَلَٰكِن تَصْدِيقَ ٱلَّذِي بَيْنَ يَدَيْهِ وَتَفْصِيلَ ٱلْكِتَٰبِ لَا رَيْبَ فِيهِ مِن رَّبِّ ٱلْعَٰلَمِينَ ۩﴾ (سورة يُونُس : ٣٧)

﴿This Qur'an is not such as can be produced by other than Allah; on the contrary it is a confirmation of [revelations] that went before it, and a fuller explanation of the Book — wherein there is no doubt — from the Lord of the Worlds.﴾   *(Qur'an 10: 37)*

﴿نَزَّلَ عَلَيْكَ ٱلْكِتَٰبَ بِٱلْحَقِّ مُصَدِّقًا لِّمَا بَيْنَ يَدَيْهِ وَأَنزَلَ ٱلتَّوْرَىٰةَ وَٱلْإِنجِيلَ ۩ مِن قَبْلُ هُدًى لِّلنَّاسِ وَأَنزَلَ ٱلْفُرْقَانَ إِنَّ ٱلَّذِينَ كَفَرُواْ بِـَٔايَٰتِ ٱللَّهِ لَهُمْ عَذَابٌ شَدِيدٌ وَٱللَّهُ عَزِيزٌ ذُو ٱنتِقَامٍ ۩﴾ (سورة آل عِمرَان : ٣-٤)

❮It is He Who sent down to you, in truth, the Book, confirming what went before it; and He sent down the Torah and the Gospel. Before this, as a guidance to humankind, and He sent down the Criterion [the Qur'an]. Then those who reject faith in the verses of Allah, will suffer the severest penalty, and Allah is Exalted in Might, Lord of Retribution.❯

(Qur'an 3: 3-4)

Furthermore, Muslims claim that the Qur'an principally accepts and confirms the scriptures that were revealed before, but it also criticizes the corruption that was done to those scriptures. As such, the Bible that the Christians possess today is not the original scripture mentioned in the Qur'an, but rather the Bible has a corrupted form of the original scriptures. In support of their position, Muslims often quote both the Qur'an and the Bible as follows:

﴿فَوَيْلٌ لِّلَّذِينَ يَكْتُبُونَ ٱلْكِتَابَ بِأَيْدِيهِمْ ثُمَّ يَقُولُونَ هَٰذَا مِنْ عِندِ ٱللَّهِ لِيَشْتَرُواْ بِهِۦ ثَمَنًا قَلِيلًا فَوَيْلٌ لَّهُم مِّمَّا كَتَبَتْ أَيْدِيهِمْ وَوَيْلٌ لَّهُم مِّمَّا يَكْسِبُونَ ۝﴾ (سورة البَقَرَة: ٧٩)

❮Then woe to those who write the 'scripture' with their own hands, and then say: "This is from Allah," to exchange it for a small price. Woe to them for what their hands do write, and for the gain they make thereby.❯

(Qur'an 2: 79)

﴿فَبِمَا نَقْضِهِم مِّيثَٰقَهُمْ لَعَنَّٰهُمْ وَجَعَلْنَا قُلُوبَهُمْ قَٰسِيَةً يُحَرِّفُونَ ٱلْكَلِمَ عَن مَّوَاضِعِهِۦ وَنَسُواْ حَظًّا مِّمَّا ذُكِّرُواْ بِهِۦ وَلَا تَزَالُ تَطَّلِعُ عَلَىٰ خَائِنَةٍ مِّنْهُمْ إِلَّا قَلِيلًا مِّنْهُمْ فَٱعْفُ عَنْهُمْ وَٱصْفَحْ إِنَّ ٱللَّهَ يُحِبُّ ٱلْمُحْسِنِينَ ۝ وَمِنَ ٱلَّذِينَ قَالُوٓاْ إِنَّا نَصَٰرَىٰٓ أَخَذْنَا مِيثَٰقَهُمْ فَنَسُواْ حَظًّا مِّمَّا ذُكِّرُواْ بِهِۦ فَأَغْرَيْنَا بَيْنَهُمُ ٱلْعَدَاوَةَ وَٱلْبَغْضَاءَ إِلَىٰ يَوْمِ ٱلْقِيَٰمَةِ وَسَوْفَ يُنَبِّئُهُمُ ٱللَّهُ بِمَا كَانُواْ يَصْنَعُونَ ۝﴾ (سورة المَائدة: ١٣-١٤)

❨So for their breaking the covenant we cursed them and made their hearts hard. They distort words from their proper places [usages] and have forgotten a portion of that of which they were reminded. And you will observe their deceit among them, except a few of them. But pardon them and over look [their misdeeds], indeed, Allah loves those doers of good. And from those who say, "We are Christians," We took their covenant but they forgot a portion of that which they were reminded. So We caused among them animosity and hatred until the Day of Resurrection. And Allah is going to inform them about what they used to do.❩   *(Qur'an 5: 13-14)*

> How do you say, we are wise, and the law of the Lord is with us? Lo, certainly he made it falsely; the pen of the scribes made it a lie. (Jeremiah 8:8 KJV)

> And it came to pass, that when Jehudi had read three or four columns, he cut it with the penknife, and cast it into the fire that was on the hearth, until the entire scroll was consumed in the fire that was on the hearth. (Jeremiah 36:23 KJV)

> Since many have taken in hand to set forth in order a declaration of those things which are most surely believed among us, even as they delivered them unto us, who from the beginning were eyewitnesses, and ministers of the word; it seemed good to me also, having had perfect understanding of all things from the very first, to write unto you in order, most excellent Theophilus. (Luke 1:1-3 KJV)

From the aforementioned, it follows that the truth of either claim can only be solved by looking at not only the accuracy of the claims but also the accuracy with which both scriptures have been recorded and the preservation of their textual purity. If the acclaimed message that was revealed by God to a prophet did not reach its followers in exactly the same purity in which it was delivered to the prophet, but instead underwent misreporting and alteration, then to the same extent, the religion may be regarded as having deviated from the truth.

Theories and methods of authenticity

The question of authenticity of any scripture claiming to be from the Almighty Allah (ﷻ) is of utmost importance since it touches on almost all aspects of a true religion; in fact it is the basis of true religion. It verifies the truthfulness of the claimant of the message, whether he is a true prophet or an impostor, and consequently whether the religion he is preaching is true or false.

In other words, if a person is a true prophet, then the scripture he brought, by necessity, must be accepted as truly coming from Allah (ﷻ), as long as the revelation has not been interfered with. Therefore, the religion he is calling to must be the true religion and vice versa. From time immemorial, there have been many claimants to prophethood, some even in modern times. The question that arises therefore, is: how can anyone distinguish a true prophet from a false one in order to determine the truth of any person's claim to have brought a divine authentic revealed scripture?

It is therefore necessary to establish some rigorous criteria that are generally acceptable in terms of logic and reason. These criteria should be such that in light of them, anyone may searchingly examine any scripture, be it the Qur'an, the Old and New Testaments, the Hindu Bhagavad-Gita, or any other religious text, and decide for himself or herself whether or not it deserves serious consideration as coming from the Lord of the universe.[5]

The generally acceptable, logical and reasonable criteria for objective analysis of any scripture may be as follows:[6]

1. The person claiming to have received revelation should be known as an individual of unblemished character and morals, of whom no evil or sin is known; in particular he must be of the strictest standard of honesty and truthfulness.
2. The words of the alleged scripture should be recorded exactly as they were received from the divine source, without the slightest interference or change on the part of anyone, including the one who claimed to have received the revelation. The original scripture should remain intact and accessible to anyone who wishes to read it.
3. The message contained in the scripture should be totally consistent throughout; no part should contradict any other part.
4. There should be no confusion among its concepts, beliefs, and teachings.
5. Nothing in it should be contrary to the objectively observed facts of the natural world.
6. It should appeal to people's reason and rational faculties, rather than to irrationality, superstition, and the like.
7. It should provide spiritual insight and moral guidance of the highest order.
8. It should not attribute to Allah (﷾), the Creator of the universe, anything that is contrary to His unique, exalted, and transcendent nature, nor to any created being anything that pertains exclusively to Allah (﷾).
9. It should explicitly and emphatically deny to anyone other than Allah (﷾) the right to be worshipped and obeyed.
10. It should emphasize brotherhood and equality among human beings, and should not uphold the domination of some people by others based on color, race, tribe or socio-economic status.
11. It should not attribute major sins or vices to the persons that Allah (﷾) singled out for the task of conveying His guidance (the prophets), for this is tantamount to attributing a lack of knowledge

or stupidity to Allah. Allah forbid.

12. Its language should be eloquent and sublime, and of the highest order of literary style and expression, beyond human imitation.

13. Although not an essential proof of its truthfulness, the scripture should contain objectively verifiable information such as could not have been known by other than the creator, Allah. It would be considered a further testimony to its truth and authenticity.

With the above criteria, the two scriptures can be looked at critically for one to make a fair, unbiased informed decision.

The New Testament — divine or human?

More often than not most Christians do not refer to the Old Testament, instead they always refer to the New Testament for their everyday theology and understanding. The reason being that they claim to have a new covenant with Christ which the church ratified and which subsequently abrogated the old covenant (the Old Testament). Therefore, looking at the New Testament and analyzing the four canonical Gospels, as well as the Epistles, to ascertain the divine authority and the authenticity of the Bible, may not be an over exaggeration in deciding the authenticity of the Bible.

There are four canonical Gospels in the New Testament. They are the Gospels according to: Matthew, Mark, Luke and John. There are many inspiring sayings of Jesus (ﷺ) in these Gospels. They were composed between forty to eighty years after the departure of Jesus Christ (ﷺ), the son of Virgin Mary on the basis of some earlier documents which are now lost. Biblical scholars have identified some of these earlier documents as follows:

1. 'Q' (German Quelle — meaning Source) — a lost document in Aramaic, which reached the Gospel writers in a Greek translation.

2. 'Urmarcus' — meaning 'primitive Mark' — an earlier draft of Mark's Gospel written on the basis of Peter's discourses about Jesus (﷽).

3. 'L', a collection of reports about Jesus (﷽) used only by Luke.

A comparison of the four Gospels reveals that their authors used these documents in a somewhat free manner, not even hesitating to change some of the things contained therein to suit their own purpose.

Biblical scholars agree that the first of these Gospels was that of Mark. It was written in Rome at least forty years after the so-called crucifixion of Jesus Christ (﷽). The Gospel, as it is today, is considered an expanded version of Urmarcus, about which Papias, an early Christian writer said:

> The elder John used to say, Mark having become Peter's interpreter, wrote down accurately whatsoever he remembered. It was not, however, in exact order that he related the sayings or deeds of Christ. For he neither heard the Lord nor accompanied him, but subsequently as I said he attached himself to Peter who used to meet the wants of his hearers, and not as making a connected narrative of the Lord's discourses.[7]

Dr. C. J. Cadoux, who was a Mackennal Professor of Church History at Oxford, sums up the conclusions of eminent Biblical scholars with regard to the nature and composition of Mark's Gospel in these words:

> It was written after Peter's martyrdom (65 C. E.), and at a time when Mark, who had not himself been a disciple of Jesus apparently had none of the personal disciples of Jesus within reach by whose knowledge he could check his narrative. These circumstances of its composition account for the existence in it, side by side, of numerous signs of accuracy and a certain number of signs of ignorance and inaccuracy.[8]

The Gospel of Matthew was written in Greek at Antioch in about 90 CE. The author made extensive use of both 'Q' and 'Urmarcus'. No independent scholar regards this Gospel as the work of Matthew, the apostle of Jesus. If Matthew composed anything it must have been only 'Q'. Regarding the liberties taken by the unknown author of this Gospel with the original material, the learned author, C. J. Cadoux again writes:

> But a close examination of the treatment he gives to his borrowings from Mark shows that he allowed himself great freedom in editing and embroidering his material in the interest of what he regarded as the rightful honouring of the great Master. The same tendencies are often visible else where when he is producing 'Q' or providing matter peculiar to himself. Anything therefore, strictly peculiar to 'Matthew' can be accepted as historical only with great caution.[9]

The third Gospel, the Gospel according to Luke, was written in Greece about the year 80 CE, for the benefit of someone known as Theophilus ('the friend of God'), who, according to one opinion, was a high official of the Roman Empire. It is an apologetic addressed to the non-Jews. The writer, who was the friend and travelling companion of St. Paul, made use of at least three lost documents, two of which are identical to those used by the author of Matthew's Gospel, and the third was peculiar to himself. Luke wished to bring his Gospel in line with the Pauline point of view and therefore he took even greater liberties with his sources than the writer of Matthew's Gospel had done.

The Gospels of Mark, Matthew, and Luke are traditionally known as 'the Synoptic Gospels' meaning originating from the same lost document and having much in common. The Gospel of John is rather very different from these. In it, the divinity and pre-existence of Jesus are affirmed, though not as a claim put by Jesus (ﷺ) himself. In the first chapter and beginning lines, the writer of this Gospel claims that the divine Logos, the Word or Reason of God, Who created the world, had become incarnate in Jesus (ﷺ). The Gospel of John was written at or near Ephesus between the years 110 and 115 CE by some unknown writer who was anti-semitically inclined and represented the Jews as the enemies of Jesus Christ (ﷺ). No independent scholar regards it as the work of John, the son of Zebedee, who according to R. H. Charles, Alfred Loisy, Robert Eisler, and other scholars, was beheaded by Agrippa I in the year 44 CE, long before the fourth Gospel was written. In fact modern Biblical scholars doubt the genuineness not only of the writer's own views in this Gospel, but also the words he puts in the mouth of Jesus Christ (ﷺ). The learned author C. J. Cadoux again writes:

> The speeches in the Fourth Gospel (even apart from the early messianic claim) are so different from the synoptic, and so like the comments of the fourth Evangelist himself, that both cannot be equally reliable as records of what Jesus said: Literary veracity in the ancient times did not forbid, as it does now, the assignment of fictitious speeches to historical characters: the best ancient historians made a practice of composing and assigning such speeches in this way.[10]

The early history of the Gospels shows that they were composed when the early Christians had become divided into different factions. Hence the Gospels were composed to propagate the special teachings of various schools and factions and their authors showed no hesitation in tampering with the earlier documents and traditional material regarding the life and teaching of Jesus (ﷺ) to bring them in line with views of their schools. Rev. T. G. Tuncker has this to say:

> Thus Gospels were produced which clearly reflected the conception of the practical needs of the community for which they were written. In them the traditional material was used, but there was no hesitation in altering it or making additions to it, or in leaving out what did not suit the writer's purpose.[11]

Furthermore, the four canonical Gospels were not the only Gospels written and circulating in the early centuries of Christianity. There were many Gospels including the Gospels according to the Hebrews (an Aramaic work which was used by the Nazarenes, the early disciples of Jesus, who regarded him only as a great prophet and denied his divinity), the Gospel of Thomas, and the Gospel of Barnabas.

Towards the end of the second century of the Christian era, only four Gospels were canonized and the rest were declared to. be heretical or apocryphal by the church. Before the Gospels according to Matthew, Mark, Luke, and John were canonized and accepted as scriptures, they did not have such sanctity which they have now and no one felt any compunction in altering them if anything contained in them did not suit his purpose or the purpose of his sect. In fact even after they were included in the canon and ratified as the word of God, changes still continued to be made in them, as is clear from the different early extant manuscripts. Referring to this situation, Professor Dummelow of Cambridge writes in his famous Bible Commentary:

> A copyist would sometimes put in not what was in the text, but what he thought aught to be in it. He would trust a fickle memory, or he would make the text accord with views of the school to which he belonged. In addition to the versions and quotations from the Christian Fathers, nearly four thousand Greek manuscripts (MSS) of the Testament were known to exist. As a result the variety of reading is considerable.[12]

As for the Epistles, St. Paul wrote fourteen out of the twenty-seven books of the New Testament, which are now called the Epistles. All were his personal instructions to various groups of faithfuls, especially to the non-Jews the gentiles. It is quite amazing that such personal instructions have matured to be regarded as the inspired word of God. How could this be when it is well known that St. Paul was an anti-Christ, a persecutor of the followers of Christ, moreover he never even met Jesus (ﷺ) in his life. Then how could he have been inspired and by whom? It is found that Paul's faith was fuelled by a self-acclaimed vision in which he claims to have seen Jesus (ﷺ) who appointed him as one of the apostles; hence he started preaching to the gentiles. Yet Paul's vision is questionable for many reasons:

1. Paul did not know Jesus (ﷺ) and had never met Jesus before in order to positively identify him in the vision which he claims to have seen.

2. Paul opposed Peter to his face, and who was Peter? He was the one authorised by Jesus (ﷺ) to take over his work. (Matthew 16:13-20 also Galatians 2:11-13)

3. Barnabas sided with Peter but split from Paul. (Acts 15:36-41)

4. Paul's followers in Galatia and Corinth seriously questioned his authority. (1 Corinthians 1:10-12)

5. Paul seems to contradict his own statement regarding the vision that he saw on his way to Damascus. (Acts 22:6-9 Vs Acts 9:3-8)

6. Paul is quite crafty and tricky in his preaching. (2 Corinthians 12:16)

Even with all these reasons to doubt the authenticity of Paul, he went on to be the most influential writer of the New Testament — writing 14 letters to various communities and in the process founding Christianity by basing his theology and doctrines on the self-refuting crucified Messiah.

To sum up, in considering how far the four canonical Gospels faithfully present the inspired message or Gospel of Jesus Christ (ﷺ), the following points should be taken into consideration:

1. That no written copy was made of the inspired sayings of Jesus Christ (ﷺ) in his lifetime.

2. That the earliest records of the sayings of Jesus Christ (ﷺ), which were made shortly after his departure when his glorification had already began, have all been irretrievably lost.

3. That in the Gospels that were written between 70 CE and 115 CE on the basis of some of the lost documents, the material contained in them was handled rather freely, the Gospel writers feeling no hesitation in changing it for what they considered to be the greater glory of Jesus Christ (ﷺ) or to bring it in line with the views of their sects.

4. That none of the Evangelists had known Jesus (ﷺ) or heard him speak.

5. That the Gospels were written in Greek whereas the language spoken by Jesus Christ (ﷺ) was Aramaic.

6. That the Gospels were composed to propagate the points of view of the different factions and that they were chosen from many others which represented different viewpoints.

7. That for at least a century after they were written they had no canonical authority and were actually changed by copyists of the different sects to serve their own purposes.

8. That the earliest extant manuscripts of the Gospels — Codex Sinaiticus, Codex Vaticanus, and Codex Alexandrinus, all belong to the fourth and fifth centuries, and no one knows how much the Gospels have been changed during the centuries from which no manuscripts are available.

9. That there are a considerable number of differences at many places among the various extant manuscripts of the fourth and fifth centuries.

10. That the Gospels taken as a whole are full of many contradictions and inconsistencies.

All these facts disclosed by distinguished Western scholars quoted in this chapter make self-evident that the Gospel of Jesus Christ (ﷺ), by which is meant the original inspired message given to Jesus by God Almighty, has not reached humanity in its original form. The four Gospels, as well as the Epistles of St. Paul, cannot be considered to be identical to the inspired Gospel of Jesus Christ (ﷺ). The manner in which they were composed, as well as the circumstances through which they have passed, are such that they cannot be relied upon to give the exact knowledge of what Jesus (ﷺ) said and taught. The learned scholar C. J. Cadoux sums up the position in these words in his book:

> In the Gospels, therefore, the main documents to which we must go if we are to fill-out at all that bare sketch, which we can put together from other sources, we find material of widely differing quality as regards credibility. So far-reaching is the element of uncertainty that it is tempting to 'down tools' at once, and to declare the task hopeless. The historical inconsistencies and improbabilities in parts of the Gospels form some of the arguments advanced in favour of the Christ-myth theory. These are, however, outweighed — as we have shown — by other considerations. Still the discrepancies and uncertainties that remain are serious and consequently many moderns, who have no doubt whatever of Jesus' real existence, regard as hopeless any attempt to dissolve out the historically-true from the legendary or mythical matter which the Gospels contain, and to reconstruct the story of Jesus' mission out of the more historical residue.[13]

Shaykh Ahmed Deedat in his book, *The Choice: Islam and Christianity, Volume Two,* quotes the following Christian scholars with regard to the Bible being human or divine:
Dr. W. Graham Scroggie of the *Moody Bible Institute*, Chicago, one of the most prestigious Christian evangelical missions in the world, in answering the question, "Is the Bible the Word of God?" (also the title of his book), under the heading: *It Is Human, Yet Divine,* says:

> Yes the Bible is human, though some, out of zeal which is not according to knowledge, have denied this. These books have passed through the minds of men, are written in the language of

men, were penned by the hands of, and bear in their style the characteristics of men.

Another erudite Christian scholar, Kenneth Cragg, the Anglican Bishop of Jerusalem, says in his book, *The Call of the Minaret*:

> Not so the New Testament (as opposed to the Qur'an)... There is condensation and editing; there is choice, reproduction and witness. The Gospels have come through the mind of the Church behind the authors. They represent experience and history.

If words have any meaning, do we have to add another word of comment to prove our case? No, but the professional propagandists, after letting the cat out of the bag, still have to try to make their readers believe that they have proved beyond the shadow of any doubt that the Bible is the indisputable word of God.[14]

Amazing scientific errors in the Bible

Astronomy
1. Heavens and earth created in six days

> Thus the heavens and the earth were finished, and all the host of them. And on the seventh day God ended his work which he had made; and he rested on the seventh day from all his work which he had made. And God blessed the seventh day, and sanctified it: because that in it he had rested from all his work which God created and made. (Genesis 2:1-3 KJV)

This part of the Bible says that the heavens and the earth were created in six days of morning and evening, yet the scientists today have estimated the age of the universe to be 4.5 billion years, by using radioactive dating analyzed on terrestrial moon rocks and meteorites. Hence this is a very clear scientific contradiction in the Bible.

On the other hand, even though one finds the same parallels of the creation of the heavens and the earth in six *ayyâm* (literary days) as in Qur'an (7: 54 and 10: 3):

$$\text{﴿إِنَّ رَبَّكُمُ ٱللَّهُ ٱلَّذِى خَلَقَ ٱلسَّمَٰوَٰتِ وَٱلْأَرْضَ فِى سِتَّةِ أَيَّامٍ ثُمَّ ٱسْتَوَىٰ عَلَى ٱلْعَرْشِ}$$
$$\text{يُدَبِّرُ ٱلْأَمْرَ مَا مِن شَفِيعٍ إِلَّا مِنْ بَعْدِ إِذْنِهِ ذَٰلِكُمُ ٱللَّهُ رَبُّكُمْ فَٱعْبُدُوهُ}$$
$$\text{أَفَلَا تَذَكَّرُونَ ۝﴾}$$

(سورة يُونس : ٣)

❬Surely, your Lord is Allah Who created the heavens and the earth in six ayyâm [days] and then He rose over the Throne, disposing the affair of all things. No intercessor [can plead with Him] except after His Permission. That is Allah, your Lord; so worship Him [Alone]. Then, will you not remember?❭   *(Qur'an 10: 3)*

However, the Qur'an unlike the Bible does not speak of days of mornings and evenings mentioning first day, second day, third day, fourth day, fifth day, sixth and seventh days of 24 hour periods. Rather what is mentioned in the Qur'an is six *ayyâm* (six long periods of time known as aeons) as understood by the scholars.

2. Light appears on the first day (before the sun)

> And God said, let there be light: and there was light. And God
> saw the light, that it was good: and God divided the light from
> the darkness. (Genesis 1:3-4 KJV)

That light appears on the first day of creation, while the sun from which the light comes is created on the fourth day, is a clear scientific contradiction.

> And God said, let there be lights in the firmament of the heaven
> to divide the day from the night; and let them be for signs, and
> for seasons, and for days, and years: And let them be for lights in

the firmament of the heaven to give light upon the earth: and it was so. And God made two great lights; the greater light to rule the day, and the lesser light to rule the night: he made the stars also...and the evening and the morning were the *fourth* day. (Genesis 1:14-16, 19 KJV)

Where did the light come from if the source of light was created on the fourth day?

3. *The earth created before the sun*

And God said, let the earth bring forth grass, the herb yielding seed, and the fruit tree yielding fruit after his kind, whose seed is in itself, upon the earth: and it was so. And the earth brought forth grass, and herb yielding seed after their kind, and the tree yielding fruit, whose seed was in itself, after its kind: and God saw that it was good. And the evening and the morning were the third day. (Genesis 1:11-13 KJV)

Today it is a well-known scientific fact from the 'big bang' theory that the earth and the sun were part of a parent body. So it (the earth) could not have come before the sun, as is found in (Genesis 1:14-19) that the sun and moon were created on the fourth day, whereas the earth was created on the third day.

4. *Vegetation created on the third day (before the sun)*

And God said, let the earth bring forth grass, the herb yielding seed, and the fruit tree yielding fruit after his kind, whose seed is in itself, upon the earth: and it was so. And the earth brought forth grass, and herb yielding seed after his kind, and the tree yielding fruit, whose seed was in itself, after his kind: and God saw that it was good. And the evening and the morning were the third day. (Genesis 1:11-13 KJV)

The vegetation appears on the third day, whereas the sun, the source and means of germination and photosynthesis, being created on the fourth day, clearly goes against the fundamental laws of botany.

5. *The sun and the moon as two independent sources of light*

> And God made two great lights; the greater light to rule the day, and the lesser light to rule the night: he made the stars also. And God set them in the firmament of the heaven to give light upon the earth. (Genesis 1:16-17 KJV)

The two great lights, the sun and the moon (the Hebrew word used for lights is lamps), were created so the bigger lamp (sun) was to govern the day, while the smaller lamp (moon) was to govern the night. On a scientific note, this is very incorrect because it is a confirmed fact that the moon does not have an independent light of its own. The light that is seen from the moon is actually reflected light from the sun. To people at the time of Jesus (ﷺ), the two must have been mentioned as 'a greater and a smaller' light. Furthermore, it was only in 1969 that Neil Armstrong came back with the following information from the moon:[15]

Just like the earth has no light of its own, neither does the moon.

Therefore, to hold that the sun and the moon are two great independent sources of light is scientifically incorrect.

Contrary to the biblical account of the sun and the moon, in the Qur'an the sun is mentioned as a source of heat and light called in Arabic *sirâj,* while the moon is mentioned as a reflected or derived light in Arabic singular *noor* and plural *muneer.*

﴿تَبَارَكَ ٱلَّذِى جَعَلَ فِى ٱلسَّمَآءِ بُرُوجًا وَجَعَلَ فِيهَا سِرَٰجًا وَقَمَرًا مُّنِيرًا ۝﴾

(سورة الفُرقان : ٦١)

❨Blessed is He Who has placed in the sky great stars and placed therein a [burning] lamp and luminous moon.❩   *(Qur'an 25: 61)*

(١٦ :سورة نوح) ﴾وَجَعَلَ ٱلْقَمَرَ فِيهِنَّ نُورًا وَجَعَلَ ٱلشَّمْسَ سِرَاجًا ۝﴿

﴾And made the moon therein a [reflected] light and made the sun a burning lamp?﴿
(Qur'an 71: 16)

Consequently other verses in the Qur'an refer to the sun as a shining light and the moon as a derived or luminous light, making it very clear that the sun is a source of heat and light, while the moon only derives or reflects its light from the sun — unlike in the Bible, which talks of two great lights, one governing the day (the sun) and other governing the night (moon).

﴾هُوَ ٱلَّذِى جَعَلَ ٱلشَّمْسَ ضِيَآءً وَٱلْقَمَرَ نُورًا وَقَدَّرَهُۥ مَنَازِلَ لِتَعْلَمُواْ عَدَدَ ٱلسِّنِينَ وَٱلْحِسَابَۚ مَا خَلَقَ ٱللَّهُ ذَٰلِكَ إِلَّا بِٱلْحَقِّۚ يُفَصِّلُ ٱلْأَيَٰتِ لِقَوْمٍ يَعْلَمُونَ ۝﴿ (٥ :سورة يونس)

﴾It is He Who made the sun a shining light and the moon a derived light and determined for it phases that you may know the number of years and account [of time]. Allah has not created this except in truth. He details the signs for a people who know.﴿   *(Qur'an 10: 5)*

6. *Concordant vs conflicting approach*

If you try to take a concordant approach to the Bible with modern science and say that the six days of creation mentioned in the Bible mean long periods of time called epochs, then you will only be able to resolve point number 1. The other four or five points will still be in clear contradiction with science. If you choose to say that the six days are twenty-four hour periods, then you still have six clear scientific errors just in the first chapter of the Bible (Genesis 1:1-19).

There are some very staunch and uncompromising Christians (dogmatic) who say that plants can survive for twenty-four hours without the sun, but then one cannot have the six day epochs and twenty-four hour days at one and the same time. The argument does not hold water. You can't have your cake and eat it, too!

As mentioned earlier, the Qur'an also speaks of six days of the creation of the heavens and the earth. However the word used in the Qur'an for days is *ayyâm,* which has two meanings: the first is the usual meaning of twenty-four hour periods, and the second is days that signify long periods of time known in geological terms as eons or even astrons, which are periods of a thousand million (billion) years. As Allah (ﷻ) says in the Qur'an:

$$ \text{﴿ ... وَإِنَّ يَوْمًا عِندَ رَبِّكَ كَأَلْفِ سَنَةٍ مِّمَّا تَعُدُّونَ ﴿٤٧﴾ ﴾} $$

(سورة الحَجّ : ٤٧)

﴾...And verily, a day with your Lord is as a thousand years of what you reckon.﴿   *(Qur'an 22: 47)*

$$ \text{﴿ تَعْرُجُ ٱلْمَلَائِكَةُ وَٱلرُّوحُ إِلَيْهِ فِي يَوْمٍ كَانَ مِقْدَارُهُ خَمْسِينَ أَلْفَ سَنَةٍ ﴿٤﴾ ﴾} $$

(سورة المعَارج : ٤)

﴾The angels and the Spirit ascend unto Him in a day the measure whereof is [as] fifty thousand years.﴿   *(Qur'an 70: 4)*

Thus, Islam holds that the heavens and the earth were created in six days, but the six days are not the normal twenty-four hour periods but long periods of time of which a day in the sight of Allah (ﷻ) is equivalent to a thousand or fifty thousand years of humanity's reckoning on earth. In scientific terms, these long periods of time are called epochs or eons.

7. *Will the earth come to an end or remain forever?*

There are some scientists who have come up with theories about the end of the earth. They may be right or they may be wrong. But to hold the view that the earth will simultaneously come to an end and also last forever is illogical and unscientific. Either the earth will come to an end or it will perish; both cannot take place at the same time. Yet this is what the Bible purports to say:

> And, you, Lord, in the beginning have laid the foundation of the earth; and the heavens are the works of your hands: they shall perish; but you remain; and they shall grow old as does a garment. (Hebrews 1:10-11 KJV)

> Of old have you laid the foundation of the earth: and the heavens are the work of your hands. They shall perish, but you shall endure: yea, all of them shall grow old like a garment; as vesture shall you change them, and they shall be changed: (Psalm 102:25-26 KJV)

However, the Bible in another place also says:

> One generation passes away, and another generation comes: but the earth abides forever. (Ecclesiastes 1:4 NKJV)

> And he built his sanctuary like high palaces, like the earth which he has established forever. (Psalm 78:69 KJV)

The earth cannot perish and stay forever simultaneously; it is illogical and unscientific, yet this is what the Bible says.

8. *The earth flat or oval shaped?*

> Thus were the visions of my head in my bed; I saw, and behold, a tree in the midst of the earth, and its height was great. The tree grew, and was strong, its height reached unto heaven, and its sight to the end of all the earth. (Daniel 4:10-11 KJV)

> Again, the Devil took him up into an exceedingly high mountain, and showed him all the kingdoms of the world, and the glory of them; (Matthew 4:8 KJV)

And the Devil, taking him up into a high mountain, showed unto him all the kingdoms of the world in a moment of time. (Luke 4:5 KJV)

It was in the 15th century that Copernicus came up with the Copernican Theory, which was also later called the Heliocentric Theory, that the earth was not the centre of the solar system. Later, Galileo, upholding this theory, proved and declared that the earth moved around the sun and that it was not flat but round. This cost him life imprisonment, and he died as a blind man under house arrest, convicted by the Roman Catholic court. So the earth being flat according to the Bible is a clear scientific error.

9. The earth does not move

Fear before him, all the earth: the world also shall be stable, that it be not moved. (1 Chronicles 16:30 KJV)

The Lord reigns, he is clothed with majesty; the Lord is clothed with strength, with which he has girded himself: the world also is established, that it cannot be moved. (Psalm 93:1 KJV)

The Bible claims that the earth is stationary; it does not move, which is a clear scientific contradiction. It was in 1609, that Galileo became aware of the invention of the telescope in Holland, and he immediately designed and constructed his own telescope. Among his discoveries were: the four moons of Jupiter, he found that the moon's surface is rough (contrary to Aristotle's view), he discovered sunspots and the phases of Venus, and he showed that the Milky Way galaxy consists of an enormous number of stars. Galileo publicly defended the view of Nicholas Copernicus, the Heliocentric Theory.

The church had upheld Aristotle's viewpoint that the universe was fixed, with the earth being its centre, from that time until 1980, when the church synod accepted its error. According to the Qur'an, the earth moves. Allah (ﷻ) says:

وَتَرَى ٱلْجِبَالَ تَحْسَبُهَا جَامِدَةً وَهِىَ تَمُرُّ مَرَّ ٱلسَّحَابِ صُنْعَ ٱللَّهِ ٱلَّذِىَ أَتْقَنَ كُلَّ شَىْءٍ ﴿
(سورة النَّمل : ٨٨) ﴾ إِنَّهُۥ خَبِيرُۢ بِمَا تَفْعَلُونَ ٨٨ ﴿

❨And you will see the mountains and think them solid, but they shall pass away as the passing away of clouds. The work of Allah, Who perfected all things. Verily, He is well acquainted with what you do.❩

(Qur'an 27: 88)

The earth moves, hence there is no scientific contradiction in the Qur'an.

10. Fruit and nutrition (botanical contradiction)

> And God said, behold, I have given you every herb bearing seed, which is upon the face of all the earth, and every tree, which has seed in its fruit; to you it shall be for food. (Genesis 1:29 KJV)

That all herbs, plants, wild berries, and even poisonous plants are for mankind to eat is a very clear scientific error, because botanists have classified all plants into edible, medicinal, and poisonous plants, of which there are those that kill instantly.

According to Peter Odhiambo, a surgeon and professor at the University of Nairobi, one poisonous plant is the tobacco leaf, containing over 4000 different substances. Out of the 4000 substances, 400 are known to be very harmful to human life and health, by way of causing cancer.[16]

11. Scientific test for a true Christian

> And these signs shall follow them that believe; in my name shall they cast out demons; they shall speak with new tongues; they shall take up serpents; and if they drink any deadly thing, it shall not hurt them; they shall lay hands on the sick, and they shall

> recover. So then after the Lord had spoken unto them, he was
> received up into heaven, and sat on the right hand of God. (Mark
> 16:17-19 KJV)

If a true Christian drinks a poisonous substance like sulphuric or concentrated nitric acid, he will not die, and he will be able to speak in a foreign language that he has not heard before.

Very few Christians, in fact hardly any, have dared to try out any of these as a confirmatory test or a falsification test for his or her true faith in Jesus being God.

12. Hydrology in the Bible contradicted by the rainbow

> I do set my rainbow in the cloud, and it shall be for a token of a
> covenant between the earth and me. And it shall come to pass,
> when I bring a cloud over the earth, that the bow shall be seen in
> the cloud: And I will remember my covenant, which is between
> me and you and every living creature of all flesh; and the waters
> shall no more become a flood to destroy all flesh. And the bow
> shall be in the cloud; and I will look upon it, that I may
> remember the everlasting covenant between God and every
> living creature of all flesh that is upon the earth. And God said
> unto Noah, this is the token of the covenant, which I have
> established between me and all flesh that is upon the earth.
> (Genesis 9:13-17 KJV)

After God had destroyed the people of Noah (ﷺ) for disobedience, He promised Noah that He was not going to punish people with floods again, so he put up a rainbow as a sign to show that He (God) will not do so again. Scientifically, we know that a rainbow is a refraction of sunlight with rain or mist. To say that rain and sunlight never existed before Prophet Noah's time is illogical, since rainbows are formed by the refraction of sunlight with mist or rain. This is another clear scientific error in the Bible.

13. Blood as a disinfectant (Medicine)

Medicine is a very important and famous field of study. The following is the Bible's point of view on the disinfecting of a house from leprosy.

> And he shall take to cleanse the house two birds, and cedar wood, and scarlet, and hyssop: and he shall kill one of the birds in an earthen vessel over running water: and he shall take the cedar wood, and the hyssop, and the scarlet, and the living bird, and dip them in the blood of the slain bird, and in the running water, and sprinkle the house seven times: and he shall cleanse the house with the blood of the bird, and with the running water, and with the living bird, and with the cedar wood, and with the hyssop, and with the scarlet: But he shall let go the living bird out of the city into the open fields, and make an atonement for the house: and it shall be clean. (Leviticus 14:49-53 KJV)

It is a well-known fact today that blood is a good carrier and breeding ground for all sorts of bacteria, viruses, and germs. How can blood be used to disinfect a house, yet it breeds germs? This is another clear scientific error in the Bible.

14. In the field of zoology

> And the hare, because it chews the cud, but divides not the hoof; it is unclean unto you. (Leviticus 11:6 KJV)

A rabbit is a rodent, not a ruminant; hence it does not chew the cud.

15. Ants have no organization

> Go to the ant, you sluggard; consider her ways and be wise: who having no guide, overseer, or ruler... (Proverbs 6:6-7 KJV)

Today, it is a known scientific fact that ants are among the most sophisticated insects on earth; having specific ants assigned to specific duties, for example, soldier ants, worker ants, the Queen, and King. Allah (ﷻ) said in the Qur'an:

﴿وَمَا مِن دَآبَّةٍ فِى ٱلْأَرْضِ وَلَا طَٰٓئِرٍ يَطِيرُ بِجَنَاحَيْهِ إِلَّآ أُمَمٌ أَمْثَالُكُم مَّا فَرَّطْنَا فِى ٱلْكِتَٰبِ مِن شَىْءٍ ثُمَّ إِلَىٰ رَبِّهِمْ يُحْشَرُونَ ۝﴾   (سورة الأنعام: ٣٨)

❨There is not an animal [that lives] on the earth, nor a being that flies on its wings, but [forms part of] communities like you. Nothing have We omitted from the Register, and they [all] shall be gathered to their Lord in the end.❩   *(Qur'an 6: 38)*

16. Do serpents eat dust?

> And the Lord God said unto the serpent, because you have done this, you are cursed above all cattle, and above every beast of the field; upon your belly shall you go, and dust shall you eat all the days of your life: (Genesis 3:14 KJV)

> The wolf and the lamb shall feed together, *and the lion shall eat straw like the ox*: and dust shall be the serpent's food. They shall not hurt or destroy in all my holy mountain, says the Lord. (Isaiah 65:25 KJV)

It is a well-known fact that snakes are carnivores; they do not eat dust.

17. Winged insects walking on four legs

> All winged insects that creep, going upon all fours, shall be an abomination to you. (Leviticus 11:20 KJV)

The mention in the bible of winged insects with four legs is from the biological and scientific point of view a clear scientific error. Anyone who has passed through secondary school and read about insects knows that they are six-legged.

18. Mythical creatures in the Bible

> And the unicorns shall come down with them, and the bullocks
> with the bulls; and their land shall be soaked with blood, and
> their dust made fat with fatness. (Isaiah 34:7 KJV)

This point concerns the existence of mythical creatures in the Bible.
Unicorns are imaginary animals in the form of white horses with long
straight spiraled horns growing from their foreheads. To have such
creatures that do not exist mentioned in the 'word of God', the Bible,
is also a clear scientific error.

The Qur'an — divine or human?

Reliability and validity of scripture

One of the scientific techniques commonly used to ascertain the
authenticity of a finding or a report is to establish its **reliability** and
validity.

The Webster Dictionary defines the word 'reliable' as trustworthy,
and the word 'valid' as sound and logical, while the Oxford
Dictionary defines 'reliable' as able to be relied upon, constantly
good in quality and performance. 'Valid' is having legal force, legally
acceptable, sound, to the point and logical.

The two definitions above can be illustrated by a simple example
as follows: Several hundred people listened to a commercial on the
radio, which said that a certain shop in town was offering everything
on sale at 50% off. Those who heard this in turn passed it to others. If,
in this process of transmission, every person gave identical
information, then the information would be termed reliable.
Furthermore, if different people went to the shop and found that

everything in the shop was truly on sale at 50% off, then this information would be termed valid. If not, then the information would be untrue or invalid, hence not authentic. Thus, information can be reliable, but not authentic or valid, and vice-versa.

The same example can be related to the Qur'an. If it can be established that no change occurred during its transmission from generation to generation and from place to place, and that the Qur'an today is in the same exact form as that which was delivered by Prophet Muhammad (ﷺ) to humankind, then the reliability of the Qur'an can be established beyond any shadow of a doubt. If, at the same time, it can be established that the Qur'an is a true revelation of Allah (ﷻ), this would also prove the validity of the Qur'an.

The reliability theory

Historians have borne witness that the Muslims utilized two different methods in the preservation and transmission of the Qur'an — memorization and written form.

Prophet Muhammad (ﷺ) was the first to memorize the entire Qur'an. Whenever a verse was revealed, he would commit it to memory. Sometimes during periods of revelation, he would repeat the verses hurriedly, lest he forgot them. Allah (ﷻ) then instructed the Prophet (ﷺ) not to rush, and assured him of the preservation of the Qur'an in his memory.

(سورة القيامة : ١٦–١٩)

⟪Move not your tongue with it [O Muhammad] to hasten with it. Indeed, upon Us is its collection [in your heart] and [to make possible] its recitation. So when We have recited [through Gabriel], then follow its recitation. Then upon Us is its clarification [to you].⟫

(Qur'an 75: 16-19)

﴿ سَنُقۡرِئُكَ فَلَا تَنسَىٰٓ ۝ إِلَّا مَا شَآءَ ٱللَّهُ إِنَّهُۥ يَعۡلَمُ ٱلۡجَهۡرَ وَمَا يَخۡفَىٰ ۝ ﴾

(سورة الأعلى : ٦–٧)

◁We will make you recite, [O Muhammad], and you will not forget, except what Allah should will. Indeed, He knows what is declared and what is hidden.▷ *(Qur'an 87: 6-7)*

These verses prove that whatever was revealed to Prophet Muhammad (ﷺ) of the Qur'an was preserved in his memory by Allah (ﷻ). This enabled the Prophet Muhammad (ﷺ) to deliver the Qur'an to humankind in the same exact words as was revealed to him by Allah. There are various sayings of Muhammad (ﷺ) that show that the Prophet used to recite the whole Qur'an to Angel Gabriel during the month of Ramadan. He (ﷺ) in turn would listen to the Qur'an as Angel Gabriel recited it. It is also reported that in the year in which the Prophet died, he recited the Qur'an twice to Gabriel. In this way Allah (ﷻ) ensured the initial preservation of the Qur'an in the memory of the blessed Prophet Muhammad. In fact, whenever a verse of the Qur'an was revealed to the Prophet, he used to call his scribes among his Companions who knew how to write, and he would dictate to them exactly what was revealed to him by Angel Gabriel, after which he would tell the scribes to read back to him what they had written in order for him to authenticate what they had written of the Qur'an. In this way, the whole Qur'an was dictated by the Prophet to his scribes during his lifetime.

Furthermore, the Prophet (ﷺ) also instructed and encouraged his Companions to recite and memorize the Qur'an. There are also numerous narrations of the Prophet Muhammad (ﷺ) that describe the virtues of learning and teaching the Qur'an, for example: «The best among you is he who learns the Qur'an and teaches it to others.» (Bukhari) As a result, many Companions memorized the Qur'an exactly as it was revealed. The Qur'an was also preserved in written form in the following eras:

> During the era of the Prophet
> During Abu Bakr's time
> During the Battle of Yamamah
> During 'Uthmân's time, 24-35 AH
> During the time of Tâbi'oon (the students of the Companions)
> During the time of the fifth Umayyad Caliph 'Abdul-Mâlik, 66-86 AH.

Hajjaj ibn Yusuf, the governor of Kufah, ordered two well-known scholars of Arabic language, namely Yahya ibn Ameer and Nasr ibn Asim, to add vowel points for ease of recitation by non-Arabs. Thus, the Qur'an was faithfully transmitted by two different and independent techniques — oral and written.

Whereas no change was involved in the oral transmission of the Qur'an, several improvements were made in its written transmission to guard against change in pronunciation.

The fact that no change has occurred in the transmission of the Qur'an can be ascertained by:

1. Looking at the original copies of the Qur'an, of which there are two available, written without vowel points. One is in Istanbul, Turkey, and another in Tashkent, Uzbekistan.

   One can ascertain that these were the Qur'ans left behind 1,435 years ago by a scientific technique called carbon-14 dating using the half-life formula (radioactive carbon dating).

2. One can also compare the available copies of the Qur'an of today with the original copies so as to confirm that they are the same.

3. One can also ascertain the reliability of the originals by listening to several memorizers reciting the whole Qur'an by heart and compare it with the originals.

One will find that the Qur'an is the only divine book that meets this standard of reliability.

The validity theory

Establishing the validity of the Qur'an requires proof that the Qur'an is the revealed word of Allah (ﷻ) and thus a divine book. Mankind today does not have any tools and techniques to prove this on the basis of scientific research or technology. One can however deduce it by using common sense, reason, logic and intelligence as discussed in the generally accepted logical and reasonable criteria of analyzing any scripture.

On the same basis, when the Qur'an is analyzed to confirm its validity and authenticity, the following observation will prove that the Qur'an is authentic beyond any shadow of doubt.

1. It can be seen that the one who claimed to have been given the Qur'an, Muhammad (ﷺ), was a person of unblemished character and had morals of the highest order; he was a man known for his highest standard of truthfulness and honesty to the extent that even prior to his claim of prophethood his people had nicknamed him 'the truthful' and 'the trustworthy'. Moreover, Allah (ﷻ) Himself bore witness to his impeccable character when He said:

﴾وَإِنَّكَ لَعَلَى خُلُقٍ عَظِيمٍ ٤﴿ (سورة القَلَم: ٤)

﴾And you [O Muhammad] are on an exalted standard of character.﴿

(Qur'an 68: 4)

﴾لَّقَدْ كَانَ لَكُمْ فِى رَسُولِ ٱللَّهِ أُسْوَةٌ حَسَنَةٌ ... ٢١﴿ (سورة الأحزَاب: ٢١)

﴾You have indeed in the Messenger of Allah a beautiful pattern [of conduct]...﴿

(Qur'an 33: 21)

If Muhammad (ﷺ) was the author of the Qur'an, this would then imply that he was an impostor. But the more one studies the biography of the Prophet (ﷺ), the less one finds reason to presume this. Material gain, the desire for power and glory, the desire to unify the Arabs, the desire for moral reformation — all of these possible motives are immediately eliminated by the unbiased reader of the Prophet's biography. In fact, the entire biography of the Prophet is one of the strongest proofs of his sincerity. But perhaps one of the strongest incidents that demonstrates the truthfulness of the Prophet (ﷺ) is when his son Ibrâheem died, the last of the children to be born to the Prophet. He was less than two years old when he died. This visibly grieved the Prophet, and tears streamed down his face. Even his Companions were distressed and saddened to see the Prophet's state. A few hours after Ibrâheem's death, a solar eclipse occurred, blocking out the bright light of the sun. Immediately, word spread among the Muslims: "Even the sun and the moon are saddened by the Prophet's loss!"

What a great opportunity was this? What more can possibly be asked by an impostor? A charlatan would have seized this moment, this golden opportunity, that would be heard for generations: "Even the skies grieve with the Prophet!" Muhammad (ﷺ) could have called the people of Madinah, and told them, "Yes! Even the heavens are affected by my loss!" In fact, he did not even have to call them; he merely had to remain silent, and let the rumors spread. Already all of Madinah was marveling at this clear miracle.

Yet the true Prophet that he was, Muhammad (ﷺ) could not deceive or lie to his people. He issued a general summons to the people of Madinah, and waited until they all gathered in the mosque. Then he stood up in front of them, praised Allah (ﷻ) and thanked Him, and said the ever-so-powerful statement, «Verily the sun and the moon are two of the signs and miracle of Allah. They do not eclipse because of the death or birth of any human being.» (Bukhari) So simple the phrase, yet so full of meaning; so innocent the sentence, yet so powerful in its implications. Can there be any doubt as to the Prophet's truthfulness?

2. As for the second criterion, the words of the alleged scripture should be recorded exactly as they were received from the divine source, without the slightest interference or change on the part of anyone, including the one who claimed to have received the revelation. Allah (ﷻ) ruled out the possibility that the Prophet (ﷺ) might have tampered with the revelation deliberately, for He said:

﴿وَإِذَا تُتْلَىٰ عَلَيْهِمْ ءَايَاتُنَا بَيِّنَاتٍ قَالَ ٱلَّذِينَ لَا يَرْجُونَ لِقَآءَنَا ٱئْتِ بِقُرْءَانٍ غَيْرِ هَٰذَآ أَوْ بَدِّلْهُ قُلْ مَا يَكُونُ لِىٓ أَنْ أُبَدِّلَهُ مِن تِلْقَآئِ نَفْسِىٓ إِنْ أَتَّبِعُ إِلَّا مَا يُوحَىٰ إِلَيَّ إِنِّىٓ أَخَافُ إِنْ عَصَيْتُ رَبِّى عَذَابَ يَوْمٍ عَظِيمٍ ۝﴾

(سورة يُونس : ١٥)

﴾And when Our verses are recited to them as clear evidence, those who do not expect the meeting with Us say: Bring us a Qur'an other than this or change it. Say [O Muhammad]: It is not for me to change it on my own accord. I only follow what is revealed to me. Indeed I fear, if I should disobey my Lord, the punishment of a tremendous Day.﴿   *(Qur'an 10: 15)*

In another verse, Allah mentions that a severe punishment would be his if Muhammad (ﷺ) were to forge or change any portion of the Qur'an. So Allah (ﷻ) said:

﴿تَنزِيلٌ مِّن رَّبِّ ٱلْعَالَمِينَ ۝ وَلَوْ تَقَوَّلَ عَلَيْنَا بَعْضَ ٱلْأَقَاوِيلِ ۝ لَأَخَذْنَا مِنْهُ بِٱلْيَمِينِ ۝ ثُمَّ لَقَطَعْنَا مِنْهُ ٱلْوَتِينَ ۝ فَمَا مِنكُم مِّنْ أَحَدٍ عَنْهُ حَاجِزِينَ ۝ وَإِنَّهُ لَتَذْكِرَةٌ لِّلْمُتَّقِينَ ۝ وَإِنَّا لَنَعْلَمُ أَنَّ مِنكُم مُّكَذِّبِينَ ۝ وَإِنَّهُ لَحَسْرَةٌ عَلَى ٱلْكَافِرِينَ ۝ وَإِنَّهُ لَحَقُّ ٱلْيَقِينِ ۝﴾

(سورة الحَاقَّة : ٤٣–٥١)

﴾This is a revelation sent down from the Lord of the worlds. And if he [Muhammad] had forged a false saying concerning Us [Allah], We surely should have seized him by his right hand, And then certainly should have cut off his aorta. And none of you could withhold Us from him. And verily, it [this Qur'an] is a reminder for the righteous. And verily, We know that there are some among you that deny. And indeed it [this Qur'an] will be a source of anguish for the disbelievers. And verily, it is an absolute truth with certainty.⟫ *(Qur'an 69: 43-51)*

Therefore, the Qur'an has been preserved safely and no doubt can be cast on its authenticity. The Qur'an as the speech of Allah (﷾) existed from the beginning of creation; it was written in the Preserved Tablet (a protected and well guarded tablet). During the month in which the Prophet (ﷺ) began his mission, the Qur'an was sent down to the lowest heaven. The trustworthy Angel Gabriel, after hearing the Qur'an from Allah (﷾) brought it down and also revealed it to Prophet Muhammad (ﷺ) who preserved it faithfully without any alteration and who then passed on to humankind.[17] Thus, the original scripture (Qur'an) has always remained intact and was accessible to anyone who wished to read it.

3. The third criterion is that the message contained in the scripture should be totally consistent throughout; no part should contradict any other part. Allah (﷾) said clearly, in no uncertain terms, that the Qur'an has no contradiction or inconsistencies whatsoever. This is what has come to be known in scientific terms as the falsification or confirmatory test. Allah (﷾) said:

$$﴿أَفَلَا يَتَدَبَّرُونَ ٱلْقُرْءَانَ وَلَوْ كَانَ مِنْ عِندِ غَيْرِ ٱللَّهِ لَوَجَدُواْ فِيهِ ٱخْتِلَٰفًا كَثِيرًا ﴿٨٢﴾﴾$$

(سورة النِّسَاء: ٨٢)

⟪Do they not then consider the Qur'an carefully? Had it been from other than Allah, they would surely have found therein much contradiction.⟫
(Qur'an 4: 82)

The fact that there are no contradictions in the Qur'an, despite the fact that it was revealed over a period of twenty-three years, in different circumstances and catering to different problems, is a clear indication of its divine origin. Furthermore, the lack of contradictions in its creed and laws are further proofs of its authenticity.

4. The remaining ten criteria for authenticity of any scripture, when analyzed hand in hand with the revelation of the Qur'an, show that indeed the Qur'an is the only authentic divine revelation remaining on the face of the earth. Within the scope of this book each of these points could be summarized in the following lines.

In creed, the topic of primary importance is that of the Creator of the universe, the one who revealed the Qur'an: His Existence (*tawheed ar-ruboobiyyah*), His Names and Attributes (*tawheed al-asmâ' was-sifât*), and His sole right to be worshipped (*tawheed al-uloohiyyah*).

No other religion comes close to this Islamic concept of perfect monotheism. Jews, Christians, even Hindus all claim to be monotheistic, but the trinity of the Christians and the paganism and idolatry of the Hindus make it obvious that such a claim is a false one. The Jews, even though they are closer than many religions to monotheism, attribute to their Creator forgetfulness, weariness, ignorance, and many other indecent human attributes that do not befit His Majesty and they also do not have a firm set of spiritual beliefs. With regard to all other beliefs in the Islamic creed, they distinctly stand out from all other religions in their purity and appeal to human rationale. For example, the belief in prophets as recipients of divine revelation, and as the means of communication between Allah (ﷻ) and humankind, also implies a sense of integrity and honour for the prophets. This integrity is denied by Christian and Jewish scriptures that ascribe, among other crimes, the crimes of murder, incest and drunkenness to the prophets of Allah — allegations that the Qur'an vehemently denies.

Not only does the Qur'an contain nothing that is contrary to reason and objectively observed fact, but it repeatedly appeals to human beings to use their reason and logical faculties to verify the truth of its message. In particular it cites many examples from the natural world as a proof of Allah's limitless power and wisdom. In addition to this, it also contains matters that were not known or understood by anyone until many centuries later, such as scientific facts.[18]

The amazing scientific facts in the Qur'an

1. The coming of the universe into existence

﴿بَدِيعُ ٱلسَّمَوَٰتِ وَٱلۡأَرۡضِ أَنَّىٰ يَكُونُ لَهُۥ وَلَدٌ وَلَمۡ تَكُن لَّهُۥ صَٰحِبَةٞ وَخَلَقَ كُلَّ شَيۡءٖ وَهُوَ بِكُلِّ شَيۡءٍ عَلِيمٞ ١٠١﴾ (سورة الأنعام: ١٠١)

❴[Allah is] Originator of the heavens and the earth. How could He have a son when He does not have a companion [wife] and He created all things? And He is, of all things, Knowing.❵ *(Qur'an 6: 101)*

﴿أَوَلَمۡ يَرَ ٱلَّذِينَ كَفَرُوٓاْ أَنَّ ٱلسَّمَوَٰتِ وَٱلۡأَرۡضَ كَانَتَا رَتۡقٗا فَفَتَقۡنَٰهُمَاۖ ...﴾ (سورة الأنبياء: ٣٠)

❴Have those who disbelieved not considered that the heavens and the earth were a joined entity, and We separated them...❵ *(Qur'an 21: 30)*

﴿ٱللَّهُ ٱلَّذِي خَلَقَ ٱلسَّمَوَٰتِ وَٱلۡأَرۡضَ وَمَا بَيۡنَهُمَا فِي سِتَّةِ أَيَّامٖ ثُمَّ ٱسۡتَوَىٰ عَلَى ٱلۡعَرۡشِۖ مَا لَكُم مِّن دُونِهِۦ مِن وَلِيٍّ وَلَا شَفِيعٍۚ أَفَلَا تَتَذَكَّرُونَ ٤ يُدَبِّرُ ٱلۡأَمۡرَ مِنَ ٱلسَّمَآءِ إِلَى ٱلۡأَرۡضِ ثُمَّ يَعۡرُجُ إِلَيۡهِ فِي يَوۡمٖ كَانَ مِقۡدَارُهُۥٓ أَلۡفَ سَنَةٖ مِّمَّا تَعُدُّونَ ٥﴾ (سورة السجدة: ٤-٥)

❴It is Allah Who created the heavens and the earth and whatever is between them in six days; then He established Himself above the

Throne. You have not besides Him any protector or any intercessor; so will you not be reminded? He arranges [each] matter from the heaven to the earth; then it will ascend to Him in a Day, the extent of which is a thousand years of those, which you count.》

(Qur'an 32: 4-5)

Islam holds that the heavens and the earth were created in six days. The six days are not the normal twenty-four hour days but long periods of time of which a day in the sight of Allah (ﷻ) is equivalent to a thousand or fifty thousand years of humanity's reckoning on earth. In scientific terms, these long periods of time are called epochs.

This information given in the Qur'an is in full agreement with the findings of contemporary science. The conclusion that astrophysics has reached today is that the entire universe, together with the dimensions of matter and time, came into existence as a result of a great explosion that occurred in no time. This event, known as "The Big Bang," proved that the universe was created from nothingness as the result of the explosion of a single point. Modern scientific circles are in agreement that the Big Bang is the only rational and provable[19] explanation of the beginning of the universe and of how the universe came into being. Before the Big Bang, there was no such thing as matter. From a condition of non-existence in which neither matter, nor energy, nor even time, existed, and which can only be described metaphysically, matter, energy, and time were all created. This fact, only recently discovered by modern astrophysics, was given in the Qur'an 1,400 years ago.[20]

2. *The expansion of the universe*

﴿وَٱلسَّمَآءَ بَنَيۡنَٰهَا بِأَيۡيْدٍ وَإِنَّا لَمُوسِعُونَ ﴿٤٧﴾﴾   (سورة الذاريات: ٤٧)

《And the heaven We constructed with strength, and indeed, We are steadily expanding it.》   *(Qur'an 51: 47)*

The word 'heaven', as stated in this verse, is used in various places in the Qur'an to mean sky, space, and universe. Here again, the word is used with the meaning of space and universe. In other words, in the Qur'an it is revealed that the universe 'expands'. This is the very conclusion that science has reached today. Until the dawn of the 20th century, the only view prevailing in the world of science was that the universe had a constant nature, and it had existed forever. The research, observations, and calculations carried out by means of modern technology, however, have revealed that the universe, in fact, had a beginning, and that it is constantly expanding. At the beginning of the 20th century, the Russian physicist Alexander Friedmann and the Belgian cosmologist Georges Lemaitre theoretically calculated that the universe is in constant motion and that it is expanding. This fact was proved also by observational data in 1929. While observing the sky with a telescope, American astronomer Edwin Hubble, with his 100-inch radio telescope at Mount Wilson Observatory in California, discovered that the stars and galaxies were constantly moving away from each other. A universe where everything constantly moves away from everything else implied a constantly expanding universe. The observations carried out in the following years verified that the universe is constantly expanding and in 1937 it became an established fact. Astronomers have now presented the Hubble Constant Theorem, which gives the equation currently used to calculate the rate at which the universe is expanding as: $V=HD$,

where $V=$ Velocity of receding star or planet
   $D=$ Distance of planet or receding star
   $H=$ Hubble constant of proportionality

The issue now is not whether the universe is expanding, but rather at what rate is it expanding. This fact was explained in the Qur'an when this was still unknown to anyone. This is because the Qur'an is the word of God, the Creator, and the Ruler of the entire universe.

3. *The earth is round, neither flat nor square*

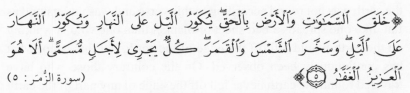

(سورة الزُّمَر : ٥)

❨He created the heavens and earth in truth. He wraps the night up into the day and wraps the day up into the night and has subjected the sun and the moon, each running [its course] for a specified term. Unquestionably, He is the Exalted in Might, the Perpetual Forgiver.❩

(Qur'an 39: 5)

In the above verses of the Qur'an, the words used for describing the universe are quite remarkable. The Arabic word translated as 'to wrap' in the above verse is *takweer*. In English, it means, means to make one thing lap over another, folded up as a garment that is laid away. In Arabic dictionaries this word is used for the action of wrapping one thing around another, in the way that a turban is put on. The information given in the verse about the day and the night wrapping each other up includes accurate information about the shape of the world. This can be true only if the earth is round. This means that in the Qur'an, which was revealed in the 7th century, the roundness of the world was hinted at.

(سورة الذاريَات : ٤٨)   ❨وَٱلْأَرْضَ فَرَشْنَٰهَا فَنِعْمَ ٱلْمَٰهِدُونَ ❨٤٨❩❩

❨And the earth We have spread out, and excellent is the preparer.❩

(Qur'an 51: 48)

(سورة النَّازعَات : ٣٠)   ❨وَٱلْأَرْضَ بَعْدَ ذَٰلِكَ دَحَىٰهَآ ❨٣٠❩❩

❨And the earth, moreover, has He extended [spread out to a wide expanse].❩

(Qur'an 79: 30)

In the second and third verse above, the Arabic words used are *farashnahâ* and *dahâhâ* which mean to spread out continuously. If the earth was not round according to this verse and was understood as flat, like one spreads a bed sheet or blanket then one who is walking on the earth would fall off the edge of the earth, but this is not what has continuously been observed. On the contrary those who have traveled round the earth never fell off the edge of any part of the earth but rather confirmed that the earth was round-shaped.

Surely, at the time the Qur'an was revealed, humankind did not possess today's telescopes or advanced observation technologies to observe that the planet earth is round-shaped. That is why all the speculative scientific knowledge of astronomy as conducted by the Greeks during the period from about 300 BC to CE 300 understood and perceived the world differently. It was then thought by both scientists and lay people that the world was a flat plane fixed as the center of the universe and all scientific calculations and explanations were based on this belief. This geocentric model was accepted by such notables as Aristotle (384 to 322 BC) and Claudius Ptolemy (90-168 CE) and largely because of the authority of Aristotle, the geocentric model became the officially accepted theory of the universe. This position was maintained until the 17th century. However, the Polish astronomer Nicolas Copernicus (1473 -1543) suggested that the earth and the other planets revolved around the sun as in the heliocentric model. It is this early knowledge that laid the foundation for the work of Galileo (1564 -1642), who made many discoveries in astronomy. As a result of his observations in astronomy, Galileo publicly defended Copernicus' viewpoint which was totally against what the church had upheld, which was Aristotle's view. It is for the same reason of lack of experimental science that the church had upheld Aristotle's viewpoint that the universe was fixed with the earth being its center. Following many skirmishes with the church, which declared the Copernican view as heretical, Galileo went ahead and published *Dialogue Concerning the Two Chief World Systems* to support his view. Consequently, he was taken to Rome in 1633 on the charges of heresy and sentenced to life imprisonment. The sentence was commuted to house arrest and he was confined to his villa at Arcetri near Florence for the rest of his life. In his last years he summed up his life's work in a manuscript entitled *Discourses and Mathematical Discoveries Concerning Two New Sciences*, which was smuggled out of Italy and published in Holland in 1638. After completing his work, Galileo became blind and died in his home in Arcetri in 1642 under house arrest.[21] Thus, the Catholic Church had adamantly insisted that the earth was flat and fixed as the center of the universe from that time until 1980, when the Church synod accepted its error.

The verses of the Qur'an, however, included information that has only been learned as recently as the 17th century. Since the Qur'an is God's word, the most correct words were used in describing the shape of the earth and the universe as well as the fact that the earth and all other planets and stars are all swimming in their own orbits without any collision.

4. The protected roof (canopy)

﴿وَجَعَلْنَا ٱلسَّمَآءَ سَقْفًا مَّحْفُوظًا وَهُمْ عَنْ ءَايَٰتِهَا مُعْرِضُونَ ۝﴾

(سورة الأنبياء: ٣٢)

﴿We made the sky a preserved and protected roof yet still they turn away from Our Signs.﴾

(Qur'an 21: 32)

﴿يَٰٓأَيُّهَا ٱلنَّاسُ ٱعْبُدُوا۟ رَبَّكُمُ ٱلَّذِى خَلَقَكُمْ وَٱلَّذِينَ مِن قَبْلِكُمْ لَعَلَّكُمْ تَتَّقُونَ ۝ ٱلَّذِى جَعَلَ لَكُمُ ٱلْأَرْضَ فِرَٰشًا وَٱلسَّمَآءَ بِنَآءً وَأَنزَلَ مِنَ ٱلسَّمَآءِ مَآءً فَأَخْرَجَ بِهِۦ مِنَ ٱلثَّمَرَٰتِ رِزْقًا لَّكُمْ فَلَا تَجْعَلُوا۟ لِلَّهِ أَندَادًا وَأَنتُمْ تَعْلَمُونَ﴾

(سورة البَقَرة: ٢١–٢٢)

❝O people, worship your Lord, Who created you and those before you, that you may become righteous — [He] Who made for you the earth a bed [spread out] and the sky a ceiling [canopy] and sent down from the sky, rain and brought forth thereby fruits as provision for you. So do not attribute to Allah equals while you know [that there is nothing similar to Him].❞   *(Qur'an 2: 21-22)*

This attribute of the sky has been proven by scientific research carried out in the 20th century. The atmosphere surrounding the earth serves crucial functions for the continuity of life. While destroying many meteors, big and small, as they approach the earth, it prevents them from falling to earth and harming living things. In addition, the atmosphere filters the light rays coming from space that are harmful to living things. Interestingly, the atmosphere lets only harmless and useful rays, visible light, near ultraviolet light, and radio waves, pass through. All of this radiation is vital for life. Near ultraviolet rays, which are only partially let in by the atmosphere, are very important for the photosynthesis of plants and for the survival of all living beings. The majority of the intense ultraviolet rays emitted from the sun are filtered out by the ozone layer of the atmosphere and only a limited, and essential, part of the ultraviolet spectrum reaches the earth.

The protective function of the atmosphere does not end here. The atmosphere also protects the earth from the freezing cold of space, which is about negative 270°C. The atmosphere is not the only thing that protects the earth from harmful effects. In addition to the atmosphere, the magnetosphere, also called the Van Allen belt, a layer caused by the magnetic field of the earth, serves as a shield against the harmful radiation that threatens our planet. This radiation, which is constantly emitted by the sun and other stars, is deadly to living things. If the Van Allen belt did not exist, the massive outbursts of energy, called solar flares, that frequently occur in the sun, would destroy all life on earth.

Dr. Hugh Ross has this to say on the importance of the Van Allen belt to our lives:

> In fact, the Earth has the highest density of any of the planets in our Solar System. This large nickel-iron core is responsible for our large magnetic field. This magnetic field produces the Van-Allen radiation shield, which protects the Earth from radiation bombardment. If this shield were not present, life would not be possible on the Earth. The only other rocky planet to have any magnetic field is Mercury — but its field strength is 100 times less than the Earth's. Even Venus, our sister planet, has no magnetic field. The Van-Allen radiation shield is a design unique to the Earth.[22]

The energy transmitted in just one of these bursts detected in recent years was calculated to be equivalent to 100 billion atomic bombs similar to the one dropped on Hiroshima. Fifty-eight hours after the burst, it was observed that the magnetic needles of compasses displayed unusual movement, and 250 kilometres above the earth's atmosphere, the temperature suddenly increased to 2,500°C. In short, a perfect system is at work high above the earth. It surrounds our world and protects it against external threats. Scientists only learned about it recently, yet centuries ago, Allah (﷾) informed mankind in the Qur'an of the world's atmosphere functioning as a protective shield. Thus, mankind should only direct all their worship to none but Allah (﷾), who is protecting humankind in ways that were hardly known to him until the 21st century.

5. The returning sky

(سورة الطّارق: ١١)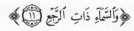

❨By the sky, which returns [with its cyclic system].❩ *(Qur'an 86: 11)*

Allah (ﷻ), in a single verse, has encompassed so much scientific knowledge that has only come to light in very recent times. In this verse Allah (ﷻ) did not specify what the sky returns so that all that will be discovered is automatically accounted for. The verse conveniently is translated to mean cyclical system as well as that which returns and sends back.

As known today, the atmosphere surrounding the earth consists of many layers. Each layer serves an important purpose for the benefit of life. Research has revealed that these layers have the function of turning the materials or rays they are exposed to back into space or back down to the earth. Here is a look at these layers with a few examples of this 'recycling' function of the layers encircling the earth.

(i) The troposphere, thirteen to fifteen kilometers above the earth, enables water vapour rising from the surface of the earth to be condensed and turn back as rain.

(ii) The ozone layer, at an altitude of twenty-five kilometers, reflects harmful radiation and ultraviolet light coming from space and turns both back into space.

(iii) The ionosphere reflects radio waves broadcast from the earth back down to different parts of the world, just like a passive communications satellite, and thus makes wireless communication, radio, and television broadcasting possible over long distances.

(iv) The magnetosphere layer turns the harmful radioactive particles emitted by the sun and other stars back into space before they reach the earth.

The fact that this property of the atmosphere's layers, which was only demonstrated in recent years, was announced centuries ago in the Qur'an once again demonstrates that the Qur'an is the word of God.

6. *The seven layers of the atmosphere*

﴿هُوَ ٱلَّذِى خَلَقَ لَكُم مَّا فِى ٱلْأَرْضِ جَمِيعًا ثُمَّ ٱسْتَوَىٰٓ إِلَى ٱلسَّمَآءِ
فَسَوَّىٰهُنَّ سَبْعَ سَمَٰوَٰتٍ وَهُوَ بِكُلِّ شَىْءٍ عَلِيمٌ ۝﴾   (سورة البقرة: ٢٩)

﴿It is He Who created for you all of that which is on earth. Then He
directed Himself to the heaven, [His being above all creation], and
made them seven heavens, and He is Knowing of all things.﴾

(Qur'an 2: 29)

﴿فَقَضَىٰهُنَّ سَبْعَ سَمَٰوَٰتٍ فِى يَوْمَيْنِ وَأَوْحَىٰ فِى كُلِّ سَمَآءٍ أَمْرَهَا وَزَيَّنَّا ٱلسَّمَآءَ ٱلدُّنْيَا
بِمَصَٰبِيحَ وَحِفْظًا ذَٰلِكَ تَقْدِيرُ ٱلْعَزِيزِ ٱلْعَلِيمِ ۝﴾   (سورة فصّلت: ١٢)

﴿And He completed them as seven heavens within two days and
inspired [made known] in each heaven its command. And We
adorned the nearest heaven with lamps [stars, for beauty] and as
protection. That is the determination of the Exalted in Might, the All-
Knowing.﴾

(Qur'an 41: 12)

The word 'heavens' appears in many verses in the Qur'an with
different shades of meaning according to the issue being addressed.
In this context, it may be used to refer to the sky above the earth, as
well as the entire universe. Given this meaning of the word, the best
information for the moment that the scientists have discovered with
regard to the seven heavens is that the earth's sky, or the atmosphere,
is made up of seven layers. Furthermore, it consists, just as is
described in the Qur'an, of exactly seven layers. In a scientific
source, the subject is described as follows:

> Scientists have found that the atmosphere consists of several
> layers. The layers differ in such physical properties as pressure
> and the types of gasses. The layer of the atmosphere closest to
> Earth is called the troposphere. It contains about 90% of the total
> mass of the atmosphere. The layer above the troposphere is

called the stratosphere. The ozone layer is the part of the stratosphere where absorption of ultraviolet rays occurs. The layer above the stratosphere is called the mesosphere. The thermosphere lies above the mesosphere. The ionized gases form a layer within the thermosphere called the ionosphere. The outermost part of Earth's atmosphere extends from about 480 km out to 960 km. This part is called the exosphere.[23]

Counting the number of layers cited in this source, shows that the atmosphere consists of exactly seven layers, just as stated in the verse.

1. Troposphere
2. Stratosphere
3. Ozonosphere
4. Mesosphere
5. Thermosphere
6. Ionosphere
7. Exosphere

Another important miracle on this subject is mentioned in the statement ❨and inspired in each heaven its command❩. This is in the second verse quoted above. In this verse, Allah (ﷻ) states that He assigned each heaven its own duty. As was seen in the previous heading, each one of these layers has vital duties for the benefit of humankind and all other living things on the earth. Each layer has a particular function, ranging from forming rain to preventing harmful rays, from reflecting radio waves, to averting the harmful effects of meteors. For example, the lowest layer is the troposphere. Rain, snow and wind take place only in that layer.

It is a great miracle that these facts, which could not possibly be discovered without the technology of the 20th century, were explicitly stated in the Qur'an fourteen centuries ago.

7. The function of the mountains as pegs

$$﴾وَجَعَلْنَا فِي ٱلْأَرْضِ رَوَاسِيَ أَن تَمِيدَ بِهِمْ وَجَعَلْنَا ... ۝﴾$$

(سورة الأنبياء: ٣١)

﴾And We placed within the earth firmly embedded mountains, lest it should shift with them...﴿
(Qur'an 21: 31)

$$﴾أَلَمْ نَجْعَلِ ٱلْأَرْضَ مِهَٰدًا ۝ وَٱلْجِبَالَ أَوْتَادًا ۝﴾$$

(سورة النبإ: ٦-٧)

﴾Have We not made the earth as a wide expanse, And the mountains as pegs?﴿
(Qur'an 78: 6-7)

In these two verses the Qur'an again draws humankind's attention to a very important geological function of mountains, which is that mountains have deep roots under the surface of the ground which keep the earth stable lest it shifts with those on it. This fact has only come to light very recently with findings of modern geology and seismic research proving that the Qur'an is the word of Allah.

According to these findings, mountains emerge as a result of the movements and collisions of massive plates forming the earth's crust. When two plates collide, the stronger one slides under the other, and the one on the top bends and forms heights and mountains. The layer beneath proceeds under the ground and makes a deep extension downward. That means that mountains have a portion stretching downwards, as large as their visible parts on the earth. In a scientific text, the structure of mountains is described as follows:

> Where continents are thicker, as in mountain ranges, the crust sinks deeper into the mantle.[24]

In the second verse above, the vital role of mountains has been likened to pegs. In other words, mountains clench the plates in the earth's crust together by extending above and beneath the earth's surface at the conjunction points of these plates. In this way, they fix the earth's crust, and prevent it from drifting over the magma stratum or among its plates. Briefly, mountains may be likened to nails that keep pieces of wood together. This fixing function of the mountains is described in scientific literature by the term

> isostasy, which is defined as 'the general equilibrium of the Earth's crust maintained by a yielding flow of rock material beneath the surface under gravitational stress.'[25]

8. The miracle of iron in the field of chemistry

﴿ ... وَأَنزَلْنَا ٱلْحَدِيدَ فِيهِ بَأْسٌ شَدِيدٌ وَمَنَـٰفِعُ لِلنَّاسِ ... ﴿٢٥﴾ ﴾

(سورة الحَديد: ٢٥)

﴿...And We sent down iron, wherein is great military might and many benefits for the people...﴾   *(Qur'an 57: 25)*

This verse appears in soorat al-Ḥadeed, which means 'iron'. When the literal meaning of the verb and object (*anzalnâ* and *al-ḥadeed*), meaning 'sent down iron from the sky', are taken into consideration together with the latest cosmological information about heavy elements, it becomes obvious that this verse implies a very significant scientific miracle in the Qur'an.

This is because modern astronomical findings have disclosed that the iron found in our world has come from the giant stars in outer space. The heavy metals in the universe are produced in the nuclei of big stars. Our solar system, however, does not possess a suitable structure for producing iron on its own. Iron can only be produced in much bigger stars than the sun, where the temperature reaches a few hundred million degrees. When the amount of iron exceeds a certain level in a star, the star can no longer accommodate it, and eventually it explodes in what is called a 'nova' or a 'supernova'. As a result of this explosion, meteors containing iron are scattered around the universe, and they move through the void until the gravitational force of a celestial body attracts them. All this shows that iron did not form on earth, but was carried from exploding stars in space via meteors, and was 'sent down to earth', in exactly the same way as stated in the verse. It is clear that this fact could not have been scientifically known in the seventh century, when the Qur'an was revealed.

9. *The relativity of time and timeless time*

﴿وَيَسْتَعْجِلُونَكَ بِالْعَذَابِ وَلَن يُخْلِفَ اللَّهُ وَعَدَهُ وَإِنَّ يَوْمًا عِندَ رَبِّكَ كَأَلْفِ سَنَةٍ مِّمَّا تَعُدُّونَ ﴿٤٧﴾﴾ (سورة الحَجّ : ٤٧)

﴿Yet they ask you to hasten the Punishment! But Allah will not fail in His promise. Verily a Day in the sight of your Lord is like a thousand years of your reckoning.﴾
(Qur'an 22: 47)

﴿قَلَ كَمْ لَبِثْتُمْ فِي الْأَرْضِ عَدَدَ سِنِينَ ﴿١١٢﴾ قَالُوا لَبِثْنَا يَوْمًا أَوْ بَعْضَ يَوْمٍ فَسْئَلِ الْعَادِّينَ ﴿١١٣﴾ قَلَ إِن لَّبِثْتُمْ إِلَّا قَلِيلًا لَّوْ أَنَّكُمْ كُنتُمْ تَعْلَمُونَ ﴿١١٤﴾﴾ (سورة المؤمنون: ١١٢-١١٤)

﴿[Allah] will say: What number of years did you stay on earth? They will say: We stayed a day or part of a day: but ask those who keep account. He will say: You stayed not but a little, if you had only known!﴾
(Qur'an 23: 112-114)

﴿يُدَبِّرُ الْأَمْرَ مِنَ السَّمَاءِ إِلَى الْأَرْضِ ثُمَّ يَعْرُجُ إِلَيْهِ فِي يَوْمٍ كَانَ مِقْدَارُهُ أَلْفَ سَنَةٍ مِّمَّا تَعُدُّونَ ﴿٥﴾﴾ (سورة السَّجْدَة: ٥)

﴿He arranges each matter from the heavens to the earth: it will ascend to Him in a Day, the the extent of which is a thousand years of your reckoning.﴾
(Qur'an 32: 5)

﴿وَمَا أَمْرُنَا إِلَّا وَاحِدَةٌ كَلَمْحٍ بِالْبَصَرِ ﴿٥٠﴾﴾ (سورة القَمَر : ٥٠)

❴And Our Command is but one, like the twinkling of an eye.❵

(Qur'an 54: 50)

$$﴿تَعْرُجُ ٱلْمَلَـٰٓئِكَةُ وَٱلرُّوحُ إِلَيْهِ فِى يَوْمٍ كَانَ مِقْدَارُهُ خَمْسِينَ أَلْفَ سَنَةٍ ﴾$$

(سورة المعارج: ٤)

❴The angels and the Spirit ascend unto Him in a Day the measure whereof is [as] fifty thousand years.❵   *(Qur'an 70: 4)*

All the five passages of the Qur'an quoted above point to the fact that time is relative with respect to the perceiver; while time may seem long to one person, it may seem shorter for another and to judge which is correct requires clocks, stopwatches and calendars. Today, the relativity of time is a proven scientific fact. This was revealed by Einstein's theory of relativity in the early years of the twentieth century. Until then, people did not know that time was a relative concept, and that it could change according to the environment. Yet, the great scientist Albert Einstein openly proved this fact with the theory of relativity. He showed that time is dependent on the perceiver and his environment.

A good example of this relative nature of time is one of the passages quoted above of an account of the conversation of people held during their judgement in the hereafter, wherein one perceives a very short period of time as a lengthy one.

The fact that the relativity of time is so clearly mentioned in the Qur'an, long before it was discovered at the beginning of the 20th Century, is further evidence that it is a holy book that has come from Allah, Lord of all creation.

10. The region in the forehead (Cerebrum) that controls human behavior

﴿كَلَّا لَئِن لَّمْ يَنتَهِ لَنَسْفَعًۢا بِٱلنَّاصِيَةِ ۝ نَاصِيَةٍ كَاذِبَةٍ خَاطِئَةٍ ۝﴾(سورة العَلق: ١٥-١٦)

❴No indeed! If he does not stop, We will grab him by the forelock, a lying, sinful forelock.❵

(Qur'an 96: 15-16)

Before the scientific discovery of the functions of the prefrontal lobe of the cerebrum, the above verse could not be fully understood because it was logically understood that it is the tongue that lies and the sinful is the person himself. However, with the very most recent discoveries in the field of human anatomy and physiology, the verse became fully understood.

Indeed the expression 'the lying, sinful forelock' in the above verse is most interesting. Research carried out in recent years revealed that the prefrontal area, which is responsible for the management of particular functions of the brain, lies in the frontal part of the skull. Scientists only discovered the functions of this area, which the Qur'an pointed out 1,400 years ago, in the last sixty years. If one looks inside the skull at the front of the head, you will find the frontal area of the cerebrum. A book entitled *Essentials of Anatomy and Physiology*, which includes the results of research on the functions of this area, says:

> The motivation and the foresight to plan and initiate movements occur in the anterior portion of the frontal lobes, the prefrontal area. This is a region of association cortex...[26]

In yet another place the book also says:

> In relation to its involvement in motivation, the prefrontal area is also thought to be the functional center for aggression...[27]

This area of the cerebrum is responsible for planning, motivation, and initiating good and sinful behaviour, and is responsible for telling lies and the truth. It is clear that the statement 'the lying, sinful forelock' corresponds completely to the above explanations. Allah (ﷻ), in the Qur'an long ago, stated this fact, which scientists have only discovered recently.

Any objective person, looking at the above and many more scientific verses that are found in the Qur'an in the light of the seventh century Arabia, will see that they are extraordinary, for no one in Muhammad's (ﷺ) time had the remotest understanding of the processes by which the universe came to being — astrophysics, relativity of time, neither of geology nor of the minute details of the atmospheric layers and their functions. These are modern scientific facts that have only been discovered and understood fairly recently.

Moreover, the Qur'an exhibits an extraordinary depth of insight into human nature, particularly in relation to the contrasting state of mind of one who is deeply grounded in faith in Allah (ﷻ), and one who is in a state of disbelief or rebellion against Him. In this regard, the Qur'an outshines the subtlest contemporary research into human psychology, dwelling on the state of peace, balance, direction and contentment of the believer on the one hand, and the inner emptiness, anxiety, depression and confusion of the non-believer, on the other hand.[28]

Even though many orientalists, who are biased against Islam, have tried to explain away the Qur'an by different plausible theories, such as by alleging that Muhammad (ﷺ) imagined that he was a prophet or that he was taught by others, that he was going through epileptic seizures or further still that he forged the Qur'an from other sources, it is quite evident that there has never been in human history an instance of a person in the grips of epileptic seizures, insanity or any other form of mental aberration, producing anything so consistent and coherent, of such a profound depth and wisdom, something which was beyond the knowledge of any human being and that was beyond the capacity of the sanest and wisest of men to produce. The pagans of Makkah too, tried the same allegation, which has been inherited by the orientalists to discredit the Qur'an and to avoid coming to grips with the truth of what Muhammad (ﷺ) had brought of the Qur'an. They claimed he was gripped by poetic frenzy, that he was a soothsayer or that he was possessed; they even went as far as saying that he was being taught by someone learned in Christian doctrines.

In fact, Muhammad (ﷺ) had no such knowledge of composing poetry, nor did he have any of the well-known bizarre characteristics of a soothsayer or one possessed. As for the 'teacher' theory, it could not be carried very far because Muhammad (ﷺ) was a well-known person in the constant full view of his enemies as well as his followers. Furthermore, he often received the divine revelations in their presence. Hence these charges were soon dropped and even his most visible enemies were forced to come to the conclusion that what Muhammad (ﷺ) brought was indeed from Allah (ﷻ). The only other way to oppose his revolutionary message of humankind's accountability to Allah (ﷻ) and the brotherhood and equality of all Muslims, which threatened to destroy the entire edifice of their power, prestige and decadent life-style, was to physically fight him and drive him out of Makkah.

Consequently, when one returns to the message of the Qur'an and looks at the sublime concepts and ideas it embodies; its total consistency from beginning to the end; the lofty standard of morality and human interaction it lays down; its profound, self-evident wisdom and depth; the extremely noble, earnest, moving quality of its tone and language; and what it contains relating to matters unknown to any human beings on earth (least of all to an illiterate Arabs) concerning the physical universe as well as the unseen realities, it becomes impossible to deny the authenticity of the Qur'an and try to ascribe it to human authorship.[29] Every logical, open minded, sincere and objective seeker cannot but conclude that the Qur'an is an authentic revelation from Allah (ﷻ) given to Muhammad (ﷺ) as a proof of his prophethood. As Allah (ﷻ) said:

﴿وَمَا كَانَ هَٰذَا الْقُرْءَانُ أَن يُفْتَرَىٰ مِن دُونِ اللَّهِ وَلَٰكِن تَصْدِيقَ الَّذِي بَيْنَ يَدَيْهِ وَتَفْصِيلَ الْكِتَٰبِ لَا رَيْبَ فِيهِ مِن رَّبِّ الْعَٰلَمِينَ ٣٧﴾ (سورة يُونس: ٣٧)

❰This Qur'an is not such as can be produced by other than Allah; on the contrary it is a confirmation of [revelations] that went before it, and a fuller explanation of the [former] scripture — about which there is no doubt — from the Lord of the Worlds.❱ *(Qur'an 10: 37)*

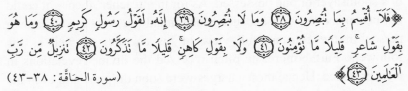

(سورة الحاقّة: ٣٨-٤٣)

❰So I swear by whatsoever you see. And by whatsoever you see not, that this is verily the word of an honoured Messenger. It is not the word of a poet, little is it that you believe! Nor is it the word of a soothsayer [or a foreteller], little is it that you remember! This is the revelation sent down from the Lord of the worlds.❱ *(Qur'an 69: 38-43)*

The glorious Qur'an also posed a number of challenges to humankind as a proof of its authenticity. In other words, Allah (ﷻ) says that if you doubt the authenticity of the Qur'an, then produce a book similar to it, yet if you cannot, then what excuse do you have for not submitting to Allah (ﷻ) by believing in Prophet Muhammad (ﷺ) and all that he brought from Allah, the Qur'an and Sunnah? Allah said:

﴿قُل لَّئِنِ ٱجْتَمَعَتِ ٱلْإِنسُ وَٱلْجِنُّ عَلَىٰٓ أَن يَأْتُوا۟ بِمِثْلِ هَٰذَا ٱلْقُرْءَانِ لَا يَأْتُونَ بِمِثْلِهِۦ وَلَوْ كَانَ بَعْضُهُمْ لِبَعْضٍ ظَهِيرًا ۝﴾

(سورة الإسراء: ٨٨)

❰Say: If all of mankind and the jinn were to come together to produce the like of this Qur'an, they could not produce the like thereof, even if they helped one another.❱   *(Qur'an 17: 88)*

﴿أَمْ يَقُولُونَ ٱفْتَرَىٰهُ قُلْ فَأْتُوا۟ بِعَشْرِ سُوَرٍ مِّثْلِهِۦ مُفْتَرَيَٰتٍ وَٱدْعُوا۟ مَنِ ٱسْتَطَعْتُم مِّن دُونِ ٱللَّهِ إِن كُنتُمْ صَٰدِقِينَ ۝ فَإِلَّمْ يَسْتَجِيبُوا۟ لَكُمْ فَٱعْلَمُوٓا۟

أَنَّمَآ أُنزِلَ بِعِلْمِ ٱللَّهِ وَأَن لَّآ إِلَهَ إِلَّا هُوَ فَهَلْ أَنتُم مُّسْلِمُونَ ۝

(سورة هُود: ١٣-١٤)

◖Or they say: He forged it [the Qur'an]. Say: Bring you then ten forged chapters like unto it, and call whomsoever you can, other than Allah [to your help], if you speak the truth! If then they answer you not, know then that it [this Qur'an] is sent down with the Knowledge of Allah and that none has the right to be worshipped but He! Will you then be Muslims?◗

(Qur'an 11: 13-14)

The similitude and contrast between Jesus and Muhammad

Perhaps nothing brings out the similarity and contrast between Islam and Christianity as much as the Islamic attitude towards Jesus (🕮), and the Christian attitude towards Muhammad (🕮). Whereas Muslims believe in Jesus Christ (🕮), the son of Mary, as one the five major prophets and messengers of God, and love and respect him as they love and respect Muhammad (🕮), Christians not only reject Muhammad (🕮) but are never weary of speaking of him in the most disparaging manner possible. However, an impartial study and inquiry into their lives will show that the prophets of Islam and Christianity were both godly men who completely devoted themselves to the task of preaching Allah's religion, of delivering humanity from error and sin and making Allah's will prevail in the world.[30]

Many learned Christian historians say that there is very little historical evidence available to inform us about the personality of Jesus (🕮) and even about his message. The official historical documents of that time contain virtually no record of Jesus (ﷺ). Biblical scholar R. T. France wrote in *Time* magazine on December 18, 1995 that:

> No first century inscription mentions him and no object or building has survived which has a specific link to him.

This fact has even led some Western historians to mistakenly claim that Jesus Christ (ﷺ) never actually existed. Therefore, our inquiry has to be primarily based on the scriptures, which address the person and mission of Jesus Christ (ﷺ). The scriptures in question are those known by both Christians and Muslims: the Holy Bible and the glorious Qur'an.[31]

It has been shown by many scholars, both Muslims and Christians, that the Biblical scriptures, both the New and the Old Testaments that are in existence today, are not reliable sources of divine authority. Dr. Bilal Philips says, in his book, *The True Message of Jesus Christ*: 'It has been documented by many scholars from various branches and sects of Christianity that much of the material in the Bible is of doubtful authenticity.' He then goes on to quote the author of *The Myth of God Incarnate*. In the preface to *The Myth of God Incarnate*, the editor wrote the following:

> In the 19th century, Western Christianity made two major new adjustments in response to important enlargements of human knowledge: it accepted that man is a part of nature and has emerged within the evolution of the forms of life on this earth: and it accepted that the books of the Bible were written by a variety of human beings in a variety of circumstances, and cannot be accorded Divine authority.[32]

In view of the complete unreliability of the Biblical scriptures which have to be used as a means of knowing the truth about Prophet Jesus (ﷺ), his mission and message, there is need to have a close examination of these Biblical Scriptures in the light of the Qur'anic verses. The Qur'an is the only authentic divine scripture left on the face of the earth today, hence the Qur'anic verses will reveal to all true seekers the truths about Jesus (ﷺ) that have survived in the Bible.

Jesus Christ: Life and mission

Jesus Christ (ﷺ) was born about 7-5 BC in a humble home in Palestine. Very little is known about the early years of his life. Easton's commentary has the following to say about his early life:

> The life of Jesus on earth may be divided into two great periods, (1) that of his private life, till he was about thirty years of age; and (2) that of his public life, which lasted about three years.

> In the "fullness of time" he was born at Bethlehem, in the reign of the emperor Augustus, of Mary, who was betrothed to Joseph, a carpenter (Matthew 1:1; Luke 3:23; comp. John 7:42). His birth was announced to the shepherds (Luke 2:8-20). Wise men from the east came to Bethlehem to see him who was born "King of the Jews," bringing gifts with them (Matthew 2:1-12). Herod's cruel jealousy led to Joseph's flight into Egypt with Mary and the infant Jesus, where they tarried till the death of this king (Matthew 2:13-23), when they returned and settled in Nazareth, in Lower Galilee (2:23; comp. Luke 4:16; John 1:46, etc.). At the age of twelve years he went up to Jerusalem to the Passover with his parents. There, in the temple, "in the midst of the doctors," all that heard him were "astonished at his understanding and answers" (Luke 2:41, etc.).

> Eighteen years pass, of which we have no record beyond this that he returned to Nazareth and "increased in wisdom and stature, and in favour with God and man" (Luke 2:52).

He entered on his public ministry when he was about thirty years of age. It is generally reckoned to have extended to about three years. "Each of these years had peculiar features of its own. (1) The first year may be called the year of obscurity, both because the records of it, which we possess, are very scanty, and because he seems during it to have been only slowly emerging into public notice. It was spent for the most part in Judea. (2) The second year was the year of public favour, during which the country had become thoroughly aware of him; his activity was incessant, and his fame range through the length and breadth of the land. It was almost wholly passed in Galilee. (3) The third was the year of opposition, when the public favour ebbed away. His enemies multiplied and assailed him with more and more pertinacity, and at last he fell a victim to their hatred. The first six months of this final year were passed in Galilee, and the last six in other parts of the land." Stalker's Life of Jesus Christ, p. 45.

The only reliable sources of information regarding the life of Christ on earth are the Gospels, which present in historical detail the words and the work of Christ in so many different aspects.[33]

The Gospels record that when Jesus Christ (﷽) was about thirty-three years of age, a prophet by the name of John the Baptist appeared in the wilderness of Palestine preaching 'the baptism of repentance for the remission of sins.' Jesus (﷽) went and was baptized by him. It was at that time that it was revealed to him that he had been chosen by God as the Messiah of the Jews to revive the spirit of the true religion as taught by all the prophets and complete the long line of Israelite prophets. Of course what he preached was not strange or unknown to the children of Israel, rather the problem at hand was that the spirit of the true religion had been stifled by the material worldliness and ritual formalism of the Sadducees as well as the trivial legalism of the Pharisees. Again and again Jesus (﷽) rebuked them for their self-styled show of righteousness in trivialities in the following words:

> Then spake Jesus to the multitude, and to his disciples, Saying,
> The scribes and the Pharisees sit in Moses' seat: All therefore
> whatsoever they bid you observe, that observe and do; but do
> not ye after their works: for they say, and do not. For they bind
> heavy burdens and grievous to be borne, and lay them on men's
> shoulders; but they themselves will not move them with one of
> their fingers. But all their works they do for to be seen of men:
> they make broad their phylacteries, and enlarge the borders of
> their garments, And love the uppermost rooms at feasts, and the
> chief seats in the synagogues, And greetings in the markets, and
> to be called of men, Rabbi, Rabbi. But be not ye called Rabbi:
> for one is your Master, even Christ; and all ye are brethren. And
> call no man your father upon the earth: for one is your Father,
> which is in heaven. Neither be ye called masters: for one is your
> Master, even Christ. But he that is greatest among you shall be
> your servant. And whosoever shall exalt himself shall be abased;
> and he that shall humble himself shall be exalted. But woe unto
> you, scribes and Pharisees, hypocrites! for ye shut up the
> kingdom of heaven against men: for ye neither go in yourselves,
> neither suffer ye them that are entering to go in. Woe unto you,
> scribes and Pharisees, hypocrites! for ye devour widows'
> houses, and for a pretence make long prayer: therefore ye shall
> receive the greater damnation. Woe unto you, scribes and
> Pharisees, hypocrites! for ye compass sea and land to make one
> proselyte, and when he is made, ye make him twofold more the
> child of hell than yourselves. Woe unto you, ye blind guides,
> which say, Whosoever shall swear by the temple, it is nothing;
> but whosoever shall swear by the gold of the temple, he is a
> debtor! Ye fools and blind: for whether is greater, the gold, or the
> temple that sanctifieth the gold? And, Whosoever shall swear by
> the altar, it is nothing; but whosoever sweareth by the gift that is
> upon it, he is guilty. Ye fools and blind: for whether is greater,

the gift, or the altar that sanctifieth the gift? Whoso therefore shall swear by the altar, sweareth by it, and by all things thereon. And whoso shall swear by the temple, sweareth by it, and by him that dwelleth therein. And he that shall swear by heaven, sweareth by the throne of God, and by him that sitteth thereon. Woe unto you, scribes and Pharisees, hypocrites! for ye pay tithe of mint and anise and cummin, and have omitted the weightier matters of the law, judgment, mercy, and faith: these ought ye to have done, and not to leave the other undone. Ye blind guides, which strain at a gnat, and swallow a camel. Woe unto you, scribes and Pharisees, hypocrites! for ye make clean the outside of the cup and of the platter, but within they are full of extortion and excess. Thou blind Pharisee, cleanse first that which is within the cup and platter that the outside of them may be clean also. Woe unto you, scribes and Pharisees, hypocrites! for ye are like unto whited sepulchres, which indeed appear beautiful outward, but are within full of dead men's bones, and of all uncleanness. Even so ye also outwardly appear righteous unto men, but within ye are full of hypocrisy and iniquity. Woe unto you, scribes and Pharisees, hypocrites! because ye build the tombs of the prophets, and garnish the sepulchres of the righteous, And say, If we had been in the days of our fathers, we would not have been partakers with them in the blood of the prophets. Wherefore ye be witnesses unto yourselves, that ye are the children of them which killed the prophets. (Matthew 23:1-31 KJV)

Therefore, the essence of his religion was total submission to the will of God by loving and obeying God and loving and being kind-hearted to fellow humans, which he tried to instill into the hearts of his fellow people through his inspiring sermons and beautiful illustrative parables.

Yet instead of the Sadducees and Pharisees acknowledging him as their Messiah, about whose coming so many earlier Israelite prophets had foretold, they turned to be his mortal enemies. From the very beginning of his ministry, the Pharisees showed themselves as bitter and persistent enemies. They could not bear his doctrines, and they sought by every means to destroy his influence among the people. They went ahead and pressed the Roman prosecutor to pass the sentence of crucifixion against him. The man who led such a pure, noble, and righteous life, was denied by his own people. It is all but a pity for Jesus (﷽); he showed a rare combination of mildness and courage in doing the will of God and in dealing with his misguided compatriots. He was filled with gentleness, selflessness, and humility; serving his friends and praying for his enemies. He worked many wonderful miracles yet never took pride of them, but only ascribed them to the power of God and even admitted that others also had the ability to do the same. His compassion for the sinners and sufferers was truly admirable. About him it may well be said that he had conquered the devil.

Jesus Christ (﷽) as a Messenger of Allah

Throughout the Qur'an, Jesus (﷽) is consistently identified fundamentally as a Messenger of God. In the Qur'an, Jesus (﷽) is quoted to have said:

$$﴿وَإِذْ قَالَ عِيسَى ٱبْنُ مَرْيَمَ يَٰبَنِىٓ إِسْرَٰٓءِيلَ إِنِّى رَسُولُ ٱللَّهِ إِلَيْكُم مُّصَدِّقًا لِّمَا بَيْنَ يَدَىَّ مِنَ ٱلتَّوْرَىٰةِ وَمُبَشِّرًا بِرَسُولٍ يَأْتِى مِنۢ بَعْدِى ٱسْمُهُۥٓ أَحْمَدُ فَلَمَّا جَآءَهُم بِٱلْبَيِّنَٰتِ قَالُوا۟ هَٰذَا سِحْرٌ مُّبِينٌ ۞﴾$$

(سورة الصَّف : ٦)

﴿And Jesus, the son of Mary, said: "O Children of Israel! I am the Messenger of Allah to you, confirming the Torah which came before me, and giving glad tidings of a messenger to come after me, whose name shall be Ahmad." But when he came to them with clear signs they said, "This is evident sorcery!"⟩   *(Qur'an 61: 6)*

There are also many places in the Bible, in the New Testament, supporting the messengership and prophethood of Jesus (﷽).

> When Jesus entered Jerusalem, the whole city was stirred and asked, "Who is this?" The crowds answered, "This is Jesus, the prophet from Nazareth in Galilee" (Matthew 21:10-11 NIV)

The people of his time are recorded as referring to Jesus (﷽) as a prophet:

> After the people saw the miraculous sign that Jesus did, they began to say: "Surely this is the prophet who is to come into the world." Jesus, knowing that they intended to come and make him into king by force, withdrew again into the hills by himself. (John 6:14-15 NIV)

Jesus (﷽) also referred to himself as a prophet of God:

> And Jesus said to them "only in his home town, among his relatives and in his own house is a prophet without honour" He could not do any miracles there, except laying his hands on a few sick people and heal them. And he was amazed at their lack of faith. (Mark 6:4-6 NIV)

Jesus (﷽) referred to himself as a messenger of God and he is quoted to have said:

> Now this is eternal life that they may know you the only true God, and Jesus Christ, whom you have sent. (John 17:3 NIV)

Jesus Christ (﷽) as a man

The Qur'an not only affirms the prophethood of Jesus (﷽), but it also clearly denies the divinity of Jesus (﷽) by showing that he and his mother both ate food, which is a human act, obviously not befitting God.

﴿مَّا ٱلْمَسِيحُ ٱبْنُ مَرْيَمَ إِلَّا رَسُولٌ قَدْ خَلَتْ مِن قَبْلِهِ ٱلرُّسُلُ وَأُمُّهُ صِدِّيقَةٌ كَانَا يَأْكُلَانِ ٱلطَّعَامَ ٱنظُرْ كَيْفَ نُبَيِّنُ لَهُمُ ٱلْآيَـٰتِ ثُمَّ ٱنظُرْ أَنَّىٰ يُؤْفَكُونَ ۝ ﴾ (سورة المائدة: ٧٥)

❨The Messiah, son of Mary, was no more than a messenger; many were the messengers that passed away before him. His mother was a woman of truth. They had both to eat food. See how We make the signs clear to them; yet see in what ways they are deluded.❩

(Qur'an 5: 75)

There are numerous accounts in the New Testament that also deny Jesus' divinity. Some of those are as follows:

> A certain ruler asked him, "Good master, what must I do to inherit eternal life (salvation)?" "Why do you call me good?", Jesus answered. "No one is good except God alone. You know the commandments. Do not commit adultery, do not murder, do not steal, and do not give false testimony, honour you father and mother..." (Luke 18:18-20 NIV)

So if Jesus (ﷺ) rejected being called 'good'[34] and stated that only God is truly good, this then is a clear indication that he is not God. Among the many verses of the Bible that show the humanity of Jesus (ﷺ) are: John 5:30-31, John 8:40, John 12:49-50, John 13:16, John 14:28, and John 20:17.

> "Abraham is our father," they answered. "If you were Abraham's children" said Jesus, "then you would do the things Abraham did. As it is, you are determined to kill me, a man who has told you truth that I heard from God." (John 8:39-40 NIV)

> Jesus told Mary Magdalene to tell his followers: "I am returning

to my Father and your Father, to my God and your God." (John
20:17 NIV)

Even in some of the writings of Paul especially, when Paul is writing
to those who have knowledge of the oneness, unity, and uniqueness
of God Almighty, he writes:

> For there is one God and one mediator between God and men,
> the man Christ Jesus. (1 Timothy 2:5 NIV)

Just like in the case of Jesus' manliness, there are many verses in
the Qur'an which confirm Prophet Muhammad's humanity, in order
to prevent his followers from elevating him to a divine or semi-divine
status, as was done to Prophet Jesus (ﷺ) by some of his followers.

﴿قُلْ إِنَّمَآ أَنَا۠ بَشَرٌ مِّثْلُكُمْ يُوحَىٰٓ إِلَىَّ أَنَّمَآ إِلَٰهُكُمْ إِلَٰهٌ وَٰحِدٌ فَمَن كَانَ يَرْجُواْ لِقَآءَ رَبِّهِۦ
فَلْيَعْمَلْ عَمَلًا صَٰلِحًا وَلَا يُشْرِكْ بِعِبَادَةِ رَبِّهِۦٓ أَحَدًۢا ﴾ ﴿١١٠﴾   (سورة الكهف: ١١٠)

﴾Say [O Muhammad]: "I am but a man like yourselves, the
inspiration has come to me, that your god is one God: whoever
expects to meet his Lord, let him work righteousness, and, in the
worship of his Lord, admit no one as partner.﴿   *(Qur'an 18: 110)*

Also in chapter Al-A'râf, Allah directed Prophet Muhammad (ﷺ)
to acknowledge that Allah (ﷻ) alone knows the time of judgement.

﴿يَسْـَٔلُونَكَ عَنِ ٱلسَّاعَةِ أَيَّانَ مُرْسَىٰهَا قُلْ إِنَّمَا عِلْمُهَا عِندَ رَبِّى لَا يُجَلِّيهَا لِوَقْتِهَآ إِلَّا هُوَ
ثَقُلَتْ فِى ٱلسَّمَٰوَٰتِ وَٱلْأَرْضِ لَا تَأْتِيكُمْ إِلَّا بَغْتَةً يَسْـَٔلُونَكَ كَأَنَّكَ حَفِىٌّ عَنْهَا قُلْ إِنَّمَا
عِلْمُهَا عِندَ ٱللَّهِ وَلَٰكِنَّ أَكْثَرَ ٱلنَّاسِ لَا يَعْلَمُونَ ﴾ ﴿١٨٧﴾   (سورة الأعراف: ١٨٧)

﴾They ask you about the Hour, when will be its appointed time? Say:
The knowledge thereof is with my Lord alone: none but He can
reveal as to when it will occur. Heavy were its burden through the
heavens and the earth. Only, all of a sudden will it come to you. They
ask you as if you are familiar with it. Say: The knowledge thereof is
with Allah alone, but most men know not.﴿   *(Qur'an 7: 187)*

Jesus (ﷺ) also denied having the knowledge of the hour of judgement.

> Heaven and earth will pass away but my words will not pass away, but of that day and that hour knoweth no man, neither the angels in the heaven nor the son but the Father. (Mark 13:31-32 KJV)

One of the attributes of Allah (ﷻ) is omniscience, knowledge of all things. Therefore, neither Jesus (ﷺ) nor Muhammad (ﷺ) can have divinity, for one who does not know the final hour cannot possibly be God.

Jesus: The most misunderstood personality in the world

Jesus (ﷺ), who forms the link between Judaism, Christianity, and Islam, is probably the most misunderstood personality in world history. Dr. Murad Hofmann, former ambassador to Algeria and Morocco, has this to say in his book:

> Readers of the recent 'biographies' of God — Karen Armstrong's "A History of God" and Jack Miles' "God: A Biography" — have led many to assume that there are about as many different individual images of God as there are Jews, Christians and Muslims. If this analysis is correct, it is safe to assume that the variety of views on Jesus must be enormous as well. One can therefore argue that the Jesus who unites people cannot possibly be the very Jesus who separates them from each other. Historical concepts of Jesus essentially boil down to three major categories. Jesus was said to be:
>
> ❖ *A Jewish apostate who wrongly considered himself to be the Messiah; this is the Jewish interpretation.*

❖ *Simultaneously God and man; this is the orthodox Christian interpretation.*

❖ *A Jewish reform-prophet; this is the Islamic view.*

Until about 200 years ago, there was no openly anti-dogmatic systematic rebellion against Christian teachings apart from a handful of skeptics. In the 19th century, however, a real rebellion began as Christianity's main textual sources were critically examined from a historical perspective. This work, conducted by professional theologians, had devastating consequences. Leading the new trend of demythologizing Christ were both Protestant and Catholic authorities like Rudolf Bultmann, Hans Camphausen, Adolf von Harnack, John Hick, Emanuel Hirsch, Hans Kung, Gerd Ludemann, Paul Tillich, Karl Rahner, Adolf Schlatter, Hans Joachim Schoeps, Wilfred Cantwell Smith and Wolfhart Pannenberg. Yet, as usual, the Christian rank and file could hardly notice this revisionist process as the local parish priests did their best to keep the result of modern theological research in the dark.[35]

So many people in the world have gone to many extremes with regard to Jesus (ﷺ). Some of the factors that led people to take such extreme positions regarding Jesus (ﷺ) are:

1. The way he was born without a father.
2. Lack of enough information regarding his early life.
3. The many miracles he performed.
4. His short life span on this earth, hardly more than 33 years.
5. His ascension to heaven.

6. His staying unmarried throughout his life on earth.
7. His wonderful and powerful preaching without fear.
8. His title of Christ.
9. His stern criticism of the Scribes and the Pharisees.
10. His apparent death and resurrection.

The renowned Muslim scholar of the Christian Bible, Ahmed Deedat in his book, *Christ in Islam,* says about this extreme position taken by emotionally worked up Christians:

> The Jews made certain insinuations about the legitimacy of Jesus (ﷺ) and charged him of blasphemy by twisting his words. The Christians read other meanings into his words, wrench words out of context to make him God. The modern day Christian the hot gospeller, the Bible thumper uses harsh words and crude approaches to win a convert to his blasphemies. The hot-gospeller says, 'Either Jesus is a God or a lunatic,' 'Either Jesus is a God or a liar,' 'Either Jesus is a God or an imposter'. These are his words, culled from Christian literature. Since no men of charity, Muslim or otherwise can condemn Jesus so harshly as such Christians who challenge Christ to make his choice between one or the other of these silly extremes. It does not seem to occur to him that there is an alternative to this Christian conundrum.[36]

Ahmed Deedat goes on to say, regarding this Christian attitude:

> Is it not possible that Jesus is simply what he claimed to be — a prophet like so many other prophets that passed away before him? Even that he is one of the greatest among them, a mighty miracle worker, a great spiritual teacher and a guide — the messiah! Why only God or a lunatic? Is 'Lunacy' the opposite of 'Divinity' in Christianity? The Qur'an lays bare and clarifies the true position of Christ in a single verse:

﴿يَٰٓأَهْلَ ٱلْكِتَٰبِ لَا تَغْلُواْ فِى دِينِكُمْ وَلَا تَقُولُواْ عَلَى ٱللَّهِ إِلَّا ٱلْحَقَّ إِنَّمَا ٱلْمَسِيحُ عِيسَى ٱبْنُ مَرْيَمَ رَسُولُ ٱللَّهِ وَكَلِمَتُهُۥٓ أَلْقَىٰهَآ إِلَىٰ مَرْيَمَ وَرُوحٌ مِّنْهُ فَـَٔامِنُواْ بِٱللَّهِ وَرُسُلِهِۦ وَلَا تَقُولُواْ ثَلَٰثَةٌ ٱنتَهُواْ خَيْرًا لَّكُمْ إِنَّمَا ٱللَّهُ إِلَٰهٌ وَٰحِدٌ سُبْحَٰنَهُۥٓ أَن يَكُونَ لَهُۥ وَلَدٌ لَّهُۥ مَا فِى ٱلسَّمَٰوَٰتِ وَمَا فِى ٱلْأَرْضِ وَكَفَىٰ بِٱللَّهِ

وَكِيلًا ﴿١٧١﴾   (سورة النِّسَاء: ١٧١)

﴾O People of the Scripture, do not commit excess in your religion or say about Allah except the truth, The Messiah, Jesus, the son of Mary, was but a messenger of Allah and His word which He directed to Mary and a soul [created at a command] from Him. So believe in Allah and His messengers. And do not say, 'Three'; desist — it is better for you. Indeed, Allah is but one God. Exalted is He above having a son. To Him belongs whatever is in the heavens and whatever is on the earth. And sufficient is Allah as Disposer of affairs.﴿   *(Qur'an 4: 171)*

In contrast to the old Christian view that Jesus (ﷺ) is 'God-Man' or rather God incarnating Himself into man in order to feel like us to know our problems and be able to solve them, the post-modern view of Christ as represented by John Hick and Paul Schwarzenau gives a more realistic and attainable position. Hoffmann says that the Christology of John Hick (Birmingham) has a more realistic chance of prevailing church-wide one of these days.

This Anglican professor emeritus realized long ago that Jesus (ﷺ) could either be only human or not human at all. Eventually he took the radical step to opt for Jesus' unadulterated humanity. According to Hick, Jesus (ﷺ) was just a man, chosen by God for a divine mission, but neither free from error, nor free from sin. His major mission was to compliment the stern Biblical image of Yahweh (God the sovereign) with the image of a kind and loving God. In other words, Jesus (ﷺ) was to spiritualize the Mosaic ritual and to humanize the Talmudic obsession with legal trivialities.

Hick explains the subsequent elevation of Jesus (ﷺ) to divine status and to being the second person of a divine trinity, as a mythical or poetic way of expressing his significance for us. According to Hick, the Jewish monotheistic image of Jesus (ﷺ) as a 'created son of God' had been transformed from a mere metaphor into a Grecopolytheistic theological construct. Hick's 'Theology of De-incarnation' proceeds from the fact that Jesus (ﷺ) never spoke of himself as God and never mentioned God as Trinitarian.[37]

The true mission and message of Jesus Christ

The message of Jesus (ﷺ) is perhaps the most important point to consider when looking at the attitude of Muslims to Christianity. For if Jesus (ﷺ) was not God incarnate, but a prophet of God, then the message, which he brought from God, is the essence of his mission. The message of Jesus Christ (ﷺ), son of Mary, was not different from, or contradictory to, that of the previous prophets who came before him. As Jesus (ﷺ) himself testifies in the New Testament:

> Do not think that I have come to abolish the law or the prophets;
> I have not come to abolish them but to fulfill them. I tell you the
> truth until heaven and earth disappear not the smallest letter, nor
> the least stroke of the pen, will by any means disappear from the
> law until everything is accomplished. (Matthew 5:17-18 NIV)

The foundation of Jesus' message was submission to the will of Allah (ﷻ) because that was the foundation of the religion that Allah had prescribed for humankind right from the beginning. Allah (ﷻ) said:

وَمَن يَرْغَبُ عَن مِّلَّةِ إِبْرَٰهِـۧمَ إِلَّا مَن سَفِهَ نَفْسَهُۥۚ وَلَقَدِ ٱصْطَفَيْنَٰهُ فِى ٱلدُّنْيَاۖ وَإِنَّهُۥ فِى ٱلْءَاخِرَةِ لَمِنَ ٱلصَّٰلِحِينَ ۞ إِذْ قَالَ لَهُۥ رَبُّهُۥٓ أَسْلِمْۖ قَالَ أَسْلَمْتُ لِرَبِّ ٱلْعَٰلَمِينَ ۞ وَوَصَّىٰ بِهَآ إِبْرَٰهِـۧمُ بَنِيهِ وَيَعْقُوبُ يَٰبَنِىَّ إِنَّ ٱللَّهَ ٱصْطَفَىٰ لَكُمُ ٱلدِّينَ فَلَا تَمُوتُنَّ إِلَّا وَأَنتُم مُّسْلِمُونَ ۞ أَمْ كُنتُمْ شُهَدَآءَ إِذْ حَضَرَ يَعْقُوبَ ٱلْمَوْتُ إِذْ قَالَ لِبَنِيهِ مَا تَعْبُدُونَ مِنۢ بَعْدِىۖ قَالُوا۟ نَعْبُدُ إِلَٰهَكَ وَإِلَٰهَ ءَابَآئِكَ إِبْرَٰهِـۧمَ

وَإِسْمَعِيلَ وَإِسْحَقَ إِلَهًا وَاحِدًا وَنَحْنُ لَهُۥ مُسْلِمُونَ ۝

(سورة البَقَرَة: ١٣٠-١٣٣)

*And who would be averse to the religion of Abraham except one
who makes a fool of himself. And We had chosen him in this world,
and indeed he, in the hereafter, will be among the righteous. When
his Lord said to him, "Submit," he said, "I have submitted [in Islam]
to the Lord of the worlds." And Abraham instructed his sons [to do
the same] and [so did] Jacob, [saying], "O my sons, indeed Allah has
chosen for you this religion, so do not die except while you are
Muslims." Or were you witnesses when death approached Jacob,
when he said to his sons, "What will you worship after me?" They
said, "We will worship your God and the God of your fathers,
Abraham and Ishmael and Isaac — one God. And we are Muslims [in
submission] to Him."*   *(Qur'an 2: 130-133)*

إِنَّ ٱلدِّينَ عِندَ ٱللَّهِ ٱلْإِسْلَـٰمُ وَمَا ٱخْتَلَفَ ٱلَّذِينَ أُوتُوا۟ ٱلْكِتَـٰبَ إِلَّا مِنۢ
بَعْدِ مَا جَآءَهُمُ ٱلْعِلْمُ بَغْيَۢا بَيْنَهُمْ وَمَن يَكْفُرْ بِـَٔايَـٰتِ ٱللَّهِ فَإِنَّ ٱللَّهَ سَرِيعُ
ٱلْحِسَابِ ۝ فَإِنْ حَآجُّوكَ فَقُلْ أَسْلَمْتُ وَجْهِىَ لِلَّهِ وَمَنِ ٱتَّبَعَنِ وَقُل لِّلَّذِينَ أُوتُوا۟
ٱلْكِتَـٰبَ وَٱلْأُمِّيِّـۧنَ ءَأَسْلَمْتُمْ فَإِنْ أَسْلَمُوا۟ فَقَدِ ٱهْتَدَوا۟ وَّإِن تَوَلَّوْا۟ فَإِنَّمَا
عَلَيْكَ ٱلْبَلَـٰغُ وَٱللَّهُ بَصِيرٌۢ بِٱلْعِبَادِ ۝   (سورة آل عِمرَان: ١٩-٢٠)

*Indeed, the religion in the sight of Allah is Islam. And those who
were given the Scripture did not differ except after knowledge had
come to them — out of jealous animosity between them. And
whoever disbelieves in the verses of Allah, then indeed, Allah is swift
in [taking] account. So if they argue with you, say, "I have submitted
myself to Allah [in Islam], and [so have] those who follow me." And
say to those who were given the Scripture and [to] the unlearned,
"Have you submitted yourselves?" And if they submit [in Islam],*

they are rightly guided; but if they turn away then upon you is only the [duty of] notification. And Allah is Seeing of [His] servants.❫
(Qur'an 3: 19-20)

In Arabic, submission to God's will is expressed by the word *Tasleem*, meaning Islam. In the Bible, Jesus (ﷺ) is reported to have taught people to submit to the will of Allah and that there was no entry into paradise without total submission to the will of Allah (ﷻ).

> Not every one who says to me Lord, Lord, shall enter the kingdom of heaven, but the one who does the will of my Father who is in heaven. (Matthew 7:21 RSV)

> Jesus said, "By myself I can do nothing; I judge only as I hear, and my judgment is just because I seek not my own will but the will of the one that sent me." (John 5:30 RSV)

In the above two statements and many others in the Bible, Jesus (ﷺ) places the emphasis on the 'will of the Father', in other words, submission of the human will to the will of God. Obviously the will of God can only be contained in the divinely revealed laws, which the prophets taught their followers. Consequently, obedience to divine law is the foundation of worship. The Qur'an affirms the need for obedience to the divinely revealed laws.

$$﴿إِنَّا أَنزَلْنَا ٱلتَّوْرَىٰةَ فِيهَا هُدًى وَنُورٌ يَحْكُمُ بِهَا ٱلنَّبِيُّونَ ٱلَّذِينَ أَسْلَمُواْ لِلَّذِينَ هَادُواْ وَٱلرَّبَّٰنِيُّونَ وَٱلْأَحْبَارُ بِمَا ٱسْتُحْفِظُواْ مِن كِتَٰبِ ٱللَّهِ وَكَانُواْ عَلَيْهِ شُهَدَآءَ فَلَا تَخْشَوُاْ ٱلنَّاسَ وَٱخْشَوْنِ وَلَا تَشْتَرُواْ بِـَٔايَٰتِى ثَمَنًا قَلِيلًا وَمَن لَّمْ يَحْكُم بِمَآ أَنزَلَ ٱللَّهُ فَأُوْلَٰٓئِكَ هُمُ ٱلْكَٰفِرُونَ ﴿٤٤﴾﴾$$

(سورة المَائدة: ٤٤)

❴It was We Who revealed the Torah; therein was guidance and light. By its standard have been judged the Jews, by the Prophets who bowed [as in Islam] to Allah's will, by the rabbis and the scholars: for to them was entrusted the protection of Allah's Book, and they were witnesses thereto: therefore fear not men, but fear Me, and sell not My Signs for a small price. If any do fail to judge by what Allah has revealed, then it is those who are disbelievers.﴿   *(Qur'an 5: 44)*

Jesus (ﷺ) was reported in the gospels to have made obedience to the divine laws the key to paradise and not the blood on the cross as alleged by Christianity.

> Now behold one came and said to him "Good teacher, what good thing shall I do that I may have eternal life?" Jesus said, "why do you call me good? No one is good except one, that is God, but if you want to enter life keep the commandments." (Matthew 19:16-17 NIV)

> Whoever therefore breaks one of the least of these commandments, and teaches men to do so, shall be called least in the kingdom of heaven but whoever does and teaches them he shall be called great in the kingdom of heaven. (Matthew 5:19 NIV)

Divine law represents guidance for humankind in all walks of life. It defines right and wrong for them and offers human beings a complete system governing all of their affairs. Only Allah (ﷻ), the Creator, Cherisher, and Sustainer, knows what is beneficial for His creation and what is not. Thus the divine laws command and prohibit various acts and substances to protect the human spirit, the human body, and the human society from harm. In order for human beings to fulfill their potential by living righteous lives, they need to worship God through obedience to His commandments.[38]

This was the religion conveyed in the message of Jesus (ﷺ): submission to the will of the one true God by obedience to His commandments. Jesus (ﷺ) stressed that he had not come to do away with the laws given to the prophets but to fulfill them just like the prophets who came before him also followed the law given to Moses.

Allah (ﷻ) says:

وَقَفَّيْنَا عَلَىٰٓ ءَاثَـٰرِهِم بِعِيسَى ٱبْنِ مَرْيَمَ مُصَدِّقًا لِّمَا بَيْنَ يَدَيْهِ مِنَ ٱلتَّوْرَىٰةِ
وَءَاتَيْنَـٰهُ ٱلْإِنجِيلَ فِيهِ هُدًى وَنُورٌ وَمُصَدِّقًا لِّمَا بَيْنَ يَدَيْهِ مِنَ ٱلتَّوْرَىٰةِ وَهُدًى
وَمَوْعِظَةً لِّلْمُتَّقِينَ ﴿٤٦﴾ (سورة المائدة: ٤٦)

And in their footsteps We sent Jesus the son of Mary, confirming the Torah that had come before him: We gave him the Gospel: therein was guidance and light, and confirmation of the Torah that had come before him: a guidance and an admonition to those who fear Allah.

(Qur'an 5: 46)

However, Paul the self-acclaimed apostle of Jesus (ﷺ), who had never met Jesus in his lifetime, systematically cancelled the law. In his letter to the Romans, he stated:

> But now we are discharged from the law, dead to that which held us captive, so that we do not serve under the old written code but in the new life of the spirit. (Romans 7:6 NIV)

The true message of Jesus (ﷺ), as a prophet of God, called people to the worship of only one true God, just like the messages of previous prophets.

وَلَقَدْ بَعَثْنَا فِي كُلِّ أُمَّةٍ رَّسُولًا أَنِ ٱعْبُدُوا۟ ٱللَّهَ وَٱجْتَنِبُوا۟ ٱلطَّـٰغُوتَ
فَمِنْهُم مَّنْ هَدَى ٱللَّهُ وَمِنْهُم مَّنْ حَقَّتْ عَلَيْهِ ٱلضَّلَـٰلَةُ فَسِيرُوا۟ فِي ٱلْأَرْضِ
فَٱنظُرُوا۟ كَيْفَ كَانَ عَـٰقِبَةُ ٱلْمُكَذِّبِينَ ﴿٣٦﴾ (سورة النحل: ٣٦)

And verily, We have sent among every nation a messenger [proclaiming]: "Worship Allah, and avoid all false deities." Then of them were some whom Allah guided and of them were some upon whom the straying was justified. So travel through the land and see what was the end of those who denied [the truth]. *(Qur'an 16: 36)*

وَمُصَدِّقًا لِّمَا بَيْنَ يَدَيَّ مِنَ ٱلتَّوْرَىٰةِ وَلِأُحِلَّ لَكُم بَعْضَ ٱلَّذِى حُرِّمَ
عَلَيْكُمْ وَجِئْتُكُم بِـَٔايَةٍ مِّن رَّبِّكُمْ فَٱتَّقُوا۟ ٱللَّهَ وَأَطِيعُونِ ۞ إِنَّ ٱللَّهَ رَبِّى
وَرَبُّكُمْ فَٱعْبُدُوهُ ۚ هَٰذَا صِرَٰطٌ مُّسْتَقِيمٌ ۞ ۞ فَلَمَّآ أَحَسَّ عِيسَىٰ مِنْهُمُ
ٱلْكُفْرَ قَالَ مَنْ أَنصَارِىٓ إِلَى ٱللَّهِ ۖ قَالَ ٱلْحَوَارِيُّونَ نَحْنُ أَنصَارُ ٱللَّهِ ءَامَنَّا بِٱللَّهِ
وَٱشْهَدْ بِأَنَّا مُسْلِمُونَ ۞   (سورة آل عِمرَان: ٥٠-٥٢)

◖[I have come to you], to attest the Torah which was before me. And to make lawful to you part of what was [before] forbidden to you; I have come to you with a Sign from your Lord. So fear Allah, and obey me. "It is Allah Who is my Lord and your Lord; then worship Him. This is a Way that is straight." When Jesus found unbelief on their part he said: "Who will be my helpers to [the work of] Allah?" The disciples said: "We are supporters of Allah; we believe in Allah, and we do bear witness that we are Muslims.◗   *(Qur'an 3: 50-52)*

> The devil led Jesus to a high place and showed him in an instant
> all the kingdoms of the world. And he said to him, "I will give
> you their authority and splendor, for it has been given to me, and
> I can give it to whomever I want to. So if you worship me it will
> be all yours." Jesus answered, "It is written: 'Worship the Lord
> your God and serve Him alone.'" (Luke 4:5-8 NIV)

Thus, the essence of the message of Jesus (ﷺ) was that only God deserves to be worshipped and that the worship of anyone or anything other than Allah (ﷻ) or alongside with Allah is false and is the greatest sin that one can commit. Jesus (ﷺ) not only called people to this message, but also practically demonstrated the worship of God alone, by bowing down and prostrating in the worship of Allah (ﷻ) alone as recorded in many places in the Bible.[39] But this pure, simple and clear message of Jesus (ﷺ) was distorted after his departure by later followers, beginning with St. Paul, who turned the message into a complicated Trinitarian philosophy, which justified the worship of Jesus (ﷺ), and then the worship of Jesus' mother Mary, the angels, and the saints.[40]

Part of the mission and message of Jesus Christ (ﷺ) was to establish the kingdom of God on earth as he always prayed for it, and told his disciples to pray for the establishment of the kingdom of God. There are many places in the New Testament where Jesus (ﷺ) spread this Gospel.

> This, then, is how you should pray: 'Our Father in heaven, hallowed be your name, your kingdom come, your will be done, on earth as it is in heaven. Give us today our daily bread. And forgive us our debts, as we also have forgiven our debtors. And lead us not into temptation, but deliver us from the evil one, for thine is the kingdom and the power and the glory forever.' Amen (Matthew 6:9-13 NIV)

No one would sensibly deny that one only prays for that which he holds very necessary, highly precious, and most dear to him. To seek the kingdom of God is, therefore, the most cherished goal of a true believer in God. The kingdom of God on earth being the establishment of the rule of God on earth, the government of God on earth, is the only type of government that can bring forth the good fruits of the equality of human rights, justice, world peace, fair and equitable distribution of wealth, and the removal of tribalism, narrow nationalism, nepotism and exploitation of the weak by the strong. This is why the kingdom of God on earth is the theme of quite a number of verses in the New Testament, of which space does not allow to discuss them all. For a full discussion of the kingdom of God on earth as prayed for by Jesus (ﷺ) one can refer to Professor Malik's book, *The Mission Of Jesus Divine Principles Of World Order.*

Jesus promises another comforter to establish the kingdom of God

Since establishing the kingdom of God requires people who love God and fear to displease God, people who are ready to sacrifice all that they have for the sake of establishing the just social, economic and political order; and since the society in the time of Jesus was so materialistic with despotic rulers of the Roman Empire; and because his disciples were very few in number (hardly more than twelve), and not strong enough to resist the Roman soldiers, he was not able to establish what he cherished most, the kingdom of God. Instead he (⌖) prayed for God to bring somebody else who would do the job.

> "Am I leading a rebellion", said Jesus, "that you have come with swords and clubs to capture me? Every day I was with you, teaching in the temple courts, and you did not arrest me. But the scripture has to be fulfilled." They all (his disciples) forsook him and fled. (Mark 14:48-50 NIV)

Therefore, naturally having gone through a very rough time within the short period of less than three years of his mission, Jesus (⌖) told the disciples of one who would come after him and guide humankind to the whole truth by establishing the kingdom of God.

> "If you love me, you will obey what I command. I will ask the Father, and He will give you another counselor to be with you forever — the spirit of truth." (John 14:15-17 NIV)

> "When the counselor comes, whom I will send to you from the Father, the spirit of truth who goes out from the Father, he will testify about me but you also must testify, for you have been with me from the beginning." (John 15:26-27 NIV)

> "Now I am going to the one who sent me, yet none of you asks me, 'where are you going?' Because I have said these things,

> you are filled with grief. But I tell you the truth: It is for your
> own good that I am going away. Unless I go away the counselor
> will not come to you; but if I go, I will send him to you. When he
> comes he will convict the world in regard to sin and
> righteousness and judgment: in regard to sin because men do not
> believe in me: in regard to righteousness because I am going to
> the Father, where you can see me no longer; and in regard to
> judgment, because the prince of this world now stands
> condemned. 'I have much more to say to you but you cannot
> bear them now. But when he the spirit of truth comes, he will
> guide you into all truth. He will not speak on his own; he will
> speak only what he hears, and he will tell you what is to come.
> He will bring glory to me by taking what is mine and making it
> known to you.'" (John 16:5-14 NIV)

As for the Sadducees and Pharisees, including the Israelites who
had refused to accept the mission and message of Jesus Christ (ﷺ),
he told them in no uncertain terms that their term was over and that
no more prophets would come from the house of Israel, but rather
God was going to raise a final prophet from the house of the
bondswoman, the Ismaelites.

> "Therefore I tell you that the kingdom of God will be taken away
> from you and given to a people who will produce its fruit.
> Anyone who falls on this stone will be broken to pieces; anyone
> on whom it falls will be crushed." When the chief priests and the
> Pharisees heard Jesus' parables, they knew he was talking about
> them. They looked for a way to arrest him, but they were afraid
> of the crowd because the people held that he was a prophet.
> (Matthew 21:43-46 NIV)

Therefore, it could be argued from the aforementioned, that the
true followers of Jesus (ﷺ) today are those who uphold his message
and mission in this regard. The author of *Islam between East and
West* says:

When discussing the question of the feasibility of pure religion in the world, a crucial example cannot be overlooked, namely the historical failure of Christianity. To explain Christianity and to understand its historical development, we have to distinguish the life of Jesus from the history of Christianity. From the very beginning, Jesus was on one side, while Christianity was on the other. As time has passed, this difference has been transformed into the difference between the divine and the human. This fact could also explain the emergence of the dogma of Jesus as the Son of God. In the Christian myth about the god-man lies the silent admission that pure Christianity is not possible in real life.[41]

Furthermore, Jesus (ﷺ), in his preaching, clearly explained that his true followers would be those with the following qualities:

✓ They will sincerely believe in the one true God and in Jesus (ﷺ) as the messenger of God.

✓ They will love God and Jesus Christ (ﷺ), the son of Mary, with all their hearts, with all their soul, with their entire mind, and with all their strength by implementing his message.

✓ They will totally submit to the will of Allah (ﷻ) by worshipping Him alone.

✓ They will follow the footsteps of Jesus (ﷺ) by not only paying lip service to his mission and message but also being a living example of that.

✓ They will struggle in this worldly life to make the prayer of Jesus (ﷺ), establishing the kingdom of God, a reality.

Jesus said to him, 'I am the way, the truth, and the life; no one comes to the Father, except through me.' (John 14:6 NIV)

This verse should be understood in the context of other verses as clarified by Jesus (﷽) himself. Some Christians misunderstand this verse to mean worshipping Jesus (﷽) is the way to reach God. But Jesus Christ (﷽) said:

> These people honour me with their lips, but their hearts are far from me. They worship me in vain; their teachings are but the rules taught by men. (Matthew 15:8-9 NIV)

> Not every one who says to me Lord, Lord, shall enter into the kingdom of heaven, but he who does the will of my father who is in heaven (meaning one who submits to Allah as a Muslim) many will say to me on that day (the day of resurrection). "Lord, Lord have we not prophesied in your name? And in your name cast out devils? And in your name done many wonderful works." And then will I profess unto them away from me, you evildoers. Therefore whoever hears these sayings of mine and does them, I will liken him to a wise man who build his house on the rock: and the rain descended, and the floods came, and the winds blew and beat on the house; and it did not fall, for it was founded on the rock. Now every one who hears these sayings of mine and does not do them, will be like a foolish man who build his house on the sand: and the rain descended, the floods came, and the winds blew and beat on that house; and it fell. And great was its fall! (Matthew 7:21-27 NIV)

Muhammad, the promised comforter: Life and mission

The comforter, the spirit of truth, the Messenger of Allah, about whose coming Jesus (﷽) had given the good news, and whose coming the prophet John the Baptist [Yahya (﷽)] had foretold, was born in Makkah in the Arabian peninsula in the year 570 CE, when the true religion had been distorted, forgotten, and gone to oblivion all over the world. The people among whom he was born were polytheists and idolaters who used to worship 360 idols placed in the Kaaba that was built by Prophet Ibrahim (﷽). They were sunk in superstition and vices of all kinds, ranging from prostitution, idol worship, drunkenness, burying of infant daughters alive, and discrimination of women. In fact, they did not have any laws to regulate their lives except the law of the jungle and a few primitive tribal mores.

Among such people who had drifted far from the way of Allah (﷽), Muhammad (ﷺ) grew up to be a man of God, one who was unique and conspicuous with a pure and spotless character, whose love of truth and compassion for the poor and downtrodden was well known. That is why his people nicknamed him 'the truthful' and 'the trustworthy'.

As he grew older, the superstitions and evil ways of his own community caused greater sorrow to his heart. He spent many hours in communion with his Creator and in meditation about the meaning of life. He longed to bring people into the straight path. At the age of forty, the divine light shone in its full splendor in his heart and he was chosen as the last prophet and messenger for the guidance of the entire human race.

He preached that there is only one true unique God, Allah, who is the loving Creator, Cherisher, and Sustainer. He exhorted them to shun all kinds of evil ways and to love one another. He taught them that real religion was not mere spiritual formalism but the removal of want and suffering of fellow humans, and the selfless service of fellow humans. He taught that religious duties and ceremonies were entirely useless if they did not train and discipline the personality of a person to help him or her become a righteous person who works for the good of others.

﴿أَرَءَيْتَ ٱلَّذِى يُكَذِّبُ بِٱلدِّينِ ۝ فَذَٰلِكَ ٱلَّذِى يَدُعُّ ٱلْيَتِيمَ ۝
وَلَا يَحُضُّ عَلَىٰ طَعَامِ ٱلْمِسْكِينِ ۝ فَوَيْلٌ لِّلْمُصَلِّينَ ۝ ٱلَّذِينَ هُمْ عَن
صَلَاتِهِمْ سَاهُونَ ۝ ٱلَّذِينَ هُمْ يُرَآءُونَ ۝ وَيَمْنَعُونَ ٱلْمَاعُونَ ۝﴾

(سورة المَاعون: ١–٧)

﴾Have you seen one who denies the Recompense? Then such is the one who repulses the orphan, and does not encourage the feeding of the poor. So woe to those who pray but are heedless of their prayer, those who show [of their deeds], and withhold [simple] assistance.﴿
(Qur'an 107: 1-7)

The Prophet struck at the root of false superiority based on color, caste, race, or nationality, thus, declaring that all human beings are brothers and equal in the sight of Allah (ﷻ). The treatment meted out to Prophet Muhammad (ﷺ) by his own people was not different from that meted out to the earlier prophets. He was rejected by the rich Makkan rulers who had vested interests in maintaining their hold on power, and subjected him and his Companions to all kinds of torture and persecution.

Furthermore, a combined attempt was made by all the seven clans of Makkah to put an end to his life. After bearing all the tortures and cruelties for thirteen long, lingering years with unparalleled patience and perseverance, Prophet Muhammad (ﷺ) migrated to Madinah where a large number of people had accepted Islam and had become his followers, eagerly awaiting him.

The migration to Madinah thus became the turning point in his life because the people of Madinah not only believed in him and his message but also made him their head of state. In Madinah, the Prophet (ﷺ) used the opportunity as head of state to establish a strong Islamic state, uniting the two warring tribes of Aws and Khasraj with the immigrants in a strong bond of brotherhood, as well as going into an alliance with the Jewish tribes in Madinah who were living under the Islamic state.

Among the many revolutionary changes, which he introduced in the newly created Islamic state were: the raising of the status of women to a position of equality with men, steps to abolish slavery, the total prohibition of all forms of intoxicants and gambling, putting an end to every kind of exploitation and doing away with priesthood, thus, granting religious freedom to all individuals and communities, bringing into force the most enlightened code of laws ever known to humankind, and the establishment of a welfare state with an ideal form of administration, full of justice and mercy.

As an individual, the Prophet (ﷺ) lived a life that can only be described as godly. He was the model par excellence for all humanity in all situations and walks of life, as described by Allah (ﷻ) in the glorious Qur'an. Allah (ﷻ) said about Muhammad (ﷺ):

(سورة القَلَم: ٤)   ﴿وَإِنَّكَ لَعَلَىٰ خُلُقٍ عَظِيمٍ ۝﴾

❨And you [O Muhammad] are on an exalted standard of character.❩
(Qur'an 68: 4)

﴿لَّقَدْ كَانَ لَكُمْ فِى رَسُولِ ٱللَّهِ أُسْوَةٌ حَسَنَةٌ لِّمَن كَانَ يَرْجُواْ ٱللَّهَ وَٱلْيَوْمَ ٱلْآخِرَ وَذَكَرَ ٱللَّهَ كَثِيرًا ۝﴾   (سورة الأحزَاب: ٢١)

❨You have indeed, in the Messenger of Allah, a beautiful pattern [of conduct] for any one whose hope is in Allah and the Final Day, and who engages much in the praise of Allah.❩   *(Qur'an 33: 21)*

﴿يَٰٓأَيُّهَا ٱلنَّبِىُّ إِنَّآ أَرْسَلْنَٰكَ شَٰهِدًا وَمُبَشِّرًا وَنَذِيرًا ۝ وَدَاعِيًا إِلَى ٱللَّهِ بِإِذْنِهِ وَسِرَاجًا مُّنِيرًا ۝﴾   (سورة الأحزَاب: ٤٥-٤٦)

❨O Prophet! Truly We have sent you as a witness, a bearer of glad tidings, and a warner, and as one who invites to Allah by His leave, and as a lamp spreading light.❩   *(Qur'an 33: 45-46)*

The Prophet (ﷺ) lived up to the highest ideals of the glorious Qur'an and exemplified the virtues mentioned therein to the extent that when his beloved wife 'Â'ishah (ﷺ) was questioned about his moral character her reply was, "He was the living Qur'an." (Muslim) In other words, he was the Qur'an in action. Muhammad (ﷺ) was a man of God who had conquered all temptations and passions and lived only for the sake of Allah (ﷻ), sacrificing all that he had to be in total submission to the will of Allah. He was as he is described in the Qur'an, a mercy for all creatures. He always felt extremely concerned about the depraved and corrupt state of his own people, and it grieved his heart when he had to give an order of punishment on anyone for the sake of justice or for the security of the young Islamic state. He never even lifted a finger against anyone for his own sake. One among the many moving incidents in his life was when, after losing both his most beloved wife Khadijah (ﷺ) and his beloved uncle Abu Tâlib, he decided to go out of Makkah about sixty kilometers away, to a place called Ta'if, to call them to Islam. The rulers of Ta'if commanded the children and the fools among the people to jeer, laugh, scoff at and scold him, and when he insisted on preaching to them, drove him out of the city and pelted him with stones until his shoes were full of blood. Allah (ﷻ) sent angels of destruction to come to his aid, and when the angels asked him if they should destroy these people who had pelted him with stones, he replied, according to the biographies of the Prophet (ﷺ):
I have not been sent to destroy nor to curse people but as a mercy to the entire humankind. O Lord, guide my people for they know not what they are doing, perchance from their loins will rise up a people who will worship You and sacrifice for Your sake, O Allah.[42]

Moreover, at the conquest of Makkah, the Prophet (ﷺ) entered the city full of humility, prostrating on his camel and praising Allah (ﷻ) with the words, "The truth has come, falsehood has vanished, and as a rule falsehood is bound to vanish when truth comes." He forgave all his enemies of the Quraysh who had spared no effort to annihilate him, his religion, and his followers. (The Quraysh were the dominant tribe in Makkah at the time of the Prophet's mission; their society was based on polytheism.) They were guilty of murder and persecution, yet he told them, "This day there is no reproof against you, there is no retaliation against you, you are all free." Here then, is a practical example of the maxim 'love your enemies' as preached by Jesus (ﷺ). Muhammad (ﷺ) had come to reclaim and reform the fallen humanity, and he won the hearts of the anti-social elements of his time by love and kindness. His charity and readiness to help the people in all possible ways was proverbial, for he was the greatest friend of the poor and the downtrodden.

He strove all his life to lead humankind from darkness to the light of the one true God, to make them righteous, to rescue them from error, superstition and sins. Yet he remained humble and modest, always conscious of his nothingness before God, and from the highest peak of moral and spiritual perfection which he had attained, he declared openly to the people:

$$﴿قُلْ إِنَّمَا أَنَا بَشَرٌ مِّثْلُكُمْ يُوحَى إِلَيَّ أَنَّمَا إِلَهُكُمْ إِلَهٌ وَاحِدٌ فَمَن كَانَ يَرْجُوا لِقَاءَ رَبِّهِ فَلْيَعْمَلْ عَمَلًا صَالِحًا وَلَا يُشْرِكْ بِعِبَادَةِ رَبِّهِ أَحَدًا ﴿١١٠﴾ ﴾ (سورة الكهف: ١١٠)$$

❨Say [O Muhammad]: I am only a man like you. It has been inspired to me that your god is One God. So whoever hopes for the meeting with his Lord, let him work righteousness and associate none as a partner in the worship of his Lord.❩   *(Qur'an 18: 110)*

Although on the basis of the glorious Qur'an, Muslims regard the characters of both Jesus (ﷺ) and Muhammad (ﷺ) as equally godly, pure, noble and soul inspiring, yet Jesus (ﷺ) had no opportunity to become a perfect model for men in all walks of life as did Prophet Muhammad (ﷺ), though both were prophets of the same God. For example Jesus (ﷺ) never got married so as to become an ideal

husband and father, neither did he triumph over his enemies so as to
have a chance of showing how a victor should treat vanquished foes
who have spared no effort to annihilate him and his followers. He did
not have his persecutors at his mercy and therefore had no occasion
to show real forbearance and forgiveness. In fact, Jesus (عليه السلام) did not
rise to power to become the model of a benevolent and just ruler and
judge. The closest to such a position is when he was at the verge of
establishing the kingdom of God on his way to Jerusalem, where he
is quoted to have said:

> But those mine enemies, which would not that I should reign
> over them, bring them hither, and slay them before me. (Luke
> 19:27 KJV)

Therefore, all human beings have no other alternative but to turn to
Prophet Muhammad (ﷺ) and not Jesus (عليه السلام), if they want to see the
true picture of an ideal happy and pious married life and of a wise,
just, and benevolent ruler, whom nothing could corrupt or divert from
working for the material as well as spiritual and moral well-being of
his people. Prophet Muhammad (ﷺ) witnessed both phases of
persecution as well as success and showed rare patience, fortitude,
courage, and love for his foes as a persecuted preacher of Islam. Yet
in the hours of political victory as a leader with a military force of
over ten thousand solders at his command, and his bitterest enemies
helpless before him, he showed unparalleled self-control and mercy
and forgave all.

On the other hand, Jesus (عليه السلام) was never given an opportunity to
practice many of his beautiful precepts and teachings. For instance he
advised his followers to sell their garments and buy swords in these
words:

> And he said unto them, when I sent you without purse, and scrip,
> and shoes, lacked ye any thing? And they said, nothing. Then
> said he unto them, But now, he that hath a purse, let him take it,

and likewise his scrip: and he that hath no sword, let him sell his garment, and buy one. (Luke 22:35-36 KJV)

Yet, he could not demonstrate to them the right use of the sword. To resist violence and aggression, often at times needs the right use of the sword, especially when helpless men, women, and children are being slaughtered and the freedom of belief and practice of one's religion is denied by fanatics and tyrants.

﴿وَمَا لَكُمْ لَا تُقَاتِلُونَ فِى سَبِيلِ ٱللَّهِ وَٱلْمُسْتَضْعَفِينَ مِنَ ٱلرِّجَالِ وَٱلنِّسَاءِ وَٱلْوِلْدَانِ ٱلَّذِينَ يَقُولُونَ رَبَّنَا أَخْرِجْنَا مِنْ هَـٰذِهِ ٱلْقَرْيَةِ ٱلظَّالِمِ أَهْلُهَا وَٱجْعَل لَّنَا مِن لَّدُنكَ وَلِيًّا وَٱجْعَل لَّنَا مِن لَّدُنكَ نَصِيرًا ۝﴾   (سورة النِّساء: ٧٥)

﴾And what is wrong with you that you fight not in the Cause of Allah, for those weak, ill-treated and oppressed among men, women, and children, whose cry is: "Our Lord! Rescue us from this town whose people are oppressors; and raise for us from You one who will protect, and raise for us from You one who will help."﴿ *(Qur'an 4: 75)*

It was Prophet Muhammad (ﷺ) who showed how a true soldier of God, the protector of the victims of intolerance and oppression should behave in the battlefield and in the moments of defeat and victory.

It is true that the life of Jesus (ﷺ) runs parallel to the early life of Muhammad (ﷺ), especially in the first thirteen years of Muhammad's prophethood, but Jesus (ﷺ) did not live long to exemplify his teachings and work out the social implication of his message. He did not have a chance to enlarge his teachings to cover all the situations of life and bring about the tremendous social reforms that Prophet Muhammad (ﷺ) did. The modern man today who has to lead a sophisticated life of being at one and the same time, a son, a husband, a father, a poor worker, a citizen, a neighbour, a despised advocate of new ideas and ways, a victim of religious and political bigotry, a man with authority, a successful leader of men, a soldier, a businessman, a judge, and a ruler will not find in Jesus (ﷺ), but in Prophet Muhammad (ﷺ), a perfect model in all these situations and walks of life. This is demonstrated by the poet France Lamartine, who opines in his history of the Turks:

> Never has a man set himself, voluntarily or involuntarily a more sublime aim, since this aim was superhuman: to subvert superstitions which had been interposed between man and his Creator, to render God unto man and man unto God; to restore the rational and sacred idea of divinity amidst the chaos for the material and disfigured gods of idolatry then existing. Never has a man undertaken a work so far beyond human power with so feeble means, for he had in the conception as well as in the execution of such a great design no other instrument than himself, and no other aid, except a handful of men living in the corner of the desert. Finally, never has a man accomplished such a huge lasting revolution in the world, because in less than two centuries after its appearance, Islam, in faith and arms, reigned over the whole of Arabia, and conquered in God's name Persia, Khorasan, Trasoxania, Western India, Syria, Abyssinia, all the known continent of North Africa, numerous Islands of the Mediterranean, Spain and a part of Gaul. If greatness of purpose, smallness of means and astounding results are the three criteria of human genius, who could dare to compare any great man in modern history with Muhammad? The most famous men created arms, laws and empires only. They founded, if anything at all, no more than material powers which often crumbled away before their very eyes. This man Muhammad moved not only armies, legislations, empires, people and dynasties, but millions of men; and more than that the altars, the gods, the religions, the ideas, the beliefs and the souls. On the basis of a Book, every letter of which has become law, he created a spiritual nationality, which blended together peoples of every tongue and every race. He has left us the indelible characteristic of his Muslim

nationality the hatred of false gods and the passion of one and immaterial God. This avenging patriotism against the profanation of heaven formed the virtue of the followers of Muhammad; the conquest of one-third of the earth to his dogma was his miracle; or rather it was not the miracle of a man but that of his reason. The idea of the unity of God, proclaimed amidst the exhaustion of fabulous theogenies, was in itself such a miracle that upon its utterance from his lips it destroyed all the ancient superstitions, temples of idols and set on fire one third of the world. His life, his mediations, his heroic revilings against the superstitions of his country and his boldness in defying the furies of idolatry, his firmness in enduring them for thirteen years in Mecca, his acceptance of the role of public scorn and of almost of being a victim of his own fellow country men: all these and finally his flight, his incessant preaching, his wars against all odds, his faith in his success and his super human security in misfortunes, his forbearance in victory, his ambition which was entirely devoted to one idea and in no manner, striving for an empire; his endless prayers, his mystic conversation with God, his death and his triumph after death; all these attest not to an imposter but to a firm conviction which gave him the power to restore a dogma. This dogma was two-fold, the unity of God and the immateriality of God; the former telling what God is, and the latter telling what God is not; the one over throwing false gods with swords, the other starting an idea with words. Philosopher, orator, apostle, legislator, warrior, conqueror of ideas, restorer of rational dogmas, of a cult without images, the founder of twenty terrestrial empires and of one spiritual empire, that is Muhammad. As regards all standards by which human greatness may be measured, we may ask, is there any man greater than he?[43]

So far, what has been seen of the attitude of Islam to Christianity is that the Qur'an mentions twenty-five prophets by name, some of whom are the famously known Jewish and Christian prophets: Abraham, Moses, David, Solomon, Elijah, Jacob, John the Baptist and Jesus the son of Mary (may Allah be pleased with them). Moreover, both Jews and Christians are recognized, respected, and honoured in Islam as people of the scriptures (Torah, Psalms, and Gospel).

The Qur'an principally accepts and confirms the scriptures that were revealed before it, but it also criticizes the corruption that was done to those scriptures: the Torah given to Moses, the Psalms given to David, and the Gospel given to Jesus, son of Mary.

﴿يَٰٓأَهۡلَ ٱلۡكِتَٰبِ قَدۡ جَآءَكُمۡ رَسُولُنَا يُبَيِّنُ لَكُمۡ كَثِيرًا مِّمَّا كُنتُمۡ تُخۡفُونَ مِنَ ٱلۡكِتَٰبِ وَيَعۡفُواْ عَن كَثِيرٍ قَدۡ جَآءَكُم مِّنَ ٱللَّهِ نُورٌ وَكِتَٰبٌ مُّبِينٌ ۝ يَهۡدِى بِهِ ٱللَّهُ مَنِ ٱتَّبَعَ رِضۡوَٰنَهُۥ سُبُلَ ٱلسَّلَٰمِ وَيُخۡرِجُهُم مِّنَ ٱلظُّلُمَٰتِ إِلَى ٱلنُّورِ بِإِذۡنِهِ وَيَهۡدِيهِمۡ إِلَىٰ صِرَٰطٍ مُّسۡتَقِيمٍ ۝ لَّقَدۡ كَفَرَ ٱلَّذِينَ قَالُوٓاْ إِنَّ ٱللَّهَ هُوَ ٱلۡمَسِيحُ ٱبۡنُ مَرۡيَمَ قُلۡ فَمَن يَمۡلِكُ مِنَ ٱللَّهِ شَيۡئًا إِنۡ أَرَادَ أَن يُهۡلِكَ ٱلۡمَسِيحَ ٱبۡنَ مَرۡيَمَ وَأُمَّهُۥ وَمَن فِى ٱلۡأَرۡضِ جَمِيعًا ... ۝﴾

(سورة المَائدة: ١٥-١٧)

﴿O people of the scriptures, there has come to you our messenger [Muhammad] making clear to you much of what you used to conceal of the scripture and overlooking much. There has come to you from Allah a light and a clear Book [the Qur'an]. By which Allah guides those who pursue His pleasure to the ways of peace, brings them out from darkness into the light, by His permission, and guides them to a straight path. They have certainly disbelieved who say that Allah is Christ, the son of Mary. Say: "Who then has the least power against Allah, if His will were to destroy Christ, the son of Mary, his mother, and all, everyone that is on the earth?..."﴾   *(Qur'an 5: 15-17)*

1. The Qur'an mentions Jesus (ﷺ), son of Mary, twenty-five times by name, saying that:

1.a. He was a true prophet of Allah (ﷻ).

1.b. He was born miraculously to the virgin Mary.

1.c. He was given many miracles, among was that he spoke as a child from the cradle to defend his mother from false accusations of adultery.

1.d. He raised the dead back to life by Allah's leave to prove that he was a true prophet.

1.e. He was given the Gospel, which was a guidance to the children of Israel.

2. The Qur'an declares and honours Mary as a virtuous, truthful woman who was chosen above women of all nations (see *Qur'an 3: 42-46*).

3. Mary is honoured in the Qur'an with a whole chapter dedicated to her virtuous historical background. This chapter, the nineteenth, is called Maryam.

4. The Qur'an clearly states that Jesus (ﷺ), son of Mary, taught the message of Islam, that God was uniquely one, and that all forms of worship should be directed to God alone.

5. The Qur'an also emphatically states that when Jesus (ﷺ) reached the climax of his mission and message of the kingdom of God to be established on earth, this put him in danger of being killed by his own people. But Allah, the All-Mighty and All-Wise, the Just and the Most Merciful, saved him from his own people by lifting him up to heaven alive (see *Qur'an 4: 158*).

6. The Qur'an, in no uncertain terms, makes it very clear that the Jews did not kill Jesus (ﷺ) by crucifixion (see *Qur'an 4: 157*).

7. Allah (ﷻ) does not mince His words in the Qur'an. He emphatically, in many passages in the Qur'an, rebukes and criticizes the false invented concepts and doctrines of humankind.

On the human-made doctrine of attributing divinity to Jesus (﷽), the Qur'an says that Jesus is not God, Jesus is not the Son of God, Jesus is not part of God, and that the doctrine of trinity is a blasphemous concept *(Qur'an 5: 72-76)*.

8. Islam does not accept the notion that Jesus (﷽) died on the cross for the sins of humankind to save humankind.

9. Islam does not accept the notion of original sin.

10. Islam therefore affirms that every human being comes into this world innocent and sinless. A newborn baby does not bear the burden of a sin committed by an ancestor. This would be a negation of Allah's attributes of justice, compassion, and mercy.

11. To further claim that the taint of this sin is certain to put human beings into Hell for all eternity unless the deity (God) sacrifices himself for His creatures is also a denial of the justice and good will of the Creator towards His creation.

12. No one can be saved except by the mercy and the grace of Allah (﷾) and by a person acknowledging and surrendering himself to the Creator and His guidance. A person can turn to His Creator in obedience and repentance without the need of any intermediary or intercessor.

On the other hand the Bible and Christianity have given a blank page of history of Islam and Muslims.

1. The Christians do not recognize or believe in Prophet Muhammad (﷾); in fact, if anything, they call him a false prophet and an anti-Christ.

2. They do not recognize or accept the Qur'an as the word of Allah (﷾) because they believe that the Bible is the last word of God.

3. The Bible even uses derogatory terms for Prophet Ishmael, saying that he will be a wild donkey of a man and his hand will be against all his brothers (see Genesis 16:12).

4. God, in the Bible, is always referred to as the God of Abraham, Isaac, and Jacob.

5. The Christians call the Muslims infidels.

6. The Christians and Jews believe that they are the children of God who deserve the blessings of heaven, while the Muslims do not deserve anything except hell.[44]

Allah (ﷻ) dedicated several chapters describing the characteristics of the people of the book (Jews and Christians), their arrogance and attitudes towards the Muslims, and the last Prophet Muhammad (ﷺ). For examples, see chapters 2, 3, 4, and 5 of the glorious Qur'an.

Thus, having inquired into both scriptures to see the contrast between Islam and Christianity and the attitude of both towards each other, it is quite obvious that Muslims are and have always been very tolerant to Christians, to the extent that Muslims are not only allowed to eat from their food but also to marry their chaste women.

Chapter 4

Socio-Political Interaction between Muslims and Christians

The Church's attitude towards Muslims, Jews and European scientists

$\mathcal{B}$ased on the quotations from the Christian world, seen in the previous chapter, what can be seen is a false foundational human-made doctrine as well as the secularized form of the teachings of Jesus (﷽) whereby to date, there is no such thing as a Christian state governed by the ten commandments and the rules and regulations given to Moses. This situation arose mostly due to the unjust theocratic rule of the Roman Catholic Church in all of Europe, with the persecution of free thinkers and European scientists like Copernicus, Johannes Kepler and Galileo, and with all forms of moral lapses and decadency. Many Christians revolted against the church and Christianity and followed the scientists' philosophy of ethics, believing that humankind could lead a happy, prosperous life without referring to God. This is what made the 'enlightened' people of Europe conclude that God is dead or that He does not exist.

Maryam Jameelah writes that the intimate relationship between the monastic ideals of Christianity and its implicit acceptance of secularism on principle is eloquently illustrated by one of the leading Christian missionaries to the Muslims, Dr. Kenneth Cragg. He said that many writers, both Muslim and non-Muslim alike, present and past, criticize Christianity for failing to discipline and check Western civilization. Rather, Christianity is implicated for allowing imperialism and its exploitation of the world, thereby aiding and abetting Western hegemony.[1]

Jameelah continues with her exposition:

> This is the kind of sophistry where the learned Christian Doctor tries to apologize for secularism. Christianity has had almost 2000 years to "regenerate" the world and convert the "natural man" into "new-man" but what have been its results? Christianity reigned unchallenged over Europe for over 1000 years, but the church proved itself more intolerant and bigoted than any other institution in history. Wherever the Catholic Church ruled, every effort was made to exterminate Jews, Muslims and Protestants and other heretics (the scientist scholars) whose legal rights to exist were not even recognized.[2]

> The blackest of the history of the Roman Catholic Church was the inquisition whose shadow, cast a virtual reign of terror over Europe for centuries. The Protestants were just as cruel and superstitious as the Catholics; it is a historical fact that the greatest leaders of the reformation — Martin Luther and John Calvin — whole-heartedly supported the white Church mania. John Calvin actually presided over the execution of this "crime". Hitler, Mussolini, Lenin and Stalin could find in a careful study of the inquisition and its methods to exterminate "heretics", and the methods of the Jesuits to indoctrinate the young, all they needed to know about secret police, spies, purges terror, propaganda and brain-washing all indispensable in the contemporary totalitarian state. No wonder religion was equated in most decent European minds with ignorance, superstitions, and fanaticism and an obstacle barring all hope of moral and material progress.[3]

This is the same kind of fear that has been cast ignorantly into the hearts and minds of the general populace of the world and especially Christians, that if the Muslims wake up from their deep slumber to re-establish the Islamic state, which governs purely by Sharia, then the same horrors that struck Europe by the Catholic Ecclesiastical will re-appear in the world. Such fears are based on erroneous conclusions and are baseless and unfounded for many reasons:

i) A majority of the Christians are very ignorant about Islam in general and more so of the aspects dealing with Islamic governance.

ii) They are falsely equating Islam with Christianity, when Islam is not a mere religion but a comprehensive way of life with authentic divine authority.

iii) The pages of history bear impeccable testimony that by and large Islam and the Muslims' rule for the past 1000 years, over half of the then known world had been the most just and tolerant rule ever seen in world history, which enabled people to progress in many fields of life.

Opening a few pages of unbiased Muslim history should suffice to see what we are talking about. A comparative study of the history of religions show that Islam has never been intolerant in the sense that it is alleged. On the contrary, Islam has been a great liberating and civilizing force for humanity. It kindled the torch of knowledge and learning. It gave room for science and technology. It introduced humankind to the true concepts of freedom, equality, and justice. It taught humankind the greatness of love, brotherhood, and at most tolerance to other faiths. Respect for other people's feelings is highly recommended in Islam. In this regard, Prince Charles of England, in 1993, while addressing a gathering at the Oxford University Centre for Islamic Studies, paid glowing tributes to Islam and its civilization and acknowledged that the West owed a lot to the Muslim world. He said:

We have underestimated the importance of 800 years of Islamic society and culture in Spain between the 8th and 15th Centuries. The contribution of Muslim Spain to the preservation of classical learning during the Dark Ages, and to the first flowerings of the Renaissance, has long been recognised. But Islamic Spain was much more than a mere larder where Hellenistic knowledge was kept for later consumption by the emerging modern Western world. Not only did Muslim Spain gather and preserve the intellectual content of ancient Greek and Roman Civilisation, it also interpreted and expanded on that civilisation, and made a vital contribution of its own in so many fields of human endeavour — in science, astronomy, mathematics, algebra (itself an Arabic word), law, history, medicine, pharmacology, optics, agriculture, architecture, theology, music... Many of the traits on which modern Europe prides itself came to it from Muslim Spain. Diplomacy, free trade, open borders, the techniques of academic research, of anthropology, etiquette, fashion, various types of medicine, hospitals, all came from this great city of cities. Medieval Islam was a religion of remarkable tolerance for its time, allowing Jews and Christians the right to practise their inherited beliefs, and setting an example which was not, unfortunately, copied for many centuries in the West...

More than this, Islam can teach us today a way of understanding and living in a world which Christianity itself is poorer for having lost. At the heart of Islam is its preservation of an integral view of the universe. Islam refuses to separate man and nature, religion and science, mind and matter, and has preserved a metaphysical and unified view of ourselves and the world around us... But the West gradually lost this integrated vision of the world with Copernicus and Descartes and the coming of the scientific revolution.[4]

The Qur'an and Hadith (Sunnah) inspired humankind with the real ideals of tolerance and history bears ample testimony to it. This part will cover the views of non-Muslim historians, most of whom do not have any sympathy for Islam, but because truth is truth by any name, they are forced to say nothing but the truth. For is it not a fact that in any court of justice, the evidence of one's own opponent holds much water and is deemed to be the most reliable?

Islam teaches that every person is answerable only to Allah (ﷻ) for his religious beliefs and no one has a right to question, much less to persecute, another for his faith. In an age of extreme religious intolerance, as has been seen in a few pages of Roman Catholic history, and in an age of absence of broad-mindedness in religious matters, when persecution for one's beliefs was regarded as a religious duty, it was the noble Prophet Muhammad (ﷺ) who, for the first time in the history of the world, not only enunciated and preached the principle of ❲no compulsion in religion❳ *(Qur'an 2: 256)*, but meticulously practiced it himself and ordered his Companions to do the same.

The Qur'an has an injunction enjoining the Muslims to say to the non-Muslims: ❲And to you your religion, and unto me my religion❳ *(Qur'an 109: 6)* as well as the injunction, ❲And had your Lord willed, those on earth would have believed — all of them entirely then [O Muhammad], would you compel the people in order that they become believers? It is not for any person to believe, except by the permission of Allah, and He will put the wrath on those who are heedless.❳ *(Qur'an 10: 99-100)*

Islam: The religion of equality

The Islamic dynamic philosophy of tawḥeed, the unity of Allah (ﷻ), is the bedrock on which the entire Islamic system of life rests, and from which the Islamic principle of the unity of humankind also springs. This tawḥeed is not a mere belief, a metaphysical philosophy; it is a dynamic belief, a revolutionary doctrine, a historic force and a communion with destiny. The Islamic stand is that all human beings are the creatures of the one unique God, Allah, who created all and sustains all and who is the guardian of all, and all human beings are equal in the sight of Allah (ﷻ). Distinctions of color, class, race, territory, socio-economic status, or worldly power are sheer illusions and ideologies which are misplaced and many times are the greatest menace for world peace.

Humanity as a single family is a creation of Allah (ﷻ). Human beings are to be respected and honoured not because they are white or black or because they are wealthy or belong to a superior race or tribe or because they are males, rather only because they are children from the same father and mother: Adam and Eve. Allah (ﷻ) says:

﴿۞ وَلَقَدْ كَرَّمْنَا بَنِىٓ ءَادَمَ وَحَمَلْنَٰهُمْ فِى ٱلْبَرِّ وَٱلْبَحْرِ وَرَزَقْنَٰهُم مِّنَ ٱلطَّيِّبَٰتِ وَفَضَّلْنَٰهُمْ عَلَىٰ كَثِيرٍ مِّمَّنْ خَلَقْنَا تَفْضِيلًا ٧﴾   (سورة الإسراء: ٧٠)

﴾We have indeed honoured the children of Adam; provided them with transport on land and sea; given them for sustenance things good and pure; and conferred on them special favours, above a great part of Our creation.﴿   *(Qur'an 17: 70)*

﴿يَٰٓأَيُّهَا ٱلنَّاسُ إِنَّا خَلَقْنَٰكُم مِّن ذَكَرٍ وَأُنثَىٰ وَجَعَلْنَٰكُمْ شُعُوبًا وَقَبَآئِلَ لِتَعَارَفُوٓا۟ إِنَّ أَكْرَمَكُمْ عِندَ ٱللَّهِ أَتْقَىٰكُمْ إِنَّ ٱللَّهَ عَلِيمٌ خَبِيرٌ ١٣﴾   (سورة الحُجُرَات: ١٣)

﴾O mankind, We have indeed created you from a male and female and made you peoples and tribes that you may know one another. Indeed the most noble of you in the sight of Allah is the most righteous of you. Indeed Allah is Knowing and Acquainted with all.﴿   *(Qur'an 49: 13)*

Sir C. P. Ramaswamy Aiyer, a leading Hindu thinker, wrote in an *Eastern Times* article on December 22, 1944:

What does Islam stand for? I regard and all thinking men
recognize Islam as the one and only democratic faith that is
actually functioning in the world today. Being a Hindu, firmly
entrenched in the Hindu faith, I yet make bold to say so. My own
religion has not succeeded, despite its fundamental philosophy
in implementing in practice the oneness of humanity. No other
religion, whatever its theory may be, has brought into practice
the essential idea of oneness of man before God as Islam has
done... It is only Islam that there can be no such problems as
those presented by Boers in South Africa or as those prevalent in
White Australia or in the southern states of America or even in
England among the several strata of society.

Sanctity of human life in Islam

As against what we saw of the plunder and slaughter of humanity
by papacy, Islam not only teaches and advocates the oneness and
equality of humankind, but it attaches the greatest importance to the
sanctity of human blood. In Islam, human life is sacred, and human
blood cannot be spilled without just cause. Allah (ﷻ) says:

﴿مِنْ أَجْلِ ذَلِكَ كَتَبْنَا عَلَى بَنِي إِسْرَائِيلَ أَنَّهُ مَن قَتَلَ نَفْسًا بِغَيْرِ نَفْسٍ
أَوْ فَسَادٍ فِي ٱلْأَرْضِ فَكَأَنَّمَا قَتَلَ ٱلنَّاسَ جَمِيعًا وَمَنْ أَحْيَاهَا
فَكَأَنَّمَا أَحْيَا ٱلنَّاسَ جَمِيعًا وَلَقَدْ جَاءَتْهُمْ رُسُلُنَا بِٱلْبَيِّنَتِ ثُمَّ إِنَّ
كَثِيرًا مِّنْهُم بَعْدَ ذَلِكَ فِي ٱلْأَرْضِ لَمُسْرِفُونَ ۝﴾ (سورة المائدة: ٣٢)

﴿Because of that, We decreed upon the children of Israel that
whoever kills a soul unless for a soul or for corruption [done] in the
land; it is as if he had slain humankind entirely. And whoever saves
one soul — it is as if he had saved humankind entirely. And Our
messengers had come to them with clear proofs. Then indeed many

of them, [even] after that, throughout the land, were transgressors.❩
                                                        (Qur'an 5: 32)

﴿وَلَا تَقْتُلُوا ٱلنَّفْسَ ٱلَّتِي حَرَّمَ ٱللَّهُ إِلَّا بِٱلْحَقِّ وَمَن قُتِلَ مَظْلُومًا فَقَدْ جَعَلْنَا لِوَلِيِّهِۦ سُلْطَٰنًا فَلَا يُسْرِف فِّي ٱلْقَتْلِ إِنَّهُۥ كَانَ مَنصُورًا ۝﴾

(سورة الإسراء : ٣٣)

❨And do not kill the soul [person] which Allah has forbidden, except by right. And whoever is killed unjustly, we have given his heir authority, but let him not exceed limits in [the matter of] taking life. Indeed, he has been supported [by the law].❩   *(Qur'an 17: 33)*

Justice and the rule of law

Islam enjoins on Muslims to decide problems which confront them with justice, whatever the consequence may be. In matters of law, all are equal and no distinction can be entertained in the execution of justice. The rule of law is supreme and administration of justice is above all. This is a matter that is very rare in this troubled world of today. Islam says that in matters of law and justice, there is no recognition of distinctions between Muslim and non-Muslim, the ruler and ruled, rich and poor, enemy and friend, or kin and stranger. Allah (ﷻ) says:

﴿۞ إِنَّ ٱللَّهَ يَأْمُرُكُمْ أَن تُؤَدُّوا ٱلْأَمَٰنَٰتِ إِلَىٰٓ أَهْلِهَا وَإِذَا حَكَمْتُم بَيْنَ ٱلنَّاسِ أَن تَحْكُمُوا بِٱلْعَدْلِ إِنَّ ٱللَّهَ نِعِمَّا يَعِظُكُم بِهِۦٓ إِنَّ ٱللَّهَ كَانَ سَمِيعًۢا بَصِيرًا ۝﴾

(سورة النِّساء : ٥٨)

❨Indeed, Allah commands you to render trusts to whom they are due and when you judge between people to judge with justice. Excellent is that which Allah instructs you. Indeed, Allah is ever Hearing and Seeing.❩   *(Qur'an 4: 58)*

﴿لَقَدْ أَرْسَلْنَا رُسُلَنَا بِالْبَيِّنَٰتِ وَأَنزَلْنَا مَعَهُمُ الْكِتَٰبَ وَالْمِيزَانَ لِيَقُومَ النَّاسُ بِالْقِسْطِ وَأَنزَلْنَا الْحَدِيدَ فِيهِ بَأْسٌ شَدِيدٌ وَمَنَٰفِعُ لِلنَّاسِ وَلِيَعْلَمَ اللَّهُ مَن يَنصُرُهُ وَرُسُلَهُ بِالْغَيْبِ إِنَّ اللَّهَ قَوِيٌّ عَزِيزٌ ﴿٢٥﴾ ﴾ (سورة الحديد: ٢٥)

﴿We have already sent Our messengers with clear evidences and sent down with them the scripture and the balance that the people may maintain [their affairs] in justice. And we sent down iron, where in is a great military might and benefits for the people and so that Allah may make evident those who support Him and His messengers unseen. Indeed Allah is Powerful and Exalted in Might.﴾

(Qur'an 57: 25)

﴿ يَٰٓأَيُّهَا الَّذِينَ ءَامَنُوا كُونُوا قَوَّٰمِينَ بِالْقِسْطِ شُهَدَآءَ لِلَّهِ وَلَوْ عَلَىٰٓ أَنفُسِكُمْ أَوِ الْوَٰلِدَيْنِ وَالْأَقْرَبِينَ إِن يَكُنْ غَنِيًّا أَوْ فَقِيرًا فَاللَّهُ أَوْلَىٰ بِهِمَا فَلَا تَتَّبِعُوا الْهَوَىٰٓ أَن تَعْدِلُوا وَإِن تَلْوُۥٓا أَوْ تُعْرِضُوا فَإِنَّ اللَّهَ كَانَ بِمَا تَعْمَلُونَ خَبِيرًا ﴿١٣٥﴾ ﴾ (سورة النِّساء: ١٣٥)

﴿O you who believe, be persistently standing firmly in justice, witnesses for Allah, even if it is against yourselves or parents and relatives. Whether one is rich or poor, Allah is more worthy of both. So follow not [personal] inclination, lest you be unjust. And if you distort [your testimony] or refuse [to give it] then indeed Allah is ever, with what you do acquainted.﴾ *(Qur'an 4: 135)*

﴿يَٰٓأَيُّهَا الَّذِينَ ءَامَنُوا كُونُوا قَوَّٰمِينَ لِلَّهِ شُهَدَآءَ بِالْقِسْطِ وَلَا يَجْرِمَنَّكُمْ شَنَـَٔانُ قَوْمٍ عَلَىٰٓ أَلَّا تَعْدِلُوا اعْدِلُوا هُوَ أَقْرَبُ لِلتَّقْوَىٰ وَاتَّقُوا اللَّهَ إِنَّ اللَّهَ خَبِيرٌۢ بِمَا تَعْمَلُونَ ﴿٨﴾ ﴾ (سورة المائدة: ٨)

﴿O you who have believed, be persistently standing firm for Allah witnesses in justice, and do not let the hatred of the people prevent you from being just. Be just, that is nearer to righteousness. And fear Allah, indeed, Allah is acquainted with what you do.❫ *(Qur'an 5: 8)*

And the history of Islam bears ample testimony that Muslims translated this ideal edict into practice.

The noble Prophet (ﷺ), in a case of theft by a very influential woman, decided the case against her and awarded the penalty of cutting off her hand for theft. On being approached by some dignitaries of the city to pardon the culprit, he declared that if his own daughter Fatimah had committed the crime, she would have received the same punishment without fail.

In the days of the second Caliph, 'Umar (ﷺ), a person of the tribe of Bakr ibn Wa'il killed a non-Muslim of Hirah. The Caliph ordered that the murderer be handed over to the kith and kin of the deceased. This was done and the successors of the assassinated executed him.[5]

During the reign of the third Caliph, Uthman (ﷺ), a verdict was given to execute one of the sons of Caliph 'Umar (ﷺ) because he was said to have killed a Hurmuzan (a Persian) who was the daughter of Abu Lu'lu', the murderer of 'Umar (ﷺ), under the impression that she too was involved in the murder of his illustrious father.[6]

In the days of the fourth Caliph, 'Ali (ﷺ), a Muslim was accused of murdering a *dhimmi* (a non-Muslim citizen of the Islamic state). The charge being proved, 'Ali (ﷺ) ordered the execution of the Muslim. The brother of the deceased, however, submitted that he had forgiven him. However, 'Ali was not satisfied, and only after his insistence and the assurance that he had received the blood money, did 'Ali consent to release the murderer. On that occasion he declared:

> Whosoever is our dhimmi, his blood is as sacred as is our blood and his property is as inviolable as is our property.[7]

Even in the later periods, when the Islamic society had degenerated, the instances of unique justice are not wanting. A Hindu sued Muhammad bin Tughlaq in the court of a Qadhi and the Sultan appeared in the court to satisfy his claim.[8] Aurangzeb Alamgir punished the grandson of his Prime Minister Asad Khan, Mirza Tafakhur, who outraged the modesty of a non-Muslim woman. Alamgir wrote: "It is my duty to prevent oppression on the people who are a trust from the Creator."[9]

It was because of this justice of Muslims that even non-Muslims preferred them to the rulers of their own faith. T.W. Arnold writes in his book, *The Preaching of Islam*:

> When the Muslim Army reached the valley of the Jordan and Abu 'Ubaydah pitched his camp at Fihl, the Christian inhabitants of the country wrote to the Arabs saying: O Muslims! We prefer you to the Byzantines, though they are of our own faith, because you keep better faith with us and are more merciful to us and refrain from doing us injustice and your rule over us is better than theirs, for they have robbed us of our goods and our homes. The people of Emessa closed the gates of their city against the army of Heraclius and told the Muslims that they preferred their government and justice to the injustice and oppression of the Greeks.[10]

There is no compulsion in religion

Islam is a missionary faith and Muslims are enjoined to preach their religion and establish the word of God on His land. There are two aspects of this: forbidding evil and oppression, and commanding right and virtue. The Islamic instructions are that there should be no compulsion in religion, and people of other faiths must not be converted to Islam by force. However, force can and should be used for the banishment of hostility, aggression, and transgression, which are the mainstays of persecution, oppression and intolerance. Islam does not consent to tolerating the intolerant and the oppressor.[11]

According to Dr. Abdul Karim, the purpose for which the Muslims were permitted to have recourse to arms, was based on three grounds:

1. To oppose and expel those who attack the Muslims without any just cause. All nations and all laws allow the right of self-defense.
2. To establish freedom of conscience, it being the duty of a Muslim to fight to protect a person, even a non-Muslim, persecuted for the sake of his or her faith.
3. To protect and preserve all places intended for the worship of God.

In fact, conversion was not the aim of any Muslim war. It could not have been otherwise, as the Qur'an repeatedly proclaims perfect freedom in the matter of conscience:

$$\text{﴿وَقُلِ ٱلْحَقُّ مِن رَّبِّكُمْ فَمَن شَآءَ فَلْيُؤْمِن وَمَن شَآءَ فَلْيَكْفُرْ ... ﴾}$$

(سورة الكهف : ٢٩)

❨And say, the truth is from your Lord, so let him who wills believe; and let him, who wills, disbelieve❩ *(Qur'an 18: 29).*[12]

Furthermore, the permission to use force is based on the following injunctions of the glorious Qur'an:

1. Whoever kills a human being unless it be for murder or for spreading fitnah (mischief, corruption and persecution), it shall be as if he had killed the entire mankind. *(Qur'an 5: 32)*
2. And fight them until there is no more (fitnah) oppression and persecution (and there prevails justice), and religion is for God, but if they cease, let there be no hostility except against those who practice oppression. *(Qur'an 2: 193)*
3. Fight in the way of Allah against those who fight you, but begin not hostilities (and do not transgress the limits prescribed by

Allah). Lo! Allah loves not aggressors. *(Qur'an 2: 190)*

4. And whoever defends himself after he has suffered wrong, for such there is no way (of blame) against them. The way (of blame) is only against those who oppress mankind and wrongly rebel in the earth. For such there is a painful doom. *(Qur'an 42: 41-42)*

5. God forbids you not, with regard to those who fight you not for (your) faith, nor drive you out of your homes, from dealing kindly and justly with them: for Allah loves those who are just. God only forbids you, with regard to those who fight you for (your) faith, and drive you out of your homes, and support others in driving you out, from turning to them (for friendship and protection). And whoever befriends them, they are the people who are unjust. *(Qur'an 60: 8-9)*

6. Let there be no compulsion in religion. The right path has surely been made distinct from the wrong; then, whoever rejects false deities and believes in Allah has got hold of a firm handhold, no breaking thereof. And God hears and knows all things. *(Qur'an 2: 256)*

Ends do not justify means

Islam further asks followers to preach the faith in the best possible way and adopt those means which are good, just, and respectable. Islam refuses to attach any worth to the dictum: The end justifies the means. In this respect, the following are the teachings of the Qur'an:

﴿وَلَا تَسْتَوِى ٱلْحَسَنَةُ وَلَا ٱلسَّيِّئَةُ ٱدْفَعْ بِٱلَّتِى هِىَ أَحْسَنُ فَإِذَا ٱلَّذِى بَيْنَكَ وَبَيْنَهُ عَدَاوَةٌ كَأَنَّهُ وَلِىٌّ حَمِيمٌ ۝ وَمَا يُلَقَّىٰهَآ إِلَّا ٱلَّذِينَ صَبَرُوا۟ وَمَا يُلَقَّىٰهَآ إِلَّا ذُو حَظٍّ عَظِيمٍ ۝﴾

(سورة فُصِّلَت: ٣٤-٣٥)

❴And good and evil are not equal of each other. Repel [evil] with that which is better and thereupon, him between whom and you there was enmity, shall be as if he was [your] devoted friend. And no one will be granted such goodness except those who exercise patience and self-restraint, none but persons having a great portion of good.❵

(Qur'an 41: 34-35)

﴿ادْعُ إِلَى سَبِيلِ رَبِّكَ بِالْحِكْمَةِ وَالْمَوْعِظَةِ الْحَسَنَةِ وَجَادِلْهُم بِالَّتِي هِيَ أَحْسَنُ
إِنَّ رَبَّكَ هُوَ أَعْلَمُ بِمَن ضَلَّ عَن سَبِيلِهِۦ وَهُوَ أَعْلَمُ بِالْمُهْتَدِينَ ۝﴾

(سورة النّحل: ١٢٥)

❴Invite to the way of your Lord with wisdom and beautiful preaching; and argue with them in a way that is best and most gracious: for your Lord knows best, who have strayed from His Path, and who receive guidance.❵

(Qur'an 16: 125)

The true testimony of history

History bears ample testimony that Muslims are the people who not only preached these precepts; they also translated them into practice. Soon after their arrival at Madinah, the noble Prophet (ﷺ) gave direction for the drafting of the world's first written constitution to the people, wherein all the rights, duties, and relationships between the Muslims, the Jews, and all the tribes of Madinah in peace and war were clearly spelled out. Moreover, in this important document, the non-Muslims were granted freedom of worship and protection from persecution. Al-Mubarakpuri writes in *The Sealed Nectar*:

> Soon after emigrating to Madinah and making sure that the pillars of the new Islamic community were well established on strong bases of administrative, political and ideological unity,

the Prophet (ﷺ) commenced to establish regular and clearly defined relations with non-Muslims. All of these efforts were exerted solely to provide peace, security, and prosperity to all mankind at large, and to bring about a spirit of rapport and harmony within his region, in particular. Geographically, the closest people to Madinah were the Jews. Whilst harboring evil intentions, and nursing bitter grudge, they showed neither the least resistance nor the slightest animosity. The Prophet decided to ratify a treaty with them with clauses that provided full freedom in faith and wealth. He had no intention whatsoever of following severe policies involving banishment, seizure of wealth and land or hostility. The treaty came within the context of another one of a larger framework relating to inter-Muslim relationships.

The most important provisions of the treaty are the following:

1. The Jews of Bani 'Awf are one community with the believers. The Jews will profess their religion and the Muslims theirs.

2. The Jews shall be responsible for their expenditure and the Muslims for theirs.

3. If attacked by a third party, each shall come to the assistance of the other. Each party shall hold counsel with the other.

4. Mutual relations shall be founded on righteousness; sin is totally excluded.

5. Neither shall commit sins to the prejudice of the other. The wronged party shall be aided.

6. The Jews shall contribute to the cost of war as long as they are fighting alongside the believers.

7. Madinah shall remain sacred and inviolable for all that join this treaty.

8. Should any disagreement arise between the signatories to this treaty, then Allah, the All-High, and His Messenger shall settle the dispute.

9. The signatories to this treaty shall boycott Quraysh

commercially; they shall also abstain from extending any support to them.

10. Each shall contribute to defending Madinah, in case of a foreign attack, in its respective area.

11. This treaty shall not hinder either party from seeking lawful revenge.

Madinah and its suburbs, after the ratification of this treaty, turned into a coalition state, with Madinah proper as capital and Muhammad (ﷺ) as 'president'; authorities lay mainly in the hand of the Muslims, and consequently it was a real capital of Islam. To expand the zone of peace and security the Prophet (ﷺ) started to enter into similar treaties with other tribes living around 'his state'.[13]

The advice that Abu Bakr (رضي الله عنه), the first caliph, gave on the occasion of the Syrian expedition, shows the real Islamic spirit. He said:

Remember that you are always in the presence of God, on the verge of death, in the assurance of judgment and in the hope of paradise. Avoid injustice and oppression, consult with your brethren and struggle to preserve the love and confidence of your troops. When you fight the battles of the Lord, acquit yourselves like men, without turning your backs, but let not your victory be stained with the blood of women and children, destroy not palm trees, nor burn any fields of corn. Cut down no fruit trees, nor do any mischief to cattle or such as you kill to eat. When you make any covenant or article, stand to it and be as good as your word. As you go on, you will find some religious persons who live retired in monasteries and propose themselves to serve God that way: Let them alone, neither kill them nor destroy their monasteries.[14]

Professor T. W. Arnold, commenting on this humanitarian approach of Islam, writes:

The self-restraint of the conquerors and the humanity which they displayed in their campaigns must have excited profound respect and secured a welcome for an invading army that was guided by such principles of justice and moderation as were laid down by the Caliph Abu Bakr. When Jerusalem submitted to the Caliph Umar, the following conditions were drawn up.

In the Name of God, the Merciful, the Compassionate. The following are the terms of capitulation which I, 'Umar, the servant of God, the Commander of the faithful, grant to the people of Jerusalem. "I grant the security of lives, their possessions, and their children, their churches, the crosses, and all that appertain to them in their integrity, and their lands and to all of their religion. Their churches therein shall not be impoverished, nor destroyed, nor injured from among them neither their endowments, nor their dignity; not a thing of their property; neither shall the inhabitants of Jerusalem be exposed to violence in following their religion; nor shall one of them be injured."[15]

Caliph 'Umar (رضي الله عنه) visited the holy places in Jerusalem (Al-Quds), Palestine, but how cautious and careful he was. Again, read in the words of Arnold:

> In company with Patriarch, 'Umar visited the holy places, and it is said while they were in the church of Resurrection, as it was the appointed hour of prayer the Patriarch bade the Caliph to offer his prayers there, but he thoughtfully refused, saying that if he were to do so, his followers might afterwards claim it as a place of Muslim worship.[16]

Gibbon wrote in his book *Decline and Fall of the Roman Empire*:

> To his Christian subjects, Muhammad readily granted the security of their persons, the freedom of their trade, and the property of their goods and the tolerance of their worship.[17]

Dr. Robert Briffault says:

> Theocracy (a term he uses as synonymous with religious government) in the East (meaning particularly the Muslim world) has not been intellectually tyrannical or coercive. We do not find there the obscurantism, the holding down of thought, the perpetual warfare against intellectual revolt, which is such a familiar feature of the European world, with Greece and Rome at its back.[18]

According to Muir:

> The Islamic leniency towards the conquered and their justice and integrity presented a marked contrast to the tyranny and intolerance of the Romans... The Syrian Christians enjoyed more civil and popular liberty under the Arab invaders than they had done under the rule of Heraclius and they had no wish to return to their former state.[19]

Sir Thomas Arnold also paid the same tribute. He wrote:

> In the first century of the Arab Rule the various Christian churches enjoyed toleration and a freedom of religious life such as had been unknown for generations under the Byzantine Government. Such references can be multiplied beyond number. Every honest historian has to admit that. And this proves that Islam has not engendered intolerance. Hence, the phrase that Islam generates intolerance is a pack of lies and a tissue of falsehood; and the attempt to hurl this charge against Islam is simply nonsensical. The allegation cannot stand the test of scrutiny on any account, on inquiry it falls to the ground because it is a false allegation and has the feet of clay.[20]

The orientalist Esposito in his famous book *Islam the Straight Path* clearly portrayed the true picture of how the Christian crusaders treated Muslims and in turn how the Muslim soldiers treated the

Christians. He wrote that though Islam and Christianity, both of which claim monotheism, seem to have the same roots, their history is largely marred by confrontation rather than dialogue or peaceful coexistence. The Christian West has always seen and portrayed Islam as a religion spread by the sword, while Muslims looked at the Christian West as invaders with their crusader armies. Accordingly, both religions have been locked in a geo-political and theological struggle for ascendancy. As Islam gained ground throughout the former Christian territories — including the Eastern Roman empire, Spain, and the Mediterranean from Sicily to Anatolia — it was seen as a threat to the Christian hegemony. According to Esposito, this growth of Islam over Christian territory, which challenged their entrenched doctrines and authority, was mostly met by hostility, intolerance, and belligerency, with few exceptions. Prophet Muhammad (ﷺ) was vilified as an imposter and identified as the anti-Christ.

The Christian theologians and writers dismissed Islam as a religion of the sword led by an infidel driven by lust for power and women. This attitude was preserved and perpetuated in literature such as the *Divine Comedy,* where Dante consigned Muhammad (ﷺ) to the lowest level of hell. However, in spite of all the vilifications, Islam continued to spread and Christian fears were fully realized, as Islam became a world power and civilisation while Christianity stagnated in its Dark Ages. Esposito further admits that by the eleventh century CE, though Christendom tried to reconquer the territories taken over by Islam through their crusades, it was a total failure that ended up in two myths abiding within the perceptions of the Western world: that the crusades were inspirational and that they triumphed.[21] Our author then sums up the Muslim response that culminated in the Christian defeat and how they treated both Jews and Christians:

> Jerusalem was a sacred city for all the three Abrahamic faiths.
> When the Arab armies took Jerusalem in 638, they occupied a

centre whose shrines had made it a major pilgrimage site in Christendom. Churches and Christian population were left unmolested. Jews, long banned from living there by Christian rulers, were permitted to return, live, and worship in the city of Solomon and David. Muslims proceeded to build a shrine, the Dome of the Rock, and a mosque, the al-Aqṣâ [22] near the area formerly occupied by Herod's temple and close by the Wailing Wall, the last remnant of Solomon's temple. Five centuries of peaceful coexistence (during this Muslim control over Jerusalem) elapsed before political events and imperial-papal power play led to centuries-long series of so-called holy wars that pitted Christendom against Islam and left an enduring legacy of misunderstanding and distrust. In 1071 the Byzantine army was decisively defeated by a Seljuq (Abbasid) army. The Byzantine emperor, Alexius I, fearing that all Asia Minor would be overran, called on fellow Christian rulers and the pope to come to the aid of Constantinople by undertaking a "pilgrimage" or Crusade to free Jerusalem and its environs from Muslim rule. For Pope Urban II, the "defense" of Jerusalem provided an opportunity to gain recognition for papal authority and its role in legitimating the actions of the temporal rulers. A divided Christendom rallied as warriors from France and other parts of Western Europe (called "Franks" by Muslims) united against the "infidel" in a holy war whose ostensible goal was the holy city. This was ironic because, as one scholar has observed, "God may indeed have wished it, but there is certainly no evidence that the Christians of Jerusalem did, or that anything extraordinary was occurring to the pilgrims there to prompt such a response at that moment in history."[23]

On the other hand, while contrasting the true motivation behind the failed Christian crusades with that of the Muslim armies, Esposito writes that the Christian rulers, knights and merchants were primarily driven by political and military ambitions which they hoped would bring them enormous economic and commercial rewards that would help establish a Latin kingdom in the Middle East. Thus as the Christian knights stormed Jerusalem in their first crusade in 1099, they made sure, in their merciless destruction in the Holy Land that they left no Muslim survivor; even women and children were not spared from the sword. The Noble Sanctuary, the *Haram al-Sharif*, was desecrated as the Dome of the Rock was converted into a church, and al-Aqsâ mosque, renamed the temple of Solomon, became a residence for the King. Latin principalities were established in Antioch, Edessa, Tripoli, and Tyre. Yet this Latin kingdom of Jerusalem was short-lived, lasting for less than a century because in 1187, Ṣalâḥ ad-Deen (Saladin), having re-established the Abbasid rule over Fatimid Egypt, led his army in a fierce battle and recaptured Jerusalem. However, the Muslim armies had humanity at heart; they were not as heartless as the Christian knights. Accordingly, they were magnanimous to their opponents and civilians alike. They spared the civilians, together with their churches and shrines. Esposito writes:

> "The striking differences in military conduct were epitomized by the two dominant figures of the Crusades: Saladin and Richard the Lion-hearted. The chivalrous Saladin was faithful to his word and compassionate towards non-combatants. Richard accepted the surrender of Acre and then proceeded to massacre all its inhabitants, including women, and children, despite promises to the contrary."

By the thirteenth century, the Crusades degenerated into intra-Christian wars, papal wars against their Christian enemies, who were denounced as heretics and schismatics. The result was a weakening, rather than a strengthening, of Christendom, as Roger Savory has observed:

> An ironical but undeniable result of the Crusades was the deterioration of the position of Christian minorities in the Holy

Land. Formerly these minorities had been accorded rights and privileges under Muslim rule, but, after the establishment of the Latin Kingdom, they found themselves treated as "loathsome schismatics." In an effort to obtain relief from persecution by their fellow Christians, many abandoned their Nestorian or Monophysite beliefs, and adopted either Roman Catholicism, or — the supreme irony — Islam.[24]

Towards the end of the fifteenth century crusade-wars, the Crusaders — who were initially meant to unite Christendom and turn back the Muslim armies — had become a spent force turning against each other. This led to the fall of Constantinople in 1453 to the Turkish Muslim conquerors. The former Byzantine capital, later to be renamed Istanbul, became the seat of the Ottoman Empire, and it is now in Turkey.[25]

This then is the true picture of the attitude of Christians and how they have always mistreated Muslims whenever they had a chance of conquering Muslims. The same thing was done in Bosnia, Chechnya, Kosovo, the Inquisition in Spain, Palestine, and most recently the Jenin massacre, the Gulf wars, and the Guantanamo Bay treatment of prisoners of war. The list is ugly and long.

Chapter 5

Economic Interaction between Muslims and Christians

$\mathcal{E}$conomically, the relationship between Muslims and Christians has not been any better. The Christian West has always used her crafty and cunning methods to exploit Muslim resources. The Christians have often used their acquired military power and technology to conquer and exploit the Muslims' vast amount of natural resources, especially over the last hundred years after the discovery of large resources of oil in Muslim lands.

The Gulf wars:
A means for economic exploitation

The most prominent of the recent classical examples of such exploitation known to all in the past and present are:

a) The planned eight-year war wherein Muslims were pitted against each other, the Iran versus Iraq war, where both Russia and America exploited enough crude oil and petroleum products in exchange for weapons and the killing of two million Muslims.

b) The Gulf war between Iraq and more than thirty-two nations of the world, mostly Christian, who saw themselves in a new twentieth century crusade for filling their bellies and pockets with petro-dollars, with America leading the coalition. A war that was planned twelve years before it actually took place by the ingenious Christian West, which resulted in the killing of one and a half million Muslims, followed by economic sanctions against Muslims in Iraq, lasted for eight years thus far. And the subsequent total destruction of Baghdad under the pretext of a search for weapons of mass destruction, which were never there in the first place.

About these carefully planned events, Huntington contends that the Gulf war was not a war to bring democracy into the region, as claimed by the Bush administration; rather it was the first post Cold War conflict that was used for exploiting the large amount of strategic energy resources. In reality, at stake was whether the bulk of the world's largest oil reserves were to be controlled by regimes in both Saudi Arabia and the Emirates, directly dependent on western military power and ingenuity for their security, or by independent anti-western regimes, who might use the oil weapon against western hegemony. In the first and the second Gulf wars, the West deliberately failed to topple Saddam Hussein[1] so that they could continue with their mission of exploiting the oil resources and dramatizing the security dependence of their regimes in the Gulf, while maintaining their expanded 'peacetime' military presence in the Gulf region. Just before the war, Iran, Iraq, the Gulf Cooperation Council, and the United States all jostled for influence over the Gulf. However, after the war, the Persian Gulf became an American lake of oil.[2]

To put it another way, Huntington says that initially the Gulf War began as a war between Iraq and Kuwait but then as the events unfolded, it turned into a war between Iraq and the West, which afterwards escalated to a war between the East and the West, 'a white man's war, a new outbreak of old fashioned imperialism.'[3]

Among other examples of economic warfare perpetuated by the Christian West against the Muslim world in the past and present are:

❖ The Sudan-American war (pretext of Christian south Sudan).

❖ The twenty-three year Italian-Libyan war for liberation from imperialist exploitation of Muslim resources.

❖ The Afghani-Soviet war between 1979 and 1989; for liberation from communism, which ended the role of the Soviet Union as a contending superpower with America.

❖ The Afghan-American war, which is still going on.

In this regard, Huntington again says in his book:

> Islam is the only civilization which has put the survival of the west in doubt, and it has done that at least twice.[4]

In a nutshell, the Christians have always economically exploited Muslim resources in the past through colonization, and now through neo-colonization, otherwise coined as globalization today. Professor of Economics at the International Institute of Islamic Thought and Civilization in Kuala Lumpur, Malaysia, Amer al-Roubaie says in his book:

> Recent changes in the global monetary financial and trading systems are driven by the interest of a few countries (mainly the G-7 groups). It is unwise to think that globalization is about the freedom of the market economy. The global economy is manipulated to serve the multinational firms, big financiers and the interests of the economically powerful nations. Their control, over global finances, technology, management, communications, research and development are the main determinants behind their economic power. At present Muslim countries are neither of individually nor collectively capable of matching the forces of the new global players (75%) seventy-five percent of the world's proven oil and gas reserve is in the

Muslim countries but they exercise little say over decisions regarding the global operations of the industry. A recent survey in *The Economist* declares that the world's biggest industry is energy with a global business amounting to at least $1.7 to $2 trillion a year. Furthermore, the World Energy Council estimates that global investment in energy between 1990 and 2020 will total some $30 trillion at 1992 prices. There is an urgent need for the establishment of multinational firms similar to the Malaysian Oil Company, partners and regional institutions like the Islamic Development Bank to increase competitiveness. Factor mobility including labor, capital and goods are important components of the global economy.[5]

The state of the Muslim world: Who is to blame?

It may be all too easy to throw the blame on the Crusaders or the Christian West for the confused and troubled state in which the Muslim world finds itself, but throwing the buck to somebody else for one's mistakes does not absolve one of the blame. Yes, it is true that the Christian West has for many years exploited the situation of the Muslim world for its economic interest, but how did this situation arise in the first place?

In order to understand how the situation came about, one ought to look back two centuries, to the period when Europe and America were experiencing a profound loss of belief in religion, due in part to the irreconcilable conflict between science and what was supposed to be the 'revealed Word of God.' Also in part due to changes in people's values and outlooks, motivated by massive changes in technology and patterns of living, the Muslim world too had started experiencing a crisis in religion and values. As the complexity of interplay. of forces took its toll and weakened Christianity in the West, the influence of Islam was also becoming attenuated in the East. As a result, many Muslims lost sight of the true reality of their faith, such that masses of them took the traditions of their societies, some of which were from Islam while others were from sources other than Islam, to be Islam itself.

The Muslim's understanding of Islam as a dynamic, revolutionary system of life dwindled until all that was left was a set of confused, quasi-Islamic traditions, some faded Islamic values and behaviour, and perhaps prayers, fasting in Ramadan, reciting the Qur'an — parrot style without understanding — when someone is dead and celebrating the Eids (the two annual Islamic celebrations).

Other Muslims also went to the opposite extreme of placing great emphasis on the ritual worship aspects of Islam while ignoring all the rest of the more important teachings about seeking knowledge, developing resources, research in all fields of human life, socio-political responsibilities, and cleanliness. Muslim children living outside the Arab world learned from pious, but often ignorant, teachers to pronounce the words of the Qur'an without understanding anything of the meaning, much less living by them. In other places youngsters grew up still more ignorant about Islam, believing it to be something related to the older generation which they were supposed to respect but which had no relevance or place in their contemporary life.

With the influence of the Western onslaught in the Muslim world after the First World War, coupled with the presence of Western imperialism, Christian missionaries, and westernized, often Western-educated natives returning home from European and American universities, the Muslims became uneasily conscious of their own material backwardness and lack of modernity in comparison to the West. And of course, due to the contact with Western goods and alluring lifestyle conveyed by Western movies, media, and propaganda, the West was seen as a glamorous utopia, adoption of whose culture and way of life would produce instant modernization and progress. Unfortunately, what was adopted was not the outstanding and excellent aspects of Western culture but only the most superficial and harmful ones, which were simultaneously applauded by many onlookers in the West as obvious signs of the Muslim world beginning to wake up and come of age.

Under the impact of all these, many Muslims accepted the Western society's dictum that religion, moral values, and the pursuit of their meaning in society, be given neither serious emphasis nor any importance in society. As its criteria for being civilized, material advancement and the discarding of traditional values were accepted as the true measure of greatness of a society without their grasping the essential fact that genuine civilization must only rest on a firm base of sound spiritual and moral principles, lacking which material progress simply becomes de-civilization, dehumanization, and destruction.

Pseudo-Islam (Muslims by name)

Consequently, there emerged three types of Muslims, who have their counterparts in other faiths too. The first are individuals to whom Islam is merely a vague tradition which, more often than not, they prefer to have nothing to do with; they are registered on their passports or birth certificates as Muslim, only because they are not Christian, Hindu, Buddhist or any other religion for that matter. They may have some outward token of respect for Islam, or they may totally be indifferent. In any case, it does not occur to them to guide their lives by Islam or try to practice it faithfully, and furthermore they regard those who do so as being backward and ignorant. This may be understandable from the fact that most such individuals lack knowledge and understanding of Islam as a total worldview and system of life; moreover they may not have been close to, or even known, anyone who could provide an example of real understanding and commitment to Islam. Such Muslims may never have prayed in their lives and may not even know how to pray because they were never taught in the first place.

For these individuals, Islam is simply a relic of ancient history. They may feel occasionally a twinge of pride in the Islamic heritage when it is mentioned, and they may even at times come to the defence of Islam when it is attacked. They may think of it once in a while when someone dies ("Where have I come from and where do I go when I die?"), but they are too preoccupied with daily activities and with family and possessions and pleasures of this worldly life to follow up this trail of thought further. Many social problems and vices have by now crept into the lives of such Muslims, including an increasing incidence of divorce, sexual license, alcoholism, and total loss of values and direction. Basically, they are Muslims only in name, no different either in their concepts or behaviour from the people who have no religion, for in fact they have neither and as a result are always hostile to Islam and to Muslims who adhere to Islam.

Folk Islam (traditional Muslims)

The second group are the traditional Muslims. They may understand the basic concepts of Islam, may have some degree of Islamic knowledge and may follow Islamic teachings to some extent but they do not understand it as a complete and comprehensive dynamic system for all aspects of human life, nor do they adhere to its requirements in all aspects of their lives, consistently, as a matter of principle and obligation.

In their minds, Islam is always mixed up with many pseudo-Islamic practices common to their societies, many of which are contrary to Islamic teachings although they have acquired some sort of Islamic flavour, and with many westernized ways of thought and behaviour as well. They definitely believe in Allah (ﷻ) and Islam, but in a theoretical sort of way that does not carry enough conviction to move them steadily and consistently toward a totally Islamic oriented way of life. Because they do not conceive of Islam as a complete system for all aspects of life, they are often critical of or look down on those who do so as having gone too far in the matter of religion.

True Islam (Muslims by choice)

The third group consists of those Muslims who understand the religion they profess as a total system of life and who have consciously chosen to pattern their lives according to it. Their worldview and frame of reference is Islam; their loyalty, obedience, and devotion are for Allah (ﷻ) alone, as is found in the words of the Qur'an:

$$﴿قُلْ إِنَّ صَلَاتِي وَنُسُكِي وَمَحْيَايَ وَمَمَاتِي لِلَّهِ رَبِّ ٱلْعَٰلَمِينَ ١٦٢﴾$$

(سورة الأنعام: ١٦٢)

❨Say: "Truly, my prayer and my service of sacrifice, my life and my death, are for Allah, the Lord of the Worlds."❩   *(Qur'an 6: 162)*

Their goal is the hereafter, and their community is the community of believers. Many of them are highly educated individuals who have arrived at such a position as a result of reflection on what is happening in the world around them. They are a unique group, part of the small yet strong company of true believers in Allah (ﷻ) who have been living in submission to Him from the time the first prophet, Adam (ﷺ), walked on earth until today, in obedience to His guidance. Without a doubt, to reach such a level of Islamic commitment requires a good understanding of Islam, which, due to very faulty and inadequate approaches to Islamic education even in Muslim countries, few are able to attain, unless they go through an Islamic curriculum of education.[6]

Moreover, the appeal of westernization and modernity is so strong that few people in the Muslim world have yet grasped the fact that material advancement is not necessarily the road to either true self-respect or satisfaction, and that it has not brought real happiness and well-being to the peoples of the West. Instead it has brought a staggering array of societal and environmental problems because the West has divorced itself from the spiritual and moral dimensions which are as integral and essential a part of humankind's nature as are their material needs.

Exploitation of Muslim resources, lack of political good will

As the Muslim community sank into the pit of colonial oppression and subjugation due to its own blunders (foremost being nationalism and secularism), coupled with neo-colonialism, the community lost its bearing and ability to educate its own people. The Muslim land was fragmented into little artificial states created by Western colonial masters, the opponents of the Sharia and the Islamic state. These artificial little states were led and ruled by hungry puppets, kings and dictators, who cared less about the well-being of Islam and their own people. As a consequence, a dual system of education was imposed on the Muslim community, which created a false dichotomy between Islamic education and the so-called modern (secular) education; of course, the leadership at all levels in the newly created artificial states was naturally passed on to those who went through the secular system of education.

Soon a Western-leaning and secular-oriented elite was prepared to take over the affairs of the newly formed states. A pre-requisite for joining into the newly formed elite was a commitment not to Islam, but to Western values, Western education, and a Western worldview. This westernization and secularization of the Muslim mind, by necessity, created hostility between Islam and the Muslim community, because even after the fall of the last Islamic state (the Ottoman Caliphate), the dominant ideology in the Muslim community was still Islam.

At any rate, as indicated earlier, the aim or motive behind the conquering of the Muslim lands by the West was not to spread Christianity (because the West had already fallen out from Christianity), though Christianity was used as a motivating factor for the conquest. Rather the aim of conquering was material gain, the exploitation of the vast natural resources in the Muslim lands. Muslims needed not to be converted to Christianity, it was enough for them to abandon their ideology and imbibe secularism. A classical example is the creation of secular Turkey under Mustafa Kemal Ataturk, the man who finished and buried the last remnants of the Ottoman Caliphate. In this respect, Professor S. P. Huntington says:

> Through a carefully calculated series of reforms in the 1920s and 1930s, Mustafa Kemal Ataturk attempted to move his people away from their Ottoman and Muslim past. The basic principles or "six arrows" of Kemalism were populism, republicanism, nationalism, secularism, statism, and reformism. Rejecting the idea of a multinational empire, Kemal aimed to

produce a homogeneous nation state, expelling and killing Armenians and Greeks in the process. He then deposed the sultan and established a western type republican system of political authority. He abolished the caliphate, the central source of religious authority, ended the traditional education and religious ministries, abolished the separate religious schools and colleges, established a unified secular system of public education, and did away with the religious courts that applied Islamic law, replacing them with a new legal system based on the Swiss civil code. He also replaced the traditional (Muslim) calendar with the Gregorian calendar and formally disestablished Islam as the state religion. Emulating Peter the Great, he prohibited the use of the fez because it was a symbol of religious traditionalism, encouraged people to wear hats, and decreed that Turkish would be written in Roman rather than Arabic script. This latter reform was of fundamental importance. "It made it virtually impossible for the new generations educated in the Roman script to acquire access to the vast bulk of traditional literature; it encouraged the learning of European languages; and it greatly eased the problem of increasing literacy." Having redefined the national, political, religious, and cultural identity of the Turkish people, Kemal in 1930s vigorously attempted to promote the Turkish economic development. Westernization went hand-in-hand with and was to be the means of modernization.[7]

With this trend continuing, the Muslim world became confused and troubled, with internal political instability playing a major role in perpetuating the continued exploitation of the Muslim world's resources. In fact, in spite of the Islamic requirement of a leader elected by the people and from among the people, and who consults with them in the conduct of all state affairs, the reality is that very few countries in the Muslim world does one find governments elected by the people and responsive to their needs, or capable of providing good governance, leadership, and stability to their countries. Rather what is found is as Suzanne Haneef puts it:

> Rather there are, by and large, the ruler and the ruled. And although in most cases they (these rulers) professed Islam and often made a public show of piety, among the rulers of the Muslim world in recent years have been many who were dictators and oppressors of the most vicious sort. They stifled all criticism and dissent in their societies, whether by individuals, groups or the press, by sadistically oppressive means, making ruthless use of highly-trained secret police and intelligence services to suppress anyone they considered a threat to their unbridled power; they filled the prisons of their "Muslim" countries to overflowing with tens of thousands of sincere and committed Muslims, many belonging to the intelligentsia, who were trying to call for a revival of Islam in their societies or to question the policies or actions of the ruler. Hair-raising Nazi-style tortures were applied to countless numbers of them under which many died, and some of the best among them were executed for fabricated "crimes" in order to silence the voice of truth so the ruler might continue unimpeded in his relentless drive for absolute power.
>
> Country after country in the Muslim world has seen rulers of this kind during the past half a century or more, men who although often "Muslims" themselves, hated and feared the very name of Islam because it constituted the only real challenge to their unchecked power and ambition, and who threw all their energies into trying to suppress it by oppressing Muslims. The Islamic requirement and demand of the people for basic human freedoms, social justice and good rule were systematically and ruthlessly stifled. Any incident occurring under such conditions was blamed on Islam and "Muslim fanaticism", as if one had to be either a Muslim or a fanatic to want freedom and justice;

indeed incidents expressly manufactured by the government for the purpose of discrediting Muslims have not been unknown. But since Islam, which is deep in the life-blood of Muslims even though they may be indifferent to its requirements, could not be so easily dismissed, such rulers attempted to reduce it to mere piety and acts of worship lest it emerge as a strong, dynamic movement in which each individual feels a keen sense of responsibility for how the country is governed, what happens to its resources, which belong to all the people, the morals and behaviour of its officials, and the entire host of matters over which the governments have jurisdiction, which Almighty Allah has made the concern of every Muslim individual as a member of his society as well.[8]

This is then the real cause of continued perpetual exploitation of Muslim natural resources; and while all this is happening, the Muslims of the first type are busy living the life of the world, preoccupied with their possessions, enjoyments, relationships, and the increase of their material advantages. Meanwhile, the second type of Muslims live in some halfway house between total loss of Islamic values and adherence to them, with various forms of excuses and apologies for their lack of commitment. They say, "Leave the leaders alone! They are God-chosen; do not mix Islam with politics, only concentrate on your soul. Allah will not ask you about the leaders but about yourself!"

But the Muslims in the third category stand firm on the Islamic principles and values, serving as a counterbalancing force against random 'progress' and indiscriminate adoption of values and behaviours that are not appropriate for Muslims and can do great harm to their societies. Because of their certain and unwavering conviction of the truth of Islam, such individuals cannot be swayed in the direction of corrupt and empty ideologies such as secularism, which have become, to a majority of mankind, the opium of the people. This third category of Muslims has brought to light the realization that all the problems facing the Muslim world today, whether political, social, economical, moral, or theological are very logically and directly, the result of Muslims falling away from Islam and that they can only be solved by a sincere and whole-hearted return to true Islam. In this respect, the Prophet (ﷺ) said:

Narrated Ibn 'Umar (﵁): I heard Allah's Messenger (ﷺ) saying: «If you (1) sold goods to a person for a certain price and then bought them back from him at a far less price; (2) followed the tails of the cows; (3) indulged in agriculture and became content with it; and (4) left jihad (struggling, exerting maximum efforts for excellence in the path of Allah), Allah will cover you with humiliation, and it will not be removed until you return back to your (deen) complete way of life of Islam.» (recorded Abu Dâwood) Allah (ﷺ) also warned us of a severe torment if we overindulge ourselves in the material world and end up forgetting our true purpose in the world:

$$﴿قُلْ إِن كَانَ ءَابَآؤُكُمْ وَأَبْنَآؤُكُمْ وَإِخْوَٰنُكُمْ وَأَزْوَٰجُكُمْ وَعَشِيرَتُكُمْ وَأَمْوَٰلُ ٱقْتَرَفْتُمُوهَا وَتِجَٰرَةٌ تَخْشَوْنَ كَسَادَهَا وَمَسَٰكِنُ تَرْضَوْنَهَآ أَحَبَّ إِلَيْكُم مِّنَ ٱللَّهِ وَرَسُولِهِ وَجِهَادٍ فِى سَبِيلِهِۦ فَتَرَبَّصُوا۟ حَتَّىٰ يَأْتِىَ ٱللَّهُ بِأَمْرِهِۦ وَٱللَّهُ لَا يَهْدِى ٱلْقَوْمَ ٱلْفَٰسِقِينَ ﴿٢٤﴾﴾$$

(سورة التوبة: ٢٤)

❨Say: If it be that your fathers, your sons, your brothers, your mates, or your kindred; the wealth that you have gained; the commerce in which you fear a decline; or the dwellings in which you delight — are dearer to you than Allah, and His Messenger, or the striving in His cause — then wait until Allah brings about His decision: and Allah guides not the people who are rebellious.❩   *(Qur'an 9: 24)*

Chapter 6

Social and Moral Interaction between Muslims and Christians

Sharia law: The safety pin of civilised societies

With regard to social and moral interaction, Muslims and Christians are incompatible. Whereas both have clear moral precepts in the teachings of their respective faiths, Christians have not been as strict as Muslims in adhering to and keeping the Sharia. Often Christians believe that they are not bound by the Ten Commandments brought by Prophet Moses (ﷺ), were subsequently fulfilled by Jesus (ﷺ) when he said:

> Think not that I have come to abolish the law or the prophets; I have not come to abolish them but to fulfil them. (Matthew 5:17 NIV)

The Christians take religion to be an individual affair; as such, many of the moral precepts found in the teaching of the prophets are not at all implemented either on an individual level or on a community level in the Christian world. Rather, since they believe that the law is not binding on them, but instead that they live under the grace and love of God, it is not necessary for capital punishment to be administered for moral lapses and crimes against fellow human beings, such as theft, adultery, fornication, murder, or drunkenness. This Christian attitude has in a way encouraged irresponsibility and immorality in society because they have separated everyday life from faith by way of promoting the following:

❖ Fashion shows, dancing competitions, and beauty pageants.

❖ Music, clubs and pubs for drinking alcohol.

❖ Illegitimate children through free society where having a mistress, girlfriend or boyfriend, is no sin, dating one another by going to film shows and on outings is normal and sex before marriage is normal.

❖ Personal freedom — believing that religion is an individual affair and therefore one is free to do as he or she likes, 'minding your own business', as they say.

❖ Various festivals that spread immorality such as Valentine's Day and April Fool's Day.

On social and moral interaction between 1980 and 1990, the overall trend in most Muslim countries was anti-Western partly due to the resurgence of Islam and the backlash against the detrimental effects of Westernization seen in Muslim societies. The reaffirmation of Islam, in whatever shape and form, meant the repudiation of European and American influence upon the Muslim society, politics and morality. In the distant past, the Western puppet regimes did try to convince their local communities to westernize for the purpose of technological advancement, but not so in the recent past; if there is any Muslim leader who has done so, then he is a lonely figure. This is because in the last quarter of the twentieth century, with the deteriorating moral situation in the Western world, it became increasingly difficult to find any Muslim leaders — be they politicians, officials, academics, business persons, or even journalists — applauding Western values or institutions. They instead emphasized the differences between the Islamic civilization and the corrupt Western civilization, thereby asserting the superiority of the Islamic culture and the need to maintain it against a Western onslaught. Whereas Muslims loathe and resent Western power and the threat it poses to their society and beliefs, they also see Western culture as a seductive, materialistic, corrupt, decadent and immoral secular way of life that is out of step with human natural instincts of morality; hence they stress all the more the need to resist its impact on their way of life. Muslims always challenge the West with respect to morality, not because the Westerners are following a corrupted form of religion which is nevertheless a religion of 'the people of the book,' but because they are not being faithful to any religion at all. To the Muslims, Western secularism, irreligiosity and immorality are worse evils than the Western Christianity that produced them. Thus, in their interactions during the Cold War, the West branded their opponents as 'godless communists' while in the post-Cold War conflict, the Muslims saw the opponents as the 'godless West'.[1]

Therefore, Muslims believe that their social life should be guided and controlled by the Sharia of Allah (ﷻ), which is derived from the Qur'an and Sunnah of the Prophet Muhammad (ﷺ), as well as consensus among the Companions of the Prophet and deduction by analogy. This is because Muslims believe that Islam has a clear social and moral system, which they believe strongly to be the solution to all the tribulations facing the secularized world of today. Muslims believe that the Sharia covers every aspect of life; it means a path that leads to Allah. It is the path upon which Allah wishes humankind to proceed in this life, including every single deed without exception. Muslims believe that human beings are incapable of discriminating between right and wrong by their own unaided powers. Therefore, it for this reason that guidance was sent to them through the prophets. Muslims also believe that every prophet had a Sharia according to the needs of his people. Allah (ﷻ) says:

﴿وَأَنزَلْنَآ إِلَيْكَ ٱلْكِتَٰبَ بِٱلْحَقِّ مُصَدِّقًا لِّمَا بَيْنَ يَدَيْهِ مِنَ ٱلْكِتَٰبِ وَمُهَيْمِنًا عَلَيْهِ فَٱحْكُم بَيْنَهُم بِمَآ أَنزَلَ ٱللَّهُ وَلَا تَتَّبِعْ أَهْوَآءَهُمْ عَمَّا جَآءَكَ مِنَ ٱلْحَقِّ

لِكُلٍّ جَعَلْنَا مِنكُمْ شِرْعَةً وَمِنْهَاجًا وَلَوْ شَاءَ اللَّهُ لَجَعَلَكُمْ أُمَّةً وَاحِدَةً وَلَكِن

لِّيَبْلُوَكُمْ فِي مَا ءَاتَنكُمْ فَاسْتَبِقُوا الْخَيْرَتِ إِلَى اللَّهِ مَرْجِعُكُمْ جَمِيعًا فَيُنَبِّئُكُم

بِمَا كُنتُمْ فِيهِ تَخْتَلِفُونَ ﴿٤٨﴾   (سورة المائدة: ٤٨)

To you We sent the Scripture in truth, confirming the Scripture that came before it, and guarding it in safety. So judge between them by what Allah has revealed, and follow not their vain desires, diverging from the truth that has come to you. To each among you have We prescribed a law and an open way. If Allah had so willed, He would have made you a single people, but [His plan is] to test you in what He has given you; so strive as in a race in all virtues. The goal of you all is to Allah; it is He that will show you the truth of the matters in which you dispute.   *(Qur'an 5: 48)*

It is only Prophet Muhammad (ﷺ) who was given the complete guidance and final message for all mankind, and as such, his Sharia is the only complete and final law for all people, representing the will of Allah (ﷻ) for all humanity.

﴿ثُمَّ جَعَلْنَاكَ عَلَى شَرِيعَةٍ مِّنَ الْأَمْرِ فَاتَّبِعْهَا وَلَا تَتَّبِعْ أَهْوَاءَ الَّذِينَ لَا

يَعْلَمُونَ ﴿١٨﴾   (سورة الجاثية: ١٨)

Then We put you, [O Muhammad], on an ordained way concerning the matter [of religion]; so follow it and do not follow the inclinations of those who do not know.   *(Qur'an 45: 18)*

Muslims believe that human beings should live their private and communal life in accordance with the divine will, which implies implementing the Sharia. This includes beliefs about Allah, the prophets, the hereafter, prayers, fasting, and all other acts of worship; how and what one eats; how one dresses, procreates, sleeps and deals with neighbours; buying and selling; as well as issues of state, macroeconomics, and war and peace.[2]

The main purpose of Sharia is to regulate the social order and protect society by realizing and securing the general good or interest of people; by promoting their welfare as individuals and as a collective body and keeping harm and injury away from them.

The vital needs that the Sharia is concerned with protecting are those that are directly connected to human life, such that if any of these needs are threatened, then corruption, disorder and injustice will reign in the society. These vital needs, in order of priority are:

- ✓ The natural system of beliefs and way of life of Islam
- ✓ The life of the individual human being and human species
- ✓ The mind of the individual
- ✓ The honour and chastity of the individual
- ✓ The wealth or property

Muslims believe that whenever people reject living according to the will of Allah (ﷻ) by implementing the Sharia, and they decide to follow their desires instead, then calamities and disasters strike, as is common all over the globe.

$$﴿ظَهَرَ ٱلۡفَسَادُ فِى ٱلۡبَرِّ وَٱلۡبَحۡرِ بِمَا كَسَبَتۡ أَيۡدِى ٱلنَّاسِ لِيُذِيقَهُم بَعۡضَ ٱلَّذِى عَمِلُواْ لَعَلَّهُمۡ يَرۡجِعُونَ ۝﴾$$

(سورة الرُّوم: ٤١)

❲Corruption has appeared throughout the land and sea by [reason of] what the hands of people have earned so He [Allah] may let them taste part of [the consequence of] what they have done that perhaps they will return [to righteousness].❳   *(Qur'an 30: 41)*

Therefore, Muslims would like to:

- ❖ Live as a community under the Islamic state guided by the Sharia.
- ❖ Re-establish the Islamic brotherhood.
- ❖ Have social responsibility towards one another under the injunction of commanding good and forbidding evil.

❖ Establish family units based on Sharia guidelines and principles, since organized family units are the foundation of Muslim civilization, hence no illegitimate children.

❖ Maintain their Islamic dress code both for men and women whether at home, at school, at the workplace and virtually wherever they may be; Muslims do not want to be restricted by anybody in the way they dress according to the Sharia.

❖ Implement their Sharia principle of no free intermingling and mixing of men and women.

❖ Stay away from girlfriend and boyfriend situations and dating; stay away from sex before marriage, this being the main way of spreading the dreaded scourge of HIV/AIDS.

❖ Stay away from all celebrations and festivities, except those celebrations allowed by Sharia, from which the Muslim derives spiritual, moral, and physical benefits which harmonize the well-being of human society.

❖ Implement the Sharia criminal law because they believe that the penal codes were prescribed to protect and secure the society from different crimes. People are at different levels of faith and morality; as such, for some the promise of rewards and the threat of punishment in the hereafter is sufficient to inspire them to do good. For others, the realization that crimes will be punished in this life by the government is necessary to restrain them from evil deeds. Yet for others who still do evil in spite of the threat of legal penalties, their public punishment serves as a deterrent to those who witness it. Allah (﷾) gives the rationale behind the prescribed penalties. He says:

$$﴿وَلَكُمْ فِى ٱلْقِصَاصِ حَيَوٰةٌ يَٰٓأُوْلِى ٱلْأَلْبَٰبِ لَعَلَّكُمْ تَتَّقُونَ ۝﴾$$

(سورة البَقَرَة: ١٧٩)

﴿In the law of equity there is [saving of] life to you, O you people of understanding; that you may become righteous.﴾ *(Qur'an 2: 179)*

Islamic law places emphasis on physical punishment for major crimes in society such as murder, adultery, theft, drunkenness, and slandering of chaste people, like it is done in Nigeria, rather than imprisonment, because a prison is more of a school for crime than a means of reforming criminals. Muslims believe that this Islamic solution is more likely to change the criminal's behaviour positively and save the community from the huge expenses of a massive prison system.[3]

Because of these marked and opposing differences in the way Muslims and Christians view the divine laws, there have always been conflicts between Muslims and Christians in the area of social and moral interactions, and these may well continue into the future, because whatever the Muslim abhors is what the Christian West considers as the norm. S.P. Huntington says:

> The causes of the renewed conflict between Islam and the West thus lie in the fundamental questions of power and culture. Who is to rule and who is to be ruled? The central issue of politics defined by Lenin is the root of contest between Islam and the west. There is, however the additional conflict, which Lenin would have considered meaningless, between two versions of what is right and what is wrong, and as a consequence, who is right and who is wrong. So long as Islam remains Islam (which it will) and the west remains the west (which is more dubious) this fundamental conflict between two great civilizations and ways of life will continue to define their relations in the future even as it has defined them for the past 14 centuries.[4]

The big question is: Are the Muslims in their interaction with Christians going to ensure that Islam remains Islam so as to meet the challenges ahead? The former German Ambassador to Algeria and Morocco, who embraced Islam sometime back, Dr. Murad Hofmann, has the following to say:

...Considering the general anti-Islamic mood generated by all types of media, how could one expect things to be any different? Given the circumstances outlined above, it is not easy to keep hope alive for miraculous transformation in the media's treatment of Islam.... Muslims are practicing their faith as a religion of peace and tolerance and yet, since the crusades, the image of Islam had never been as bad as it is today. In reality Islam was a culture more beleaguered than belligerent....

Naturally, Muslims can hope for a thorough improvement of the image of the religion only if they are ready to admit without reservation that the sometimes very un-Islamic Muslim world has contributed a lot to the un-flattering impression their religion has made....

More promising are the coordinated activities like the annual "day of the open mosque" organized by the central council of Muslims in Germany on October 3rd which is a public holiday. This activity is more likely to reduce prejudice and fear, and to educate better than any Islamic television channel could. The thing to do now is not to be present with television, radio and newspapers, but to be represented in them. To make this work more, Muslims will have to learn how to get articles published in the mainstream press: Articles so concise, objective, well researched and well written as to be virtual ready-to-print. Why not profit from the fact that journalists like everybody else would rather work less than more?[5]

Islamophobia uncalled for

The recent influence of the mass media, which is totally under the control of the West, who are in many cases opposed to Islam and Muslims, has moulded the world's opinion against Islam and

Muslims. Instead of the Christian world looking at Islam from the Islamic eyes, and understanding it from authentic Islamic sources in order to live in harmony with the Muslim world, the Christians have decided to blindly follow the Western mass media in its endeavour to suppress Islam and Muslims from following and asserting their values. The West has done this and is still doing so by casting the fear of Islam, otherwise known as Islamophobia, into the hearts of Christians, by misrepresenting Islam and Muslims, saying that Islam:

1) is a backward religion that is against progress and technology
2) is a religion of the Arabs and not Africans or anyone else
3) is the religion of Muhammedans and the Arabs
4) has a Sharia that is intolerant and barbaric
5) discriminates against and oppresses women
6) has come to change your way of life by taking away your God-given freedom to do whatever you want with your life
7) is the religion of terror, and that Muslims are terrorists
8) has come to bring hostility among nations
9) was spread by the sword, and that Muslims are fanatics
10) is threatening world peace, and therefore Iraq must disarm

On the contrary, the truth of the matter is that all these are lies and misconceptions hurled at Islam and Muslims. In fact, Islam is a religion of peace and tolerance, progress, and justice, as has already been discussed in a few pages of unbiased history. It suffices to know that even the orientalists such as Esposito, Huntington, Sir Thomas Arnold and others show in their writings that all the above accusations about Islam and Muslims are a pack of lies thrown at Islam by Western propaganda machinations to perpetuate the ongoing conflict with Islam.

When most Western scholars evaluate the rapid expansion of Islam after the death of Prophet Muhammad (ﷺ), they marvel at how within less than half a century the Muslim forces overran the

Byzantine and Persian armies, conquering Iraq, Syria, Palestine and Egypt. They also admire how the momentum of the early Muslim victories were spearheaded by a series of brilliant battles under great sincere generals of the calibre of Khalid ibn Waleed (ﷺ) and 'Amr ibn al-'Âṣ (ﷺ), which then extended the Muslim boundaries to Morocco and Spain in the west and across central Asia to India in the east. These scholars also admit that Muslim armies, unlike others, proved to be formidable conquerors and effective rulers, builders rather than destroyers.

Muslim armies and their leaders replaced the indigenous rulers and armies of the conquered countries but preserved much of their government, bureaucracy and culture. For many in the conquered territories, it was no more than an exchange of masters, one that brought peace to people demoralized and disaffected by the casualties and heavy taxation that resulted from the years of Byzantine-Persian warfare. Local communities were free to continue to follow their own way of life in internal, domestic affairs. In many ways local populations found Muslim rule more flexible and tolerant than that of the Byzantines and Persians. Religious communities were free to practice their faith — to worship and be governed by their religious leaders and laws in such areas as marriage, divorce, and inheritance. In exchange, they were required to pay tribute, a poll tax (*Jizyah*) that entitled them to Muslim protection from outside aggression and exempted them from military service. They were therefore called the 'protected ones' (*dhimmis*). In effect this always meant lower taxes, greater local autonomy, rule by fellow Semites with closer linguistic and cultural ties than the Hellenized Greco-Roman elites of Byzantine, and greater religious freedom for Jews and indigenous Christians. Most of the Christian Churches, such as the Nestorian, Monophysites, Jacobites and Copts had been persecuted as heretics and schismatics by Christian orthodoxy. For these reasons, some Jewish and Christian communities aided the invading armies, regarding them as less oppressive than their imperial masters. Muslims saw the conquests as a manifestation of the promise of Allah to make Islam supreme.[6]

﴿هُوَ ٱلَّذِىٓ أَرْسَلَ رَسُولَهُۥ بِٱلْهُدَىٰ وَدِينِ ٱلْحَقِّ لِيُظْهِرَهُۥ عَلَى ٱلدِّينِ كُلِّهِۦ وَكَفَىٰ بِٱللَّهِ شَهِيدًا ۝﴾ (سورة الفَتْح: ٢٨)

❲It is He Who has sent His Messenger with Guidance and the Religion of Truth, to proclaim it [make it supreme and victorious] over all religion: and enough is Allah for a Witness.❳ *(Qur'an 48: 28)*

It was narrated that Thawbân (رضي الله عنه) said: Allah's Messenger (ﷺ) said: «Allah drew the ends of the earth together for me to see, and I saw its eastern and its western lands, and I saw that the dominion of my Ummah will reach as far as that which was drawn together for me to see. And I have been given two treasures, the red and the white.[7] I asked my Lord not to let my Ummah be destroyed by widespread famine, and not to let them be dominated by an enemy that is not of them, that would destroy them utterly. My Lord said: O Muhammad, when I decree something, it cannot be altered. I have granted you that your Ummah will not be destroyed by a widespread famine, and it will not be dominated by an enemy that is not of them, that would destroy them utterly, even if all people from all regions were to come together (to destroy them). But some of them will destroy others, and some will take others captives.» (Muslim)

According to Professor Esposito, the Muslim conquest destroyed very little. If anything, they only suppressed imperial rivalries and sectarian bloodletting among the newly conquered population while they tolerated Christianity, even though they disestablished it as the authority in the land relegating Christian life and its endowments, politics and theology to a private and personal rather than public affairs. Just as the Christians had earlier reduced the status of the Jews so did the Muslims with the exception that the Christian status was reduced merely judicially without the accompaniment of systematic persecution or blood lust and in most cases unmarred by vexatious behaviour.[8]

Notwithstanding this magnanimous attitude of Islam towards Christianity, a common misrepresentation associated with the spread of Islam is the role of jihad, so-called 'holy war'. While most Westerners are very quick to demonize Islam as a religion spread at the point of the sword, the truth of the matter, as understood by Muslims and as is becoming increasingly clear to many people, is that jihad in the Qur'an and Muslim practice refers to the obligation of all Muslims to strive (with jihad meaning striving or self-exertion) or struggle to follow God's will. This includes both the struggle to lead a virtuous life and the universal mission of the Muslim community to spread God's rule and law through teaching, preaching and, where necessary, armed struggle. Allah (ﷻ) said:

﴿وَجَٰهِدُواْ فِى ٱللَّهِ حَقَّ جِهَادِهِۦ هُوَ ٱجْتَبَىٰكُمْ وَمَا جَعَلَ عَلَيْكُمْ فِى ٱلدِّينِ مِنْ حَرَجٍ مِّلَّةَ أَبِيكُمْ إِبْرَٰهِيمَ هُوَ سَمَّىٰكُمُ ٱلْمُسْلِمِينَ مِن قَبْلُ وَفِى هَٰذَا لِيَكُونَ ٱلرَّسُولُ شَهِيدًا عَلَيْكُمْ وَتَكُونُواْ شُهَدَآءَ عَلَى ٱلنَّاسِ فَأَقِيمُواْ ٱلصَّلَوٰةَ وَءَاتُواْ ٱلزَّكَوٰةَ وَٱعْتَصِمُواْ بِٱللَّهِ هُوَ مَوْلَىٰكُمْ فَنِعْمَ ٱلْمَوْلَىٰ وَنِعْمَ ٱلنَّصِيرُ ٧٨﴾

(سورة الحَجّ: ٧٨)

❨And strive hard in Allah's cause as you ought to strive. He has chosen you, and has not laid upon you in religion any hardship, it is the religion of your father Abraham. It is He [Allah] Who has named you Muslims both before and in this [the Qur'an], that the Messenger [Muhammad] may be a witness over you and you be witnesses over the people. So establish prayer and give charity and hold fast to Allah. He is your Protector and what an Excellent Protector and what an Excellent Helper.❩

(Qur'an 22: 78)

Thus the astonishing expansion of Islam resulted not only from armed conquest but also from peaceful preaching and coexistence with communities of other faiths, thereby guaranteeing all their rights under the Islamic state. In fact, in the later centuries, in many parts of Africa, the Indian sub-continent and Southeast Asia, Islam effectively spread not by armed struggle but primarily through the magnanimity of Muslim traders and Sufi (mystic) missionaries who won converts by their good life examples and their peaceful preaching.[9]

Challenges ahead for Muslim-Christian interactions

The challenges that lie ahead for both Muslims and Christians in their interaction with each other are quite formidable, especially in the wake of the false propaganda of the fight against terrorism, which in reality is a diplomatic way of saying the fight against Islam and Muslims. In an interview with the BBC on Friday, 24, 2003, Prime Minister of Malaysia, Dr. Mahathir Muhammad, put it succinctly before handing over power to his successor:

> It is not a question of disarming Iraq, since North Korea has the said weapons of mass destruction, yet America is afraid to disarm her, rather it is a declaration of war by America against Islam and Muslims.

The challenges that lie ahead for Muslims and Christians are to solve all these lies and misconceptions hurled at Islam and Muslims, since they are some of the causes and factors that have increased the conflict between Islam and Western Christianity. S. P. Huntington adds some more causes for renewed conflicts:

Comparably mixed up factors have increased the conflict between Islam and the west in the late twentieth century (20th).

a) First, Muslim population growth has generated large numbers of unemployed and disaffected youth, people who became recruits to Islamist causes, exert pressure on neighbouring societies and migrate to the West.

b) Second, the Islamic resurgence has given Muslims renewed confidence in the distinctive character and worth of their civilization and values compared to those of the west.

c) Third, the west's simultaneous efforts to universalize its values and institutions to maintain its military and economic conflicts in the Muslim world generate intense resentment among Muslims.

d) Fourth, the collapse of communism removed a common enemy of the west and Islam and left each the perceived major threat of the other.

e) Fifth, the increasing contact between and intermingling of Muslims and westerners stimulate in each a new sense of their own identity and how it differs from that of the other. Interacting and intermingling also exacerbate differences over the rights of the members of one civilization in a country dominated by the members of the other civilization within both Muslim and Christian societies, tolerance for the other declined sharply in the 1980s and 1990s.[10]

Muslims have the burden and challenge of correcting all the misconceptions and misrepresentation of Islam and Muslims mentioned earlier in this chapter under the subtitle *Islamophobia Uncalled For*, which are broadcast daily in the Western controlled mass media, as well as those written by orientalist scholars, aimed at discrediting Islam and Muslims, and creating conflict between Muslims and Christians. They also have to display the true character of Islam as required of them.

Furthermore, Muslims should not paint all Christian people with the same brush, for is it not true that Allah (ﷻ) pointed out that they are not all of the same character? Among the Christians, there are very sincere, good-hearted people who are not proud or arrogant and who are very compassionate to Muslims. Allah says:

﴿۞ لَيْسُوا۟ سَوَآءً مِّنْ أَهْلِ ٱلْكِتَـٰبِ أُمَّةٌ قَآئِمَةٌ يَتْلُونَ ءَايَـٰتِ ٱللَّهِ ءَانَآءَ ٱلَّيْلِ وَهُمْ يَسْجُدُونَ ۝ يُؤْمِنُونَ بِٱللَّهِ وَٱلْيَوْمِ ٱلْـَٔاخِرِ وَيَأْمُرُونَ بِٱلْمَعْرُوفِ وَيَنْهَوْنَ عَنِ ٱلْمُنكَرِ وَيُسَـٰرِعُونَ فِى ٱلْخَيْرَٰتِ وَأُو۟لَـٰٓئِكَ مِنَ ٱلصَّـٰلِحِينَ ۝ ﴾

(سورة آل عِمرَان: ١١٣-١١٤)

❲Not all of them are alike: of the People of the Book are a portion that stand [for the right]; they rehearse the verses of Allah all night long, and then prostrate themselves in adoration. They believe in Allah and the Last Day; they enjoin what is right, and forbid what is wrong; and they hasten in good works: they are in the ranks of the righteous.❳
(Qur'an 3: 113-114)

﴿وَإِنَّ مِنْ أَهْلِ ٱلْكِتَـٰبِ لَمَن يُؤْمِنُ بِٱللَّهِ وَمَآ أُنزِلَ إِلَيْكُمْ وَمَآ أُنزِلَ إِلَيْهِمْ خَـٰشِعِينَ لِلَّهِ لَا يَشْتَرُونَ بِـَٔايَـٰتِ ٱللَّهِ ثَمَنًا قَلِيلًا أُو۟لَـٰٓئِكَ لَهُمْ أَجْرُهُمْ عِندَ رَبِّهِمْ إِنَّ ٱللَّهَ سَرِيعُ ٱلْحِسَابِ ۝ ﴾ (سورة آل عِمرَان: ١٩٩)

❲And there are, certainly, among the People of the Book, those who believe in Allah, in the revelation to you, and in the revelation to them, bowing in humility to Allah: they will not sell the verses of Allah for a small price. For them is a reward with their Lord, and Allah is swift in account.❳
(Qur'an 3: 199)

﴿۞ لَتَجِدَنَّ أَشَدَّ ٱلنَّاسِ عَدَٰوَةً لِّلَّذِينَ ءَامَنُوا۟ ٱلْيَهُودَ وَٱلَّذِينَ أَشْرَكُوا۟ وَلَتَجِدَنَّ أَقْرَبَهُم مَّوَدَّةً لِّلَّذِينَ ءَامَنُوا۟ ٱلَّذِينَ قَالُوٓا۟ إِنَّا نَصَـٰرَىٰ ذَٰلِكَ

بِأَنَّ مِنْهُمْ قِسِّيسِينَ وَرُهْبَانًا وَأَنَّهُمْ لَا يَسْتَكْبِرُونَ ۝ وَإِذَا سَمِعُواْ مَا

أُنزِلَ إِلَى الرَّسُولِ تَرَىٰ أَعْيُنَهُمْ تَفِيضُ مِنَ الدَّمْعِ مِمَّا عَرَفُواْ مِنَ الْحَقِّ يَقُولُونَ رَبَّنَآ

ءَامَنَّا فَاكْتُبْنَا مَعَ الشَّهِدِينَ ۝ وَمَا لَنَا لَا نُؤْمِنُ بِاللَّهِ وَمَا جَآءَنَا مِنَ الْحَقِّ

وَنَطْمَعُ أَن يُدْخِلَنَا رَبُّنَا مَعَ الْقَوْمِ الصَّلِحِينَ ۝ ﴾   (سورة المائدة: ٨٢-٨٤)

❨You will surely find the most intense of the people in animosity
toward the believers [to be] the Jews and those who associate others
with Allah; and you will find the nearest of them in affection to the
believers those who say, "We are Christians." That is because among
them are priests and monks and because they are not arrogant. And
when they hear what has been revealed to the Messenger, you see
their eyes overflowing with tears because of what they have
recognized of the truth. They say, "Our Lord, we have believed, so
register us among the witnesses."❩   *(Qur'an 5: 82-83)*

﴿ ... وَلَوْ ءَامَنَ أَهْلُ الْكِتَبِ لَكَانَ خَيْرًا لَّهُم مِّنْهُمُ الْمُؤْمِنُونَ

وَأَكْثَرُهُمُ الْفَسِقُونَ ۝ ﴾   (سورة آل عمران: ١١٠)

❨...If only the People of the Scripture [Jews and Christians] had
believed, it would have been better for them. Among them are
believers, but most of them are defiantly disobedient.❩ *(Qur'an 3: 110)*

Christians, on the other hand, have the duty of not blindly
following or believing anything that they hear from the electronic
media or read from the works of orientalists about Islam and
Muslims, but to go back to authentic sources of Islam, the Qur'an and
Sunnah [sayings of Muhammad (ﷺ)] to confirm the information.
They also have to differentiate between the religion of Islam and the
individual Muslim who is attempting to implement the teachings of
Islam, who at times may falter or not show the true picture of Islam.
In that case, the mistake of an individual Muslim should not be

blamed on Islam but on the individual himself or herself.

Christians also have to learn to be tolerant of people of other faiths and live in peace and harmony with their Muslim neighbours rather than stigmatizing their Muslim neighbours for faults that are manufactured by the mass media, for is it not true that Jesus (ﷺ) taught that one should love his neighbour as he loves himself?

> And one of the scribes came, and having heard them reasoning together, and perceiving that he had answered them well, asked him, which is the first commandment of all? And Jesus answered him, the first of all the commandments is, Hear, O Israel; The Lord our God is one Lord: And thou shalt love the Lord thy God with all thy heart, and with all thy soul, and with all thy mind, and with all thy strength: this is the first commandment. And the second is like, namely this, Thou shalt love thy neighbour as thyself. There is none other commandment greater than these. (Mark 12:28-31 KJV)

Even St. Paul taught that loving one's neighbor was part of fulfilling the law of God, when he wrote to the Romans:

> Render therefore to all their dues: tribute to whom tribute is due; custom to whom custom; fear to whom fear; honour to whom honour. Owe no man any thing, but to love one another: for he that loveth another hath fulfilled the law. For this, Thou shalt not commit adultery, Thou shalt not kill, Thou shalt not steal, Thou shalt not bear false witness, Thou shalt not covet; and if there be any other commandment, it is briefly comprehended in this saying, namely, Thou shalt love thy neighbour as thyself. Love worketh no ill to his neighbour: therefore love is the fulfilling of the law. (Romans 13:7-10 KJV)

Conclusion and word of advice

As we come to the conclusion of this work, we shall quote former American senator Paul Findley from the concluding chapter of his book *Silent No More: Confronting America's False Images of Islam*:

> As we confront America's false image of Islam, all must acknowledge that Muslims, like Christians and Jews, have blemished history when it comes to religious tolerance. No one's laundry is spotless, but historians may discover that Muslim laundry has the least stains. Over the centuries, leaders of all three monotheistic faiths have treated many non-believers with extreme brutality in gross violation of their own religious doctrines and principles. Stereotypes propagated by Christian leaders, for example led to the slaughter of Muslims in Jerusalem during the crusades and to the cruel execution of many Muslims and Jews during the inquisition in Spain and France. For nearly three centuries U.S. citizens, mostly Christians, held African-Americans, many of them Muslims, as personal property, mistreated them in despicable ways, and routinely denied them the opportunity to practice their religion. A constitutional amendment ended slavery more than a century ago, but African-Americans were terrorized by mobs and many of them murdered during the decades that followed. In all, nearly ten thousand were victims of lynching. For several generations professed Christians, many marauding under the Ku Klux Klan banner, kept the descendants of slaves segregated from other citizens and ruthlessly denied them justice in voting, housing, employment, education and public accommodation.

Paul Findley further says:

> Throughout the violent bloody Arab-Israel conflict that began with the creation of Israel in 1948 (by British Christians), the

antagonists have stereotyped each other. On one side Jews are denounced as "racists" for harsh discrimination against most Muslim Palestinians while on the other, Palestinians are excoriated as terrorists and unworthy of first class citizenship. Some of the Jews oppressed under the Nazi regime are now the oppressors in the Arab-Israel conflict. For fifty years, the leaders of Israel government — religious and secular Jews using overwhelming military power augmented by massive aid from the US government — have subjugated, dispossessed, brutalized, and stereotyped the Palestinian people both Muslims and Christians. The support provided by the United States, pledged as it is to religious tolerance, has in effect supported these intolerant policies.[11]

Paul Findley further notes in his writing, quoting Inayat I. Lalani:

At times through the years Muslim rulers have been engaged in harsh religious stereotyping on a broad scale. There have been waves of intolerance against religious minorities — or subjugated majorities, for that matter — under Islamic rule in all countries and during all ages. Unfortunately, many Muslims will vehemently deny such behavior, or somehow try to justify it. Several Muslim rulers treated their non-Muslim adversaries and subjects with utmost cruelty... The behavior of Sulaiman the Magnificent as he retreated back towards Istanbul after the failed siege of Vienna in 1529 does not inspire admiration either... At the same time, historians have noted, parenthetically but with impressive reality, that on balance Muslim rulers have been more enlightened and have accorded non-Muslims greater protection from discrimination and oppression than say, Christian conquerors up until the beginning of the Enlightenment. At no time did Muslim leaders engage in religious oppression that even approached the awful agony of death by burning at the stake and boiling in oil as inflicted against non-believers during the Christian inquisition and wholesale slaughter of Muslims in the Middle East by swords wielded by Christian crusaders. There was no such thing as ecclesiastical Muslim authority examining one's faith in ridiculous details as the inquisitors did. Muslim leaders never ordered banishment, excommunication or burning the stake... The reason for such restraint must be found in the relative liberal attitude of Muslim scholars towards dissent.[12]

The former US senator is rather positive regarding the future events between Muslims and Christians. He says:

The beginning of the third millennium may herald a promising new era for interfaith relationships in the United States (and round the world). Except for persistent anti-Muslim stereotypes and the intolerance sometimes exhibited by fundamentalist Christians... Today, Muslims are the primary targets of intolerance, and to an embarrassing degree, Muslim stereotypes are made-in-America... Only in America is Islam closely and falsely linked in the public mind with terrorism. This stereotype exists beyond our borders of course, but nowhere else has it flourished in recent years with comparable intensity and persistence.[13]

To remedy the negative image of Islam and Muslims, and the conflict between Muslims and Christians in their interactions, Paul Findley says:

Muslims must undertake two vitally important steps that they alone can accomplish. In recommending these steps, I realize that I may be venturing into sensitive areas of personal behaviour and tradition, but I take that risk because of the importance of removing stereotypes in the shortest time possible. First, Muslims should identify themselves publicly with Islam and seek to present the truth about their faith to non-Muslims. Responding to stereotypes with reactive, corrective measures is essential, but practical steps are equally important.... Muslims should not wait for a crisis to occur before offering factual information about their religion. As a first step, they should mark themselves as Muslims, so that their own good behaviour and worthy accomplishments will be identified with Islam. Exemplary conduct can be recognized by the public as Islamic only if the person is clearly identified as Muslim. Second, Muslims must defend their faith aggressively and publicly against misconceptions and misrepresentations, especially those expressed by professed Muslims. When people identified as Muslims reportedly engage in bad conduct or express false or misleading interpretations of Islam, other Muslims must break habitual silence and condemn these reports of un-Islamic behaviour. To be effective, this must be done promptly, clearly and publicly.[14]

Fourteen hundred years of interactions between Muslims and Christians all over the world is not something that can be adequately handled within the scope of such a small work because much water has flowed in the river of time. Therefore, after all is said and done by the scholars who have been quoted, from all walks of life, both Muslims and non-Muslims, we as Muslims have the following duties and responsibilities:

1. There is a need to learn our religion thoroughly and also have a good understanding of the worldviews of other people and communities who are not Muslims, with whom we interact. We need to understand their lifestyles, their needs and problems, and we need to see the dominant trends in these communities. Only then will be able to offer Islamic alternatives for their specific problems.

2. We need to focus and have priorities, now that we know the challenges ahead of us. The task of preaching the word of Allah (ﷺ) is a delicate one on our shoulders. The best preaching is

through our personal examples, to reflect in our daily life and show our good habits, which are natural values of truth, goodness, beauty, and justice, and also shun all negative values and habits condemned by Islam.

3. Our neighbourhoods and communities also need to reflect the values of Islam. Many Muslim communities are not a good advertisement of Islam today; our communities need to be clean, caring and compassionate, peaceful, safe, hardworking and disciplined, and open and welcoming.

4. Our greater priority in this secular society, which is living under the influence of the West, is to make people realize the terrible consequences of secularism and materialism, which result from the rejection of religion and of faith in Allah (ﷻ). The arrogant and limited vision of secular humankind; the constantly changing and chaotic state of its laws and values; the plundering of the earth's resources; the enormous waste of human lives drowned in alcohol, disfigured by drugs, flushed out by abortions, wiped out by HIV/AIDS; genocidal, economic greed and so forth need to be addressed by offering Islamic alternatives.

5. Today's preaching in the world should aim at putting back meaning and purpose in people's lives, burnishing their consciences so that the natural inclination of humans to believe in Allah (ﷻ) can shine forth again, reviving their power of reasoning so that they can once more acknowledge their Creator and Sustainer and their proper place in the scheme of things.

6. This can only be done if Muslims become united again by putting prejudice and differences aside and bringing their resources together for proper investment in the fields of:

❖ The press and mass media
❖ Education from kindergarten to university
❖ Business entrepreneurship to improve economic well-being

❖ Community, preaching, health and rehabilitation centres

❖ Research projects to improve upon the societal, educational, moral, and political well-being, as well as farming and small scale industry

❖ Housing for Muslim communities, to be rented at reasonable rates

❖ Payments and distribution of charity to the needy in society.

When all this is done with sincerity, professionalism and hard work, it will preserve and strengthen the integrity of the Muslim society, and hence we shall be fulfilling the divine trust that we took from Allah. Allah (ﷻ) said:

﴿إِنَّا عَرَضْنَا ٱلْأَمَانَةَ عَلَى ٱلسَّمَٰوَٰتِ وَٱلْأَرْضِ وَٱلْجِبَالِ فَأَبَيْنَ أَن يَحْمِلْنَهَا وَأَشْفَقْنَ مِنْهَا وَحَمَلَهَا ٱلْإِنسَٰنُ إِنَّهُ كَانَ ظَلُومًا جَهُولًا ۝ لِيُعَذِّبَ ٱللَّهُ ٱلْمُنَٰفِقِينَ وَٱلْمُنَٰفِقَٰتِ وَٱلْمُشْرِكِينَ وَٱلْمُشْرِكَٰتِ وَيَتُوبَ ٱللَّهُ عَلَى ٱلْمُؤْمِنِينَ وَٱلْمُؤْمِنَٰتِ وَكَانَ ٱللَّهُ غَفُورًا رَّحِيمًا ۝﴾ (سورة الأحزاب : ٧٢–٧٣)

❬Indeed, we offered the trust to the heavens and earth and mountains, but they declined to bear it and feared it but man [undertook] to bear it. Indeed he was unjust and ignorant. [It was] so that Allah may punish the hypocrite men and hypocrite women and the men and women who associate others with Him, and Allah may accept repentance from the believing men and believing women. And ever is Allah forgiving merciful.❭   *(Qur'an 33: 72-73)*

Epilogue

A brief biography of the author

$\mathcal{I}$ was born in a very strict Christian home of the SDA (Seventh Day Adventist) denomination and grew up in a place called Kisumu in Kenya, where I took my primary, secondary, and high school education, after which I joined the Kenyan Armed forces. During my childhood and teenage years, my parents always took us (my brothers, my sisters and me) to church on Saturday. Before the day of church services, on Fridays at sunset, we always stopped doing any work and dedicated all the time left until midnight to reading and studying the Bible, singing different hymns like "The Rock of Ages" and praying to God through Jesus Christ (ﷺ). My family was very strict in moral values and dietary laws. There was no smoking, drinking of alcohol, dating, listening to music, watching movies or going to film shows. My parents were intent on raising us as devout and responsible people, people who would be successful in life and care for others. As a matter of fact, our parents were so serious about Christianity that they named all of us after prophets mentioned in the Bible, and our sisters were named after the wives of the prophets. Our folks always gave their tithes, ten percent of their total earnings, to the church where we attended our Saturday services. At the end of every month, they invited the church leaders (pastors and reverends) for dinner and special prayers, and sometimes for ten o'clock tea and special prayers, after which the leaders would take the tithes.

In this way, we came to inherit the religion of our parents, who always struggled to give us the best education and spared much of their time, especially from Friday sunset up until Saturday sunset, for our spiritual development. As we continued with the church services and reading and studying the Bible, as well as attending monthly visits by the church leaders as a family, we started questioning certain discrepancies that we felt were not reasonable or logical. For example, we always questioned the pastors on the issue of the trinity, how Jesus (ﷺ) could be God and man simultaneously, why were we still sinning if Christ was crucified for our sins, or even why we should seek repentance if the price had been paid at Calvary by Jesus Christ. Believe me, they never provided any adequate answers, and when we insisted, they would retort, "You are demon-possessed; Satan has gone into your heads; you should not question the Bible or the church. Just believe!"

We were a big family, and my parents were very poor. After finishing my high school education, I decided to join the Kenyan army without the knowledge of my parents, but after consulting with my eldest brother, who approved it. By now, Father was very far out of our reach trying to make ends meet, working in the North Eastern province of Kenya (NEP), and Mother was struggling on the farm to produce food for this big family of ten. For this reason, we never informed our parents about my joining the army. Mother would never have accepted the idea, for she had always worked hard so that I could go to university, since none of her children had made it to university until then. I managed to be recruited into the military, the intention being to shoulder the burden of educating my younger brothers. I trained as an Officer Cadet for one year and graduated as a Second Lieutenant in 1986 from the Kenyan Armed Forces Training College.

Subsequently, I was posted to Nairobi Langata barracks, where they assigned me to a military outpost in the North Eastern Province (NEP) of Kenya, an area that had, and still has, a Muslim majority. This area is well known, as NEP was very notorious for bandits because it is an arid and semi-arid area with very poor infrastructure, no clean water, no electricity, and no social institutions such as good schools or hospitals. As such, there were no adequate economic activities that would support human growth and development; actually it was an area that had been forgotten by the Kenyan government and even today that is still the same. For this reason, the area was, and is, prone to banditry.[1]

The area where I was the commander, known as Takaba, was a small village almost bordering Ethiopia, near a town called Moyale. It was a very dry area, with virtually no human economic activity except for a few herds of goats, sheep and camels. Yet even these animals, like human beings, were always going far and wide in search of water for survival. I used to be supplied weekly with rations and food by the military aircraft called a buffalo, which supplied all the military camps in the whole NEP every Wednesday. Apart from these supplies, I had under my command a water buzzer (a large lorry or truck used for carrying large amounts of water to distant places), two five-ton Mercedes-Benz lorries, a Land Rover and a signal centre for communications in my camp. Actually, they nicknamed me 'the territorial commander' because I was far from other camps and I was the boss. I used to send out the water buzzer to collect water for my soldiers at least three times a week, and would also send the two lorries to collect firewood for cooking. Seeing that the village was very poor and without water, something went into my heart and I felt that it was my duty to help the villagers as much as I was able, so the same water buzzer would supply the village with water and the lorries would supply them with firewood, as well as whatever few supplies of rations we could occasionally share with the villagers.

Allah the Exalted knows best, but I think it is from this very little humanitarian help to the villagers that Allah (ﷻ) put some light of guidance into my heart.

By this time, 1986, I was still a Christian, but it is well known that the army is full of many immoralities. Many things had changed by then; I was not the same innocent young boy under the strict care of his Christian parents who had just left high school. Maybe this was the reason that my dear loving mother, in particular, despised the idea of her child joining the army in the first place. Being much wiser and wanting the best for her children, she automatically knew that the army would corrupt her child, but what was there to do, knowing it was out of her hands.

From military life to Islam

In the Kenyan army, as in most armies, we were indoctrinated to believe in the three W's: wine, women, and war. Although I was not by any means the same innocent young Christian boy, I still believed in God and kept on going to church, although only occasionally. During this time, my parents did not get as much help from me as they had expected, partly because of the type of military training I had received, and partly due to my own irresponsible behaviour. My father convinced me to get married early enough, in the hope that it would make me more responsible, which it did. At least it calmed me down a bit. In 1989, I was sent once more to NEP, but this time to a place called Mandera, a stone's throw from the Somali border.

In the mean time, my wife had had several miscarriages, and this time when I was posted to Mandera, she was two months pregnant. I had hardly stayed in NEP for four months when I received a signal message that again my dear wife had had another miscarriage. This depressed me so much; in fact I was very demoralized, especially when I came to know that it was due to the negligence of those on duty in the Medical Regimental Service (MRS). They had been called to attend to my wife but, because they were enjoying their drinking with women at the time, they did not bother to come and attend to the patient until the next day, when she had bled so much that the foetus could not be saved.

As fate would have it — maybe God was trying to compensate me for my low morale — I received another signal message from my Nairobi barracks camp during the same week. It indicated that I had been selected for a peacekeeping mission in Namibia, then South-West Africa, and that the other selected soldiers and I were to report to Nairobi as soon as possible. I came back to Nairobi, consoled my sad wife and encouraged her not to lose hope. After all, I was going out of my country for a mission that would earn better money and would help us to raise the child that we were expecting in the future.

In April 1989, we travelled to Namibia for the peace mission, which lasted for one year and three months. We made a lot of money, but many soldiers and officers wasted their money by drinking too much and going out with women; after all, they were far away from their wives for more than a year, which justified to them their immoral behavior. Somehow it dawned on me that I had to take care of my life. I said to myself, "You can't go on living like this. You must change your life. Look at your Muslim soldiers, how disciplined they are. They do not drink or go out with girlfriends like the other soldiers. They fast in their month of fasting, they are very prayerful, very kind-hearted, always united together as brothers and members of the same family. Why don't you be like them and save your money?"

Instead of joining them, I decided to go back to the Bible and read it more seriously and critically. Maybe if my soldiers had only told me something about Islam, I would have joined them immediately, for I was craving for some guidance to get hold of my life, but alas, they never did. They were too late, for I was taken over by the Christian Union. I attended church meetings every evening and grew in faith until I got baptized again, this time in the Lutheran Church, by a very friendly Dutch pastor who taught me the Bible and invited me to his home many times.

I became a strong Christian and even started preaching to my soldiers and friends. I sent letters and pictures home to my parents about my changed life and convictions about Christianity. This really depressed my elder brother, who by now had followed our father who had become Muslim from his acquaintance with Muslims in NEP. However, even though our father had long been Muslim since we were still in secondary school, his Islam was not based on knowledge but only blind imitation, due to the good lifestyle that he saw from the Muslims in NEP, where he was working as a driver. He never really told us anything about Islam, not because he never wanted to, but because he knew very little about it, perhaps only how to pray and fast in the month of fasting. My elder brother had followed my father and joined Islam, but he was not any better than Father in his knowledge about Islam. When he heard that I had been baptized in the Lutheran church in Namibia, and he saw the pictures that I had sent to Mother, he was very much disturbed, for he had hoped to convince my other brothers and me to join him. With the new revelations about my situation in Namibia, of having become a strong Christian, it seemed that his hopes had been buried in the dust. But he never lost hope. Instead he wrote me a good letter and said that the best present I could bring for him would be the videotapes of the famous Muslim scholar of the Christian Bible, Ahmed Deedat. Luckily, I sent for the tapes three days before our departure from Namibia, and just a day before leaving to return home, the tapes were delivered on my doorstep in Windhoek. They were sixty-six videotapes comprising lectures, debates, and dialogues on comparative religion.

I arrived home on June 5th, 1990 and was warmly welcomed by my parents, brothers, sisters and my dear wife. It was a great relief to be home after so long. The next day, I opened the carton with the sixty-six videotapes of Ahmed Deedat. My eldest brother was very anxious since this was the long awaited present that he had sent for, so he chose a debate about Christianity and Islam, between Ahmed Deedat and a Christian professor from a university in Pretoria. The debate was very hot and controversial, and as a Christian at the time, I was on the side of the Christian professor for the whole time when he spoke to defend the cardinal doctrines of Christianity, which by now I was well acquainted with. But when the Muslim scholar of the Christian Bible, Shaykh Ahmed Deedat, stood and started quoting the Christian Bible from his head without looking into the Bible, while at the same time disproving the cardinal doctrines of Christianity one by one, my faith was indeed shaken. Still I told my brother that maybe the professor was not well prepared or maybe he was not good enough to handle the debate. I proposed that it would be better to choose two or three more tapes from different Christian scholars dialoguing with Deedat.

This time I was the one to choose from the sixty-six videotapes. I went through virtually all the titles and chose a four-hour long dialogue between Deedat and two very experienced Christian missionaries, one American and the other British. The four-hour session was very interesting indeed; it covered virtually all important subjects on Islam and Christianity, including the authenticity of the two books, the Bible and the Qur'an, the question of the Holy Trinity, the divinity of Jesus Christ (ﷺ), original sin, and the crucifixion of Jesus Christ (ﷺ). At the end of the four-hour long dialogue, I was convinced beyond any reasonable doubt in my heart about Islam. It seemed so strange to me. I thought, "How can this be that just yesterday I was so convinced about Christianity, and after two videotapes, lasting six hours, everything about my Christian faith had fallen apart!" Yet my heart could not let go of the truth revealed to me through these two exciting debates and dialogues. "I had to make a decision," I thought, "but what about my wife, mother, and my job; and how about my Christian friends? What will I tell them?"

There were just too many questions lingering in my mind, all of which needed immediate answers. The truth about Islam was pounding in my heart; all doubts and questions about illogical issues in Christianity had been well addressed by Deedat in the question and answer sessions of the debate and dialogue. The ball was in my court. Before the end of the day that afternoon, June 6th, 1990, I made the most difficult decision in my life and took the Shahâdah[2] (embraced Islam) in front of my eldest brother, a decision that later was to change my whole worldview about life and the purpose of creation. It was indeed a momentous decision to make.

The cardinal doctrines of Christianity not taught by Jesus

I became very serious about my decision to embrace Islam, spent most of my time reading, and actually watched the sixty-six videotapes of Ahmed Deedat, making sure that I wrote down notes as I watched. Within less than a year, I became well-acquainted with comparative studies between Islam and Christianity. By then I had taught myself the basics of Islam through the famous book called *Islam in Focus* by Hammudah Abdalati. In my serious studies about Islam and Christianity, I found that in reality, the cardinal doctrines of Christianity that I had learned in the Christian church were actually never taught by Jesus Christ (ﷺ).

The Holy Trinity

I was taught by my parents and in the church that there were three separate and distinct divine persons in Godhead: God the Father, God the Son, and God the Holy Spirit. The Athanasian Creed as taught in the church read:

> There is one person of the Father, another of the Son, and another of the Holy Spirit. But the Godhead of the Father, of the Son, and of the Holy Spirit, is all one; the glory equal, the Majesty co-eternal... The Father is God, the Son is God, and the Holy Spirit is God. And yet they are not three Gods, but one God... For like as we are compelled by the Christian verity to acknowledge every person by himself to be God and Lord, so are we forbidden by the Catholic religion to say there be three Gods, or three Lords.

In time, after much reading and interaction with various books and scholars, this doctrine became obviously self-contradictory to me. It is like saying one plus one plus one is three, yet it is also one. If there are three distinct, divine persons and each is God, then logic dictates that there must be three gods. There was never any logical answer given by the church leaders about the belief in the three divine persons within the Oneness of God, hence the church, recognizing the impossibility of harmonizing the three gods into one, declared the Holy Trinity a mystery that a believer has to accept blindly without question. Rev. J. F. De Groot wrote in his book *Catholic Teaching*:

> The Most Holy Trinity is a mystery in the strictest sense of the word. For reason alone cannot prove the existence of a Triune God, Revelation teaches it. And even after the existence of the mystery has been revealed to us, it remains impossible for the human intellect to grasp how the Three Persons have but one Divine Nature.[3]

Through a thorough reading and study of the Bible, I found that Jesus Christ (ﷺ) actually never even mentioned the word trinity, let alone taught it, as purported by the church pastors. In fact, Jesus (ﷺ) said nothing about there being three divine persons in Godhead; if anything, his understanding of God was not any different from the earlier Israelite prophets, who had always preached the unity of God, and never at any time the trinity. As a matter of fact, when Jesus (ﷺ) was in the middle of reasoning with Pharisees and Herodians who were sent to catch him with his own words, one came and questioned him as follows:

> And one of the scribes came, and having heard them reasoning together, and perceiving that he had answered them well, asked him, which is the first commandment of all? And Jesus answered him, the first of all the commandments is, Hear, O Israel; The Lord our God is one Lord: And thou shalt love the Lord thy God with all thy heart, and with all thy soul, and with all thy mind, and with all thy strength: this is the first commandment. And the second is like, namely this, Thou shalt love thy neighbour as thyself. There is none other commandment greater than these. And the scribe said unto him, Well, Master, thou hast said the truth: for there is one God; and there is none other but he: (Mark 12:28-32 KJV).

So Jesus (ﷺ), like his predecessor prophets, believed in only one divine God, as we find in his reply to the devil when he came to test him with worldly luxuries, promising him the whole world as his kingdom. Jesus (ﷺ) answered him and said:

> Then saith Jesus unto him, get thee hence, Satan: for it is written, Thou shalt worship the Lord thy God, and him only shalt thou serve. (Matthew 4:10 KJV)

The truth of the matter, which today is known by many, is that the Christians coined the term 'Holy Trinity' about three hundred years after Jesus (ﷺ). The four canonical Gospels, written between 70 and 115 CE, contain virtually nothing in reference to the trinity. Even *The New Catholic Encyclopaedia* (bearing the Nihil Obstat and Imprimatur, indicating official approval) admits that the doctrine of the trinity was unknown to the early Christians and that it was formulated in the last quarter of the fourth century:

> It is difficult in the second half of the 20th century to offer a clear, objective, and straightforward account of the revelation, doctrinal evolution, and theological elaboration of the mystery of the Trinity. Trinitarian discussion, Roman Catholic as well as others, present a somewhat unsteady silhouette. Two things have happened. There is recognition on the part of exegetes and Biblical theologians, including a constant growing number of Roman Catholics that one should not speak of Trinitarianism in the New Testament without serious qualification. There is also the closely parallel recognition on the part of historians of dogma and systematic theologians that when one does speak of an unqualified Trinitarianism, one has moved from the period of Christian origins to, say, the last quarter of the fourth century. It was only then that what might be called the definitive Trinitarian dogma 'one God in three persons' became thoroughly assimilated into Christian life and thought.[4]

Elsewhere, the same Encyclopaedia asserts this more emphatically:

> The formulation 'one God in three persons' was not solidly established into Christian life and its profession of faith, prior to the end of the 4th century. But it is precisely this formulation that has first claim to the title the Trinitarian dogma... Among the Apostolic Fathers, there had been nothing even remotely approaching such a mentality or perspective.[5]

I found that the doctrine of the Holy Trinity was never taught by Jesus Christ (ﷺ); moreover, it was nowhere to be found in the Bible, neither in the Old nor the New Testament. It was completely foreign to the mentality and perspective of the early Christians, and it only became part of the Christian faith as late as the end of the fourth century. Easton's Bible Dictionary affirms this fact when it says about the trinity:

> — A word not found in Scripture, but used to express the doctrine of the unity of God as subsisting in three distinct Persons. This word is derived from the Greek word *trias*, first used by Theophilus (A.D. 168 AD - 183 AD), or from the Latin word *trinitas*, first used by Tertullian (A.D. 220 AD), to express this doctrine. The propositions involved in the doctrine are these:
> 1. That God is one, and that there is but one God (Deuteronomy 6:4; 1 Kings 8:60; Isaiah 44:6; Mark 12:29,32; John 10:30).
> 2. That the Father is a distinct divine Person (hypostasis, subsistentia, persona, suppositum intellectuale), distinct from the Son and the Holy Spirit.
> 3. That Jesus Christ was truly God, and yet was a Person distinct from the Father and the Holy Spirit.
> 4. That the Holy Spirit is also a distinct divine Person.

Therefore, rationally as well, the dogma of trinity is untenable; it is beyond reason and logic, for if there are three distinct and separate persons, then there must be three distinct separate substances, which can never be superimposed to be one. Furthermore, if the three divine persons are infinite, then it means there are three distinct infinites, three omnipotents, three eternals, and so three gods. If they are finite, then we are led to the absurdity of conceiving of an infinite being having three finite modes of subsistence or three persons who are separately finite making up an infinite conjunctly. Allah is not like an apple that can be divided into three thirds, which then form one whole. The fact is that if the three divine persons are finite, then none of them — the Father, the Son, or the Holy Spirit — is God.

Thus, the doctrine of the Holy Trinity was a later development that came as a consequence of the deification of two creatures, Jesus Christ (🕮) and the mysterious Holy Spirit, and their association with God as partners in His Godhead, a formula that was invented and used by Athanasius, an Egyptian deacon from Alexandria, and subsequently accepted and canonized by the Council of Nicaea in 325 CE. Whether considered from a historical perspective or otherwise, it is a regression from rational theology to mythology, for at the root of all mythologies lies the irrational tendency of the human mind to deify great men, to personify non-personal forces and attributes, and to present them as divine persons.

Otherwise, I found that Islam was the only religion that preached a plain, simple, rational, logical, and radical Unity of God. It presented an understanding of God that was totally free from anthropomorphic or mythological fancies. I learned in Islam that Allah (🕮) was the only unique Creator, Cherisher, Sustainer, and Governor of all that exists. He is One in His self, and One in Substance. Allah (🕮) is the only Self-Subsistent One, the Self-Sufficient Who is independent of all needs while all are dependent on Him. He is the Creator and Nourisher of all, the All-Good, the All-Mighty, the All-Knowing, All-Loving, the All-Merciful, the Eternal and Infinite. He begets not, nor is He begotten. Nothing can come out of Him and then become His equal and partner in Godhead, and whatever one conjures up in his mind as God, is not God, because there is none like unto Him.

﴿قُلْ هُوَ ٱللَّهُ أَحَدٌ ۝ ٱللَّهُ ٱلصَّمَدُ ۝ لَمْ يَلِدْ وَلَمْ يُولَدْ ۝ وَلَمْ يَكُن لَّهُ كُفُوًا أَحَدٌ ۝﴾ (سورة الإخلاص: ١-٤)

❨Say: He is Allah, the One. Allah the Self-Sufficient Master, [Whom all creatures need while He is independent of all needs]. He begets not, nor was He begotten. And there is none co-equal or comparable unto Him.❩ *(Qur'an 112: 1-4)*

۞ ٱللَّهُ لَا إِلَٰهَ إِلَّا هُوَ ٱلۡحَىُّ ٱلۡقَيُّومُ لَا تَأۡخُذُهُۥ سِنَةٌ وَلَا نَوۡمٌ لَّهُۥ مَا فِى ٱلسَّمَٰوَٰتِ وَمَا فِى ٱلۡأَرۡضِ مَن ذَا ٱلَّذِى يَشۡفَعُ عِندَهُۥٓ إِلَّا بِإِذۡنِهِۦ يَعۡلَمُ مَا بَيۡنَ أَيۡدِيهِمۡ وَمَا خَلۡفَهُمۡ وَلَا يُحِيطُونَ بِشَىۡءٍ مِّنۡ عِلۡمِهِۦٓ إِلَّا بِمَا شَآءَ وَسِعَ كُرۡسِيُّهُ ٱلسَّمَٰوَٰتِ وَٱلۡأَرۡضَ وَلَا يَـُٔودُهُۥ حِفۡظُهُمَا وَهُوَ ٱلۡعَلِىُّ ٱلۡعَظِيمُ ۝ ۞ (سورة البَقَرَة: ٢٥٥)

{Allah — there is no deity except Him, the Ever-Living, the Sustainer of [all] existence. Neither drowsiness overtakes Him nor sleep. To Him belongs whatever is in the heavens and whatever is on the earth. Who is it that can intercede with Him except by His permission? He knows what is [presently] before them and what will be after them, and they encompass not a thing of His knowledge except for what He wills. His chair/footstool extends over the heavens and the earth, and their preservation tires Him not. And He is the Most High, the Most Great.}

(Qur'an 2: 255)

The divinity of Jesus Christ (ﷺ)

The second doctrine of Christianity that I came to discover had never been taught by Jesus (ﷺ) was his own divinity. In the church, we were taught to believe that Jesus (ﷺ) was God. In fact, the Athanasian Creed stated:

> Furthermore, it is necessary for everlasting salvation that he also believes rightly in the Incarnation of our Lord Jesus Christ.

As a Protestant in the S.D.A. church we believed, just like the Roman Catholics, that Jesus Christ (ﷺ) was God from all eternity, being the second person of the Holy Trinity, and that two thousand years ago, Jesus (ﷺ) chose to appear in human body and was born of the virgin Mary. As such, we used to make all prayers and supplication to God through Jesus (ﷺ). The Godhood of Jesus was asserted in the *Catholic Teaching* in the following words:

This teaching about Christ's divinity which is bound to be found in so many places of the scripture, has always been proclaimed by the church as one of the most important truths of the Catholic Faith. The Council of Nicaea, which was the first General Council after persecutions, solemnly condemned Arius who contended that Christ was not God but a creature.[6]

Going through the words of Jesus (ﷺ) as recorded in the four canonical Gospels, I realized that Jesus (ﷺ) in many places strongly disclaimed Godhood and divinity as against what was attributed to him by the church. He said in many places as follows:

And when he was gone forth into the way, there came one running, and kneeled to him, and asked him, Good Master, what shall I do that I may inherit eternal life? And Jesus said unto him, Why callest thou me good? There is none good but one, that is, God. (Mark 10:17-18 KJV)

Jesus saith unto her, Mary. She turned herself, and saith unto him, Rabboni; which is to say, Master. Jesus saith unto her, touch me not; for I am not yet ascended to my Father: but go to my brethren, and say unto them, I ascend unto my Father, and your Father; and to my God, and your God. (John 20:16-17 KJV)

These words spake Jesus, and lifted up his eyes to heaven, and said, Father, the hour is come; glorify thy Son, that thy Son also may glorify thee: As thou hast given him power over all flesh, that he should give eternal life to as many as thou hast given him. And this is life eternal, that they might know thee the only true God, and Jesus Christ, whom thou hast sent. (John 17:1-3 KJV)

It was recorded in the Gospels that Jesus always talked of 'My Father and your Father, and my God and your God.' These words of

Jesus (ﷺ) only meant that he stood in the same relationship to God as any other man. He was a creature of God, and not a God. It was recorded in the Gospels that when he was in great agony on the cross as recorded in the Gospels, he cried out to God:

> And at the ninth hour Jesus cried with a loud voice, saying, Eloi, Eloi, lama sabachthani? Which is, being interpreted, My God, my God, why hast thou forsaken me? (Mark 15:34 KJV)

I could not imagine such words coming out of the mouth of God; rather this was the cry of a helpless man in agony addressed to his Creator and Lord seeking for help.

Moreover I found that there were so many places in the Bible where it is recorded that Jesus (ﷺ) prayed to God, therefore I thought to myself, "If Jesus was really God, how could he pray to another God?"

> And in the morning, rising up a great while before day, he went out, and departed into a solitary place, and there prayed. (Mark 1:35 KJV)

> Then cometh Jesus with them unto a place called Gethsemane, and saith unto the disciples, Sit ye here, while I go and pray yonder. And he took with him Peter and the two sons of Zebedee, and began to be sorrowful and very heavy. Then saith he unto them, My soul is exceeding sorrowful, even unto death: tarry ye here, and watch with me. And he went a little further, and fell on his face, and prayed, saying, O my Father, if it be possible, let this cup pass from me: nevertheless not as I will, but as thou wilt. (Matthew 26:36-39 KJV)

> And he came out, and went, as he was wont, to the Mount of Olives; and his disciples also followed him. And when he was at the place, he said unto them, pray that ye enter not into temptation. And he was withdrawn from them about a stone's

cast, and kneeled down, and prayed, Saying, Father, if thou be willing, remove this cup from me: nevertheless not my will, but thine, be done. And there appeared an angel unto him from heaven, strengthening him. And being in an agony he prayed more earnestly: and his sweat was as it were great drops of blood falling down to the ground. And when he rose up from prayer, and was come to his disciples, he found them sleeping for sorrow, And said unto them, Why sleep ye? Rise and pray, lest ye enter into temptation. (Luke 22:39-46 KJV)

Furthermore, I was taught in the church that Jesus (ﷺ) was born in a stable to the virgin Mary, was circumcised after eight days, was breast-fed by his mother, ate normal earthly food when hungry, cried when in agony, was a carpenter and spoke of himself as a son of man. "Then how could such a humble person be God?," I thought.

They answered and said unto him, Abraham is our father. Jesus saith unto them, if ye were Abraham's children, ye would do the works of Abraham. But now ye seek to kill me, a man that hath told you the truth, which I have heard of God: (John 8:39-40 KJV)

I found that, like the trinity, the doctrine of the incarnation [God becoming a man in the form of Jesus (ﷺ) in order to solve humankind's problems] was also developed long after Jesus (ﷺ). In fact, by going through the Gospels, I could by now trace the stages through which Jesus (ﷺ) was gradually deified. In the 'Q' source, he was regarded as a prophet of God, as a human being and nothing more; in 'Urmarcus', there was an attempt to glamorize his person and attribute many miracles to him; in the works of the first and second centuries, he was presented as a mighty angel, the firstborn of all creation, but still a creature nevertheless; and finally in the preface of the Gospel according to John, and other works of the third and fourth centuries, he was made into a God. This was affirmed in the

Nicene Creed (325 CE), contrary to the views of those early Christians who still did not believe in the divinity of Jesus (ﷺ). If they denied these words, they would face the sword:

> I believe in... one Lord Jesus Christ, the only begotten Son of God. Born of the Father before all ages. God of God, Light of Light, true God of true God. Begotten not made; being of one substance with the Father.

The reasoning I found in Islam could no longer allow me to accept a man as God who was born of a woman, had human needs, such as ignorance and limitations, and gradually grew in stature, power and wisdom, like all other human beings. Thus, to put human limitations upon God and believe in His incarnation in a human body is to deny the Perfection of God.

Islam liberated me from such illogical and irrational beliefs and dogmas. In a way, Islam opened my eyes and sharpened my reasoning capacity. The Qur'an taught me that Jesus (ﷺ) was a great prophet of God - sinless, pure, and humble, but like all prophets, he was in all respects a human being.

﴿إِنَّ مَثَلَ عِيسَىٰ عِندَ ٱللَّهِ كَمَثَلِ ءَادَمَ خَلَقَهُۥ مِن تُرَابٍ ثُمَّ قَالَ لَهُۥ كُن فَيَكُونُ ٥٩﴾ (سورة آل عِمرَان: ٥٩)

﴿The similitude of Jesus before Allah is like that of Adam; He created him from dust, then said to him "Be": and he was.﴾ *(Qur'an 3: 59)*

﴿ ... إِنَّمَا ٱلْمَسِيحُ عِيسَى ٱبْنُ مَرْيَمَ رَسُولُ ٱللَّهِ وَكَلِمَتُهُۥٓ أَلْقَىٰهَآ إِلَىٰ مَرْيَمَ وَرُوحٌ مِّنْهُ فَـَٔامِنُوا۟ بِٱللَّهِ وَرُسُلِهِۦ وَلَا تَقُولُوا۟ ثَلَٰثَةٌ ٱنتَهُوا۟ خَيْرًا لَّكُمْ ... ١٧١﴾ (سورة النِّسَاء: ١٧١)

﴿Most certainly the Messiah, Jesus, the son of Mary, was [no more than] a messenger of Allah, and His Word, which He bestowed on Mary, and a spirit proceeding from Him: so believe in Allah and His messengers. Say not "trinity": desist: it will be better for you.❩

(Qur'an 4: 171)

❨مَّا ٱلْمَسِيحُ ٱبْنُ مَرْيَمَ إِلَّا رَسُولٌ قَدْ خَلَتْ مِن قَبْلِهِ ٱلرُّسُلُ وَأُمُّهُ
صِدِّيقَةٌ كَانَا يَأْكُلَانِ ٱلطَّعَامَ ٱنظُرْ كَيْفَ نُبَيِّنُ لَهُمُ ٱلْآيَاتِ
ثُمَّ ٱنظُرْ أَنَّىٰ يُؤْفَكُونَ ﴿٧٥﴾❩   (سورة المائدة: ٧٥)

❨The Messiah, son of Mary, was no more than a messenger; many
were the messengers that passed away before him. His mother was a
woman of truth. They had both to eat food. See how Allah makes His
Signs clear to them; yet see in what ways they are deluded away from
the truth!❩

(Qur'an 5: 75)

The divine sonship of Jesus (ﷺ)

I was also taught to believe that Jesus Christ (ﷺ) is a son of God
in a special and exclusive sense, that he is the only begotten son. He
was God begotten, not made. In fact, the most famous passage of the
Bible that was used to support this belief is from the Gospel
according John:

> For God so loved the world, that he gave his only begotten Son,
> that whosoever believeth in him should not perish, but have
> everlasting life. For God sent not his Son into the world to
> condemn the world; but that the world through him might be
> saved. He that believeth on him is not condemned: but he that
> believeth not is condemned already, because he hath not
> believed in the name of the only begotten Son of God. (John
> 3:16-18 KJV)

However, after going through Shaykh Ahmed Deedat's debate
with Doctor Anis Shorrosh, the Palestinian Christian who has a
doctorate in divinity, entitled "Is Jesus God?" I found that this dogma

of Jesus (ﷺ) being the only begotten son of God was also not in conformity with the sayings and teachings of Jesus Christ (ﷺ), son of Mary. Furthermore, I found out in the Bible that this expression 'son of God' had also been used in reference to many earlier prophets such as Jacob, David, Solomon, and Adam (peace be upon them all).

> And thou shalt say unto Pharaoh, Thus saith the LORD, Israel is my son, even my firstborn. (Exodus 4:22 KJV)

> I will declare the decree: the LORD hath said unto me, Thou art my Son; this day have I begotten thee. (Psalms 2:7 KJV)

> He shall build a house for my name; and he shall be my son, and I will be his father; and I will establish the throne of his kingdom over Israel forever. (1 Chronicles 22:10 KJV)

> Which was the son of Enos, which was the son of Seth, which was the son of Adam, which was the son of God. (Luke 3:38 KJV)

Thus, the phrase 'son of God' meant nothing more than nearness to God in love and piety. Jesus (ﷺ) himself had taught in no uncertain terms that whoever was committed to God by fulfilling His will and living a devout life, acting with beautiful conduct of behaviour of kindness and mercy towards human beings, deserved the title 'son of God'. Jesus Christ (ﷺ), son of Mary, said:

> But I say unto you, Love your enemies, bless them that curse you, do good to them that hate you, and pray for them which despitefully use you, and persecute you; That ye may be the children of your Father which is in heaven: for he maketh his sun to rise on the evil and on the good, and sendeth rain on the just and on the unjust. (Matthew 5:44-45 KJV)

> Blessed are the peacemakers: for they shall be called Sons of God. (Matthew 5:9 ASV)

These Biblical sayings of Jesus Christ (ﷺ), son of Mary, left no doubt in my mind of what the phrase 'son of God' meant for Jesus (ﷺ), since before him, Adam, Israel (Jacob), David, Solomon and others had been called the 'sons of God', to mean those who were close to God in love and piety. So when, in the Bible, Jesus (ﷺ) referred to himself as 'son of God' (though most of the time he referred to himself as 'son of man'), it was no doubt in the same sense as the earlier prophets. Therefore, it was only in a metaphorical sense that Jesus (ﷺ) called himself occasionally 'son of God'.

I was taught that a very interesting incident took place in the time of Jesus (ﷺ) that is connected with the two doctrines regarding the divinity and the divine sonship of Jesus Christ (ﷺ), son of Mary. The Jews accused him of blasphemy against God, meaning that he claimed to be God, whereas as a Christian I was taught that Jesus (ﷺ) was God incarnate, meaning he had a right to be God, and therefore there was no blasphemy. So Jesus is recorded in the Bible as having clarified himself:

> It was winter; and Jesus was walking in the temple in Solomon's porch. The Jews therefore came round about him, and said unto him, "How long dost thou hold us in suspense? If thou art the Christ, tell us plainly." Jesus answered them, "I told you, and ye believe not: the works that I do in my Father's name, these bear witness of me. But ye believe not, because ye are not of my sheep. My sheep hear my voice, and I know them, and they follow me: and I give unto them eternal life; and they shall never perish, and no one shall snatch them out of my hand. My Father, who hath given (them) unto me, is greater than all; and no one is able to snatch (them) out of the Father's hand. I and the Father are one." The Jews took up stones again to stone him. Jesus answered them, "Many good works have I showed you from the Father; for which of those works do ye stone me?" The Jews answered him, "For a good work we stone thee not, but for

blasphemy; and because that thou, being a man, makest thyself
God." Jesus answered them, "Is it not written in your law, I said,
ye are gods? If he called them gods, unto whom the word of God
came (and the scripture cannot be broken), say ye of him, whom
the Father sanctified and sent into the world, Thou blasphemest;
because I said, I am (the) Son of God?" (John 10:23-36 ASV)

Our pastors in the church, while trying to prove to us that Jesus
(ﷺ) was indeed God and 'son of God', always used verse 30 of
John, Chapter 10, but this verse was never read within the context of
verses 23 to 34. When it is understood within the context, it becomes
clear that what Jesus (ﷺ) meant was neither the false accusation of
the Jews against him of blasphemy nor the Christian belief in his
being God. Jesus (ﷺ) was one with God in purpose, not in divinity;
it was a oneness of purpose rather than of Godliness. This is because
the Jews only misunderstood him claiming to be God when he said,
"I and the Father are one." In his answer, Jesus (ﷺ) obviously was
referring to these verses, which they knew very well:

I said, ye are gods, and all of you sons of the Most High.
Nevertheless ye shall die like men, and fall like one of the
princes. (Psalms 82:6-7 ASV)

Thus, as the judges and prophets of old [7] were called 'god' in the
metaphorical sense, Jesus (ﷺ), according to the Bible, also referred
to himself as 'son of God' in the same sense. It was clear that for
Jesus (ﷺ), the term 'son of God' carried no particular import or
meaning other than the idiom that the scriptures permitted. There was
no case for singling out Jesus (ﷺ) as the only 'son of God' or even
'god' in a special or literal sense, as I was taught in Christianity. This
was why Jesus (ﷺ) quoted the scriptures in answering the Jews who
accused him of claiming to be God, which would be a blasphemy
against God:

Is it not written in your law, I said, ye are gods? If he called them

gods, unto whom the word of God came (and the scripture
cannot be broken),[8] say ye of him, whom the Father sanctified
and sent into the world, Thou blasphemest; because I said, I am
(the) Son of God?

In other words, if God had addressed His prophets with the term
'god' then what contradiction[9] is there in Jesus (ﷺ) calling himself
'son of God'.

And the LORD said unto Moses, See, I have made thee a god to
Pharaoh: and Aaron thy brother shall be thy prophet. (Exodus
7:1 KJV)

Therefore, if these verses are read within the whole context, the
meaning becomes very clear. On the other hand, if the same verse,
John 10:30, is read out of context, then it may look like Jesus (ﷺ)
claimed to be God. The glorious Qur'an, the last revelation of God to
humankind, however, strongly rejects this Christian dogma that Jesus
Christ (ﷺ), son of Mary, was the son of God. Allah (ﷻ) says:

$$﴿وَقَالَتِ ٱلۡيَهُودُ عُزَيۡرٌ ٱبۡنُ ٱللَّهِ وَقَالَتِ ٱلنَّصَٰرَى ٱلۡمَسِيحُ ٱبۡنُ ٱللَّهِ ۖ
ذَٰلِكَ قَوۡلُهُم بِأَفۡوَٰهِهِمۡ ۖ يُضَٰهِـُٔونَ قَوۡلَ ٱلَّذِينَ كَفَرُواۡ مِن قَبۡلُ ۚ
قَٰتَلَهُمُ ٱللَّهُ ۚ أَنَّىٰ يُؤۡفَكُونَ ۝ ٱتَّخَذُوٓاۡ أَحۡبَارَهُمۡ وَرُهۡبَٰنَهُمۡ
أَرۡبَابٗا مِّن دُونِ ٱللَّهِ وَٱلۡمَسِيحَ ٱبۡنَ مَرۡيَمَ وَمَآ أُمِرُوٓاۡ إِلَّا لِيَعۡبُدُوٓاۡ
إِلَٰهٗا وَٰحِدٗا ۖ لَّآ إِلَٰهَ إِلَّا هُوَ ۚ سُبۡحَٰنَهُۥ عَمَّا يُشۡرِكُونَ ۝﴾$$

(سورة التَّوبَة: ٣٠-٣١)

﴿The Jews call Ezra a son of Allah, and the Christians call the
Messiah the son of Allah. That is a saying from their mouth; they but
imitate what the unbelievers of old used to say. Allah's curse be on
them: how they are deluded away from the Truth! They take their
scholars and their monks to be their lords besides Allah, and [also]
the Messiah, son of Mary; yet they were commanded to worship but

One God: there is no god but He. Exalted is He above whatever they associate with Him.❭   *(Qur'an 9: 30-31)*

❲And they say: "[Allah] Most Gracious has begotten a son!" Indeed you have put forth a thing most monstrous! The heavens almost rupture therefrom, and the earth splits open, and the mountains fall down in utter ruin. That they should attribute a son for [Allah] Most Gracious. For it is not consonant with the majesty of [Allah] Most Gracious that He should beget a son.❭   *(Qur'an 19: 88-92)*

﴾بَدِيعُ السَّمَٰوَٰتِ وَٱلْأَرْضِ أَنَّىٰ يَكُونُ لَهُۥ وَلَدٌ وَلَمْ تَكُن لَّهُۥ صَٰحِبَةٌ وَخَلَقَ كُلَّ شَىْءٍ وَهُوَ بِكُلِّ شَىْءٍ عَلِيمٌ ۝ ذَٰلِكُمُ ٱللَّهُ رَبُّكُمْ لَآ إِلَٰهَ إِلَّا هُوَ خَٰلِقُ كُلِّ شَىْءٍ فَٱعْبُدُوهُ وَهُوَ عَلَىٰ كُلِّ شَىْءٍ وَكِيلٌ ۝﴿

(سورة الأنعَام: ١٠١-١٠٢)

❲He is the Originator of the heavens and the earth: how can He have a son when He has no companion [wife]? He created all things, and He has full knowledge of all things. That is Allah, your Lord! There is no god but He, the Creator of all things; then worship Him; and He has power to dispose of all affairs.❭   *(Qur'an 6: 101-102)*

So again, I found that reason, logic, and common sense were on the side of Islam. Just as one scholar put it, "Philosophy tells us that no being from whom another being can come out, and yet exist as a separate individual, and become his equal and partner can be regarded as perfect." To attribute a son to God would be to deny the perfection of the Creator. Just as Prophet Ayyoob [Job (☸)] put it very simply and logically:

How then can man be justified with God? Or how can he be clean that is born of a woman? Behold even to the moon, and it shineth not; yea, the stars are not pure in His sight. How much less man, that is a worm? And the son of man, which is a worm? (Job 25:4-6 KJV)

The original sin (Inherited sin) and repentance

In Christianity, I was taught to believe that sin is inherited right from the first man, Adam (﷿), down to our parents and unto us. That is, by disobeying God's command not to eat of the forbidden fruit of knowledge, Adam sinned, and this sin was passed down and inherited by all the children of Adam; thus all human beings are born sinful.

Wherefore, as by one-man sin entered into the world, and death by sin and so death passed upon all men, for that all have sinned. (Romans 5:12 KJV)

For all have sinned, and come short of the glory of God; being justified freely by his grace through the redemption that is in Christ Jesus. (Romans 3:23-24 KJV)

We were also taught that the requirement of God's justice is that a price has to be paid for every sin, that God cannot and will not allow a single sin to go unpunished, and therefore the only thing that can wipe out sin is the shedding of blood.

Without the shedding of blood there is no remission. (Hebrews 9:22)

Thus in Christianity, the wage of sin is death, which came about due to the sin of our first parents. Had Adam and Eve (peace be upon them) not sinned, there would be no death, hence this death was the plan of Satan, who made Adam and Eve sin. As Christians, we regarded death as a form of destruction that was originated by Satan, not God, because God is love and not destruction or enmity.

> For the wages of sin is death; but the gift of God is eternal life through Jesus Christ our Lord. (Romans 6:23 KJV)

Therefore, according to what I was taught in Christianity, since sin came into this world through one man, Adam (ﷺ), then it was only logical for it to be removed through one man, the second Adam, Jesus Christ (ﷺ). This is how the formula for the concept of atonement was derived. We were taught that when Adam (ﷺ) sinned against God, he was cut off from God, and thus all his descendants were also cut off from God, but when Jesus (ﷺ) came and supposedly died on the cross for the sins of the world, humanity was then reconciled to God.

> And not only so, but we also rejoice in God through our Lord Jesus Christ, by whom we have now received the reconciliation. (Romans 5:11 ASV)

> Therefore as by the offense of one judgment came upon all men to condemnation; even so by the righteousness of one the free gift came upon all men unto justification of life. For as by one man's disobedience many were made sinners, so by the obedience of one shall many be made righteous. (Romans 5:18-19 KJV)

We were taught that Jesus Christ (ﷺ), the 'son of God' came from heaven, shed his holy sinless blood, suffered indescribable agony, and died on the cross to pay the penalty for the sins of humankind. This had to be so because Jesus (ﷺ) was the only candidate fit for this ordeal, due to the fact that he was the infinite God; thus he alone could pay the infinite price of sin. No one could be saved unless he or she accepted Jesus Christ (ﷺ) as his or her personal saviour and redeemer. Everyone was doomed to suffer eternally in hell, as a consequence of their sinful nature, unless they accepted the atonement, a free gift made for their sins through the blood of Jesus Christ (ﷺ) shed on the cross. In time, though, I realized that these were the teachings of St. Paul adopted by the church.

> Remember that Jesus Christ, of the seed of David, was raised from the dead according to my Gospel. (2 Timothy 2:8 KJV)

After doing enough research on this doctrine of the Christian faith, I found out that like many other Christian beliefs, the doctrine of hereditary sin also had no support. It was not found in the words of Jesus (ﷺ), and none of the earlier prophets had taught this; all the prophets taught that every person was only accountable and responsible for his or her own actions and sins. According to the Bible, Prophet Moses (ﷺ) taught:

> The fathers shall not be put to death for the children, neither shall the children be put to death for the fathers: Every man shall be put to death for his own sin. (Deuteronomy 24:16 KJV)

Prophet Jeremiah (ﷺ) also taught that sin is not inherited and that everyone is responsible for him or herself.

> In those days they shall say no more, the fathers have eaten a sour grape, and the children's teeth are set on edge. But everyone shall die for his own iniquity: every man that eats the sour grape, his teeth shall be set on edge. (Jeremiah 31:29-30 KJV)

Prophet Ezekiel (ﷺ) also rejected the dogma of the original sin in the following words:

> The soul that sins, it shall die. The son shall not bear the iniquity of the father, neither shall the father bear the iniquity of the son: the righteousness of the righteous shall be upon him, and the wickedness of the wicked shall be upon him. But if the wicked will turn from all his sins that he hath committed, and keep all

my statutes, and do that which is lawful and right, he shall surely live, he shall not die. (Ezekiel 18:20-21 KJV)

Lo, this only have I found, that God has made man upright; but they have sought out many inventions. (Ecclesiastes 7:29 KJV)

Jesus Christ (ﷺ) himself taught that children were innocent and pure; they were born sinless, and as such, if they died in their childhood, they deserved to inherit paradise.

At the same time came the disciples unto Jesus, saying, "Who is the greatest in the kingdom of heaven?" And Jesus called a little child unto him, and set him in the midst of them, and said, "Verily I say unto you, except ye be converted, and become as little children, ye shall not enter into the kingdom of heaven. Whosoever therefore shall humble himself as this little child, the same is greatest in the kingdom of heaven. And whoso shall receive one such little child in my name receiveth me. But if anyone causes one of these little ones who believe in me *to sin*, it would be better for him to have a large millstone hung around his neck and to be drowned in the depths of the sea." (Matthew 18:1-6 KJV)

The Islamic perspective

I found in the Qur'an three very explicit verses that left no doubt in my mind that Jesus Christ (ﷺ) was never crucified and that he never died, but God Almighty raised him up alive unto Himself to save him from his enemies who attempted to kill him. Allah (ﷻ) says:

﴿وَقَوْلِهِمْ إِنَّا قَتَلْنَا الْمَسِيحَ عِيسَى ابْنَ مَرْيَمَ رَسُولَ اللَّهِ وَمَا قَتَلُوهُ وَمَا صَلَبُوهُ وَلَٰكِن شُبِّهَ لَهُمْ وَإِنَّ الَّذِينَ اخْتَلَفُوا فِيهِ لَفِي شَكٍّ مِّنْهُ مَا لَهُم بِهِ مِنْ عِلْمٍ إِلَّا اتِّبَاعَ الظَّنِّ وَمَا قَتَلُوهُ يَقِينًا ﴿١٥٧﴾ بَل رَّفَعَهُ اللَّهُ إِلَيْهِ وَكَانَ اللَّهُ عَزِيزًا حَكِيمًا ﴿١٥٨﴾ وَإِن مِّنْ

أَهْلِ ٱلْكِتَٰبِ إِلَّا لَيُؤْمِنَنَّ بِهِۦ قَبْلَ مَوْتِهِۦ وَيَوْمَ ٱلْقِيَٰمَةِ يَكُونُ عَلَيْهِمْ شَهِيدًا ۝

(سورة النِّساء: ١٥٧–١٥٩)

❴That they said [in boast], "We killed Christ Jesus the son of Mary, the Messenger of Allah"; but they killed him not, nor crucified him, but so it was made to appear to them, and those who differ therein are full of doubts, with no [certain] knowledge, but only conjecture to follow, for of a surety they killed him not. Nay, Allah raised him up unto Himself; and Allah is Exalted in Power, Wise. And there is none of the People of the Book but must believe in him before his death; and on the Day of Judgment he will be a witness against them.❵

(Qur'an 4: 157-159)

Thus, these three verses made it explicitly clear to me that Jesus Christ (ﷺ) never died on the cross as I previously believed, according to the Christian doctrine of atonement and salvation. Furthermore I found another passage in the glorious Qur'an and a number of statements of Prophet Muhammad (ﷺ) that indicated to me that there would be a second coming of Jesus Christ (ﷺ) to complete part of his life that was cut short by the circumstances of his time.

۞ وَلَمَّا ضُرِبَ ٱبْنُ مَرْيَمَ مَثَلًا إِذَا قَوْمُكَ مِنْهُ يَصِدُّونَ ۝ وَقَالُوٓا۟ ءَأَٰلِهَتُنَا خَيْرٌ أَمْ هُوَ مَا ضَرَبُوهُ لَكَ إِلَّا جَدَلًۢا بَلْ هُمْ قَوْمٌ خَصِمُونَ ۝ إِنْ هُوَ إِلَّا عَبْدٌ أَنْعَمْنَا عَلَيْهِ وَجَعَلْنَٰهُ مَثَلًا لِّبَنِىٓ إِسْرَٰٓءِيلَ ۝ وَلَوْ نَشَآءُ لَجَعَلْنَا مِنكُم مَّلَٰٓئِكَةً فِى ٱلْأَرْضِ يَخْلُفُونَ ۝ وَإِنَّهُۥ لَعِلْمٌ لِّلسَّاعَةِ فَلَا تَمْتَرُنَّ بِهَا وَٱتَّبِعُونِ هَٰذَا صِرَٰطٌ مُّسْتَقِيمٌ ۝

(سورة الزّخرُف: ٥٧–٦١)

❴When [Jesus] the son of Mary is held up as an example, behold thy people raise a clamor there at [in ridicule]! And they say, "Are our gods best, or he?" This they set forth to thee, only by way of disputation: yea, they are a contentious people. He was no more than a servant: We granted Our favor to him, and We made him an example to the Children of Israel. And if it were Our Will, We could make angels from amongst you, succeeding each other on the earth. And [Jesus] shall be a Sign [for the coming of] the Hour [of Judgment]: therefore have no doubt about the [Hour], but follow Me: this is a Straight Way.❯ *(Qur'an 43: 57-61)*

Abu Hurayrah reported that the Messenger of Allah (ﷺ) said: «By Him in Whose hand is my life, the son of Mary (may peace be upon him) will soon descend among you as a just judge. He will break crosses, kill swine and abolish the jizyah (taxation taken from non-Muslims living under the protection of the Islamic state), and the wealth will pour forth to such an extent that no one will accept it.» (Muslim)

All these proved to me that Jesus (ﷺ) the son of Mary will descend among the Muslims as a just judge, ruling by the Islamic law since the Sharia of all the Prophets stands abrogated by the advent of Prophet Muhammad (ﷺ). Jesus (ﷺ) will break the cross, meaning he will break the symbol of Christianity and prove to the Christians that he never died on the cross as purported. He will also kill the swine, implying that the flesh of the pig — a favorite dish in many Christian homes, which is contrary to the law of God — will be swept out of existence symbolizing that the Sharia of Allah will prevail over the current secular law. And he will also stop the jizyah because the whole human race will be required to embrace Islam, especially since the controversy over the personality of Jesus Christ will have been cleared by Jesus the son of Mary: that he was never God and never died on the cross.

I learned from Islam that there is no such thing as original sin, and that all children are pure and sinless at birth. Sin is not something to be inherited; it is acquired by an individual when he or she goes against the law of God. In fact, according to Islam, human beings have been created with a nature to do good and inclination to do evil.

We have this characteristic of being forgetful. Adam and Eve (peace be upon them) forgot about the commandment of Allah (ﷻ), and Satan was able to deceive them to the extent that they disobeyed God, but God turned to them and taught them words of repentance. They repented and hence He forgave them once and for all.

﴿وَلَقَدْ عَهِدْنَا إِلَىٰ ءَادَمَ مِن قَبْلُ فَنَسِيَ وَلَمْ نَجِدْ لَهُ عَزْمًا ۝﴾

(سورة طه: ١١٥)

﴿And indeed We made a covenant with Adam before, but he forgot and We found on his part no firm will power [of committing sin].﴾

(Qur'an 20: 115)

﴿فَوَسْوَسَ إِلَيْهِ ٱلشَّيْطَٰنُ قَالَ يَٰٓـَٔادَمُ هَلْ أَدُلُّكَ عَلَىٰ شَجَرَةِ ٱلْخُلْدِ وَمُلْكٍ لَّا يَبْلَىٰ ۝ فَأَكَلَا مِنْهَا فَبَدَتْ لَهُمَا سَوْءَٰتُهُمَا وَطَفِقَا يَخْصِفَانِ عَلَيْهِمَا مِن وَرَقِ ٱلْجَنَّةِ وَعَصَىٰٓ ءَادَمُ رَبَّهُ فَغَوَىٰ ۝ ثُمَّ ٱجْتَبَٰهُ رَبُّهُ فَتَابَ عَلَيْهِ وَهَدَىٰ ۝﴾

(سورة طه: ١٢٠-١٢٢)

﴿Then Satan whispered to him; he said, "O Adam, shall I direct you to the tree of eternity and possession that will not deteriorate?" And they [Adam and his wife] ate of it, and their private parts became apparent to them, and they began to fasten over themselves from the leaves of paradise. And Adam disobeyed his Lord and erred. Then his Lord chose him and turned to him in forgiveness and guided [him].﴾

(Qur'an 20: 120-122)

﴿فَتَلَقَّىٰ ءَادَمُ مِن رَّبِّهِۦ كَلِمَٰتٍ فَتَابَ عَلَيْهِ إِنَّهُۥ هُوَ ٱلتَّوَّابُ ٱلرَّحِيمُ ۝﴾

(سورة البقرة: ٣٧)

﴿Then Adam received from his Lord words [of repentance]. And He pardoned him, verily He is the One Who forgives, the Merciful.﴾

(Qur'an 2: 37)

﴿وَقَالَا رَبَّنَا ظَلَمْنَا أَنفُسَنَا وَإِن لَّمْ تَغْفِرْ لَنَا وَتَرْحَمْنَا لَنَكُونَنَّ مِنَ ٱلْخَٰسِرِينَ ۝﴾

(سورة الأعرَاف: ٢٣)

﴿They said: [Adam and Eve] "Our Lord! We have wronged ourselves. If you do not forgive us and have mercy on us, then we shall certainly be the losers."﴾ *(Qur'an 7: 23)*

In Islam, there is no original sin, and sin is not inherited. Rather, there is an original lesson: that Satan should not trick you as he did your parents. Allah (ﷻ) said about this:

﴿يَٰبَنِىٓ ءَادَمَ لَا يَفْتِنَنَّكُمُ ٱلشَّيْطَٰنُ كَمَآ أَخْرَجَ أَبَوَيْكُم مِّنَ ٱلْجَنَّةِ يَنزِعُ عَنْهُمَا لِبَاسَهُمَا لِيُرِيَهُمَا سَوْءَٰتِهِمَآ ... ۝﴾

(سورة الأعرَاف: ٢٧)

﴿O children of Adam! Let not Satan deceive you, as he got your parents [Adam and Eve] out of paradise, stripping them of their clothing, to show them their private parts...﴾ *(Qur'an 7: 27)*

﴿قُلْ أَغَيْرَ ٱللَّهِ أَبْغِى رَبًّا وَهُوَ رَبُّ كُلِّ شَىْءٍ وَلَا تَكْسِبُ كُلُّ نَفْسٍ إِلَّا عَلَيْهَا وَلَا تَزِرُ وَازِرَةٌ وِزْرَ أُخْرَىٰ ثُمَّ إِلَىٰ رَبِّكُم مَّرْجِعُكُمْ فَيُنَبِّئُكُم بِمَا كُنتُمْ فِيهِ تَخْتَلِفُونَ ۝﴾

(سورة الأنعَام: ١٦٤)

﴿Say: "Shall I seek for a Lord other than Allah, while he is the Lord of all things? No person earns any sin except against himself only and no bearer of burdens shall bear the burden of another. Then unto your Lord is your return, so he will inform you of that where in you used to differ."﴾ *(Qur'an 6: 164)*

Considered rationally, it would be an extremely unjust to condemn the entire human race for the sin committed by our first parents thousands of years ago. Sin is the wilful transgression of the law of God or the law of right and wrong. Therefore, the responsibility or blame for it must lie only on the individual who has committed it, and not on his or her children. Human beings were given a free will with an inclination and ability to do evil or to fight against it and do well. It is only when a grown-up person, capable of distinguishing between right and wrong, makes the wrong use of the God-given intellect and free will, and falls prey to his or her temptation, that sin is born in him or her. Otherwise, there have lived many men and women who resisted and conquered evil inclinations and lived their lives in harmony with the will of Allah as is found in the sacred records of Prophets Enoch, Noah, Jacob, John the Baptist, Zachariah, Jesus Christ (peace be upon them) and many more. They lived righteous and upright lives as people who feared God and eschewed evil.

> That upon you may come all the righteous blood shed upon the earth, from the blood of righteous Abel unto the blood of Zacharias son of Barachias, whom ye slew between the temple and the altar. (Matthew 23:35 KJV)

> There was in the days of Herod, the king of Judaea, a certain priest named Zacharias, of the course of Abia: and his wife was of the daughters of Aaron, and her name was Elisabeth. And they were both righteous before God, walking in all the commandments and ordinances of the Lord blameless. (Luke 1:5-6 KJV)

It is the height of misanthropy and cynicism for children to be considered sinful right from birth. How unreasonable and hard-hearted a man can become by believing in the dogma of hereditary sin, is shown by the theological dictum of St. Augustine that all unbaptised infants are doomed to burn eternally in the fire of hell. Until very recently, the unbaptised infants were not buried in consecrated grounds in Christendom, because they were believed to have died with the original sin.

Atonement, repentance, and salvation

In the Christian doctrine of atonement, we were taught that God's justice requires that a price be paid for the original sin and other sins of humankind, that for God to pardon a sinner without punishing him would be a denial of His Justice. Reverend W. Goldsack wrote:

> It should be as clear as daylight to anyone that God cannot break His law: He cannot forgive a sinner without first giving him an appropriate punishment. For if He did so, who would call Him just and Equitable.[10]

From the Islamic point of view, this understanding shows a complete ignorance of the nature of God. God is not a mere judge or king; rather Allah (ﷻ) is the Master of the Day of Judgement, who is Merciful and Forgiving at the same time. If He finds some good in a person or sees that he or she is sincerely repentant, having a real urge to conquer the evil in himself or herself, He may well forgive his or her shortcomings and sins altogether. This can by no stretch of the imagination be seen as a violation of His Justice. After all, the only true motivation for punishing a person is to check the evil in him or her and to reform the offender. To punish a person for his or her past sins, even after he or she has sincerely repented and reformed himself or herself, is a sign of vengeance and not justice. A God whose justice requires compensation for every fall and sin of a person is no better than a loan shark.

The God that I learnrd about in Islam, whom we worship, is One full of love and mercy; when He prescribes a law and a way to be followed and obeyed, it is not for His benefit but for humankind's benefit. When He punishes a person for his or her faults and sins, it is not for His own satisfaction or sadistic pleasure, but only to check the evil in the person and purify him or her.

﴿مَّنْ عَمِلَ صَٰلِحًا فَلِنَفْسِهِۦ وَمَنْ أَسَآءَ فَعَلَيْهَا وَمَا رَبُّكَ بِظَلَّٰمٍ لِّلْعَبِيدِ ۝﴾

(سورة فُصِّلَت: ٤٦)

﴿Whosoever does righteous good deeds, it is for [the benefit of] his own self, and whosoever does evil, it is against his own self, and your Lord is not at all unjust to [His] slaves.﴾   *(Qur'an 41: 46)*

Hell itself is like a hospital where the spiritually ill, afflicted with the diseases of malice, hatred, selfishness, jealousy, arrogance, greed, dishonesty, drunkenness, miserliness, racism, and all sorts of impurities, are cured through the fire of suffering and remorse. Yet those who have the persistent urge to do good and are sincerely repentant will find Allah (ﷻ) Ever-Ready to forgive and pardon their failings and sins without demanding any compensation from them or from anyone else. This is exactly what Jesus (ﷺ) taught in his beautiful parables of the lost sheep, the lost coin, and the prodigal son. Moreover, the most important Biblical prayer taught by Jesus (ﷺ) shows Allah's readiness to always forgive the sinners however much they may have sinned.

> After this manner therefore pray ye: Our Father which art in heaven, Hallowed be thy name. Thy kingdom come. Thy will be done in earth, as it is in heaven. Give us this day our daily bread. And forgive us our debts, as we forgive our debtors. And lead us not into temptation, but deliver us from evil: For thine is the kingdom, and the power, and the glory, forever. Amen. (Matthew 6:9-13 KJV)

Accordingly, forgiveness of sinners after punishing them, or someone else on their behalf, is no forgiveness at all. As I have learned in Islam, Allah (ﷻ) does forgive sins without having to punish us, or any other person on our behalf for that matter, if He sees any real goodness in those who have turned away from their sins and reformed themselves. This kind of forgiveness is not against God's justice but is regarded as the true forgiveness. Allah (ﷺ) said:

﴿وَمَن يَعْمَلْ سُوءًا أَوْ يَظْلِمْ نَفْسَهُ ثُمَّ يَسْتَغْفِرِ ٱللَّهَ يَجِدِ ٱللَّهَ غَفُورًا رَّحِيمًا ۝ وَمَن يَكْسِبْ إِثْمًا فَإِنَّمَا يَكْسِبُهُ عَلَىٰ نَفْسِهِ وَكَانَ ٱللَّهُ عَلِيمًا حَكِيمًا ۝ وَمَن يَكْسِبْ خَطِيئَةً أَوْ إِثْمًا ثُمَّ يَرْمِ بِهِ بَرِيئًا فَقَدِ ٱحْتَمَلَ بُهْتَٰنًا وَإِثْمًا مُّبِينًا ۝﴾

(سورة النِّسَاء: ١١٠–١١٢)

﴿If anyone does evil or wrongs his own soul, but afterwards seeks Allah's forgiveness, he will find Allah Oft-Forgiving, Most Merciful. And if anyone earns sin, he earns it against his own soul: for Allah is Full of Knowledge and Wisdom. But if any one earns a fault or a sin and blames it on to one that is innocent, he carries [on himself] a falsehood and a flagrant sin.﴾   *(Qur'an 4: 110-112)*

﴿قُلْ يَٰعِبَادِيَ ٱلَّذِينَ أَسْرَفُوا عَلَىٰ أَنفُسِهِمْ لَا تَقْنَطُوا مِن رَّحْمَةِ ٱللَّهِ إِنَّ ٱللَّهَ يَغْفِرُ ٱلذُّنُوبَ جَمِيعًا إِنَّهُ هُوَ ٱلْغَفُورُ ٱلرَّحِيمُ ۝ وَأَنِيبُوا إِلَىٰ رَبِّكُمْ وَأَسْلِمُوا لَهُ مِن قَبْلِ أَن يَأْتِيَكُمُ ٱلْعَذَابُ ثُمَّ لَا تُنصَرُونَ ۝﴾

(سورة الزُّمَر: ٥٣–٥٤)

﴿Say: "O my servants who have transgressed against their souls! Despair not of the Mercy of Allah: for Allah forgives all sins: for He is Oft-Forgiving, Most Merciful." Turn to your Lord [in repentance] and bow to Him, before the penalty comes on you: after which you shall not be helped.﴾   *(Qur'an 39: 53-54)*

حَدَّثَنَا أَنَسُ بْنُ مَالِكٍ قَالَ سَمِعْتُ رَسُولَ اللَّهِ صَلَّى اللَّهُ عَلَيْهِ وَسَلَّمَ يَقُولُ قَالَ اللَّهُ تَبَارَكَ وَتَعَالَى يَا ابْنَ آدَمَ إِنَّكَ مَا دَعَوْتَنِي وَرَجَوْتَنِي غَفَرْتُ لَكَ عَلَى مَا كَانَ فِيكَ وَلَا أُبَالِي يَا ابْنَ آدَمَ لَوْ بَلَغَتْ ذُنُوبُكَ عَنَانَ السَّمَاءِ ثُمَّ اسْتَغْفَرْتَنِي غَفَرْتُ لَكَ وَلَا أُبَالِي

يَا ابْنَ آدَمَ إِنَّكَ لَوْ أَتَيْتَنِي بِقُرَابِ الأَرْضِ خَطَايَا ثُمَّ لَقِيتَنِي لا
تُشْرِكُ بِي شَيْئًا لأَتَيْتُكَ بِقُرَابِهَا مَغْفِرَةً .

«On the authority of Anas ibn Mâlik (ﷺ), who said: I heard the
Messenger of Allah (ﷺ) say: Allah the Almighty has said: O son of
Adam, so long as you call upon Me and ask of Me, I shall forgive you
for what you have done, and I shall not mind. O son of Adam, were
your sins to reach the clouds of the sky and were you then to ask
forgiveness of Me, I would forgive you. O son of Adam, were you to
come to Me with sins nearly as great as the earth and you then face
Me, ascribing no partners to Me, I would bring you forgiveness
nearly as great as your sins.» (a sound hadith recorded by Tirmidhi)

The Christian scheme of salvation, which I was taught in the
church, is that Jesus (ﷺ) paid for the original sins and all our sins
when he died on the cross and shed his blood at Calvary, and that
without belief in the saving power of his blood, there is no salvation.
After becoming a Muslim, when I went through this doctrine with a
critical eye, I actually discovered that this was St. Paul's theological
understanding, and it was actually on the basis of this understanding
of a crucified Messiah that Paul built his whole theology, which
became the foundation of all Christian teachings. Paul said in his
Epistles:

> For by grace are you saved through faith; and that not of
> yourselves: it is the gift of God: not of works, lest any man
> should boast. For we are his workmanship, created in Christ
> Jesus unto good works, which God has before ordained that we
> should walk in them. (Ephesians 2: 8-10 KJV)

> For Christ is the end of the law, so that there may be
> righteousness for everyone that believes. (Romans 10:4 NIV)

> So also is the free gift not like the offense. For if through the

offense of one many are dead, much more the grace of God, and the gift by grace, which is by one man, Jesus Christ, has abounded unto many. (Romans 5:15 KJV)

For as by one man's disobedience many where made sinners, so by the obedience of one shall many be made righteous. (Romans 5:19 KJV)

So Paul nailed the law and commandments on the cross and claimed that salvation could only be attained through the grace of God and believing in the death and resurrection of Jesus Christ (ﷺ). He says in his letters:

Having cancelled the written code with its regulations, that was against us and that stood opposed to us, he took it away nailing on the cross. (Colossians 2:14 NIV)

But we preach Christ crucified a stumbling block to Jews and foolishness to the Gentiles. (I Corinthians 1:23 NIV)

For all have sinned, and come short of the glory of God; Being justified freely by his grace through the redemption that is in Christ Jesus: Whom God hath set forth to be a propitiation through faith in his blood, to declare his righteousness for the remission of sins that are past, through the forbearance of God; (Romans 3:23-25 KJV).

That if you confess with your mouth, "Jesus Lord", and believe in your heart that God raised him from the dead, you will be saved. For it is with your heart that you believe and are justified and it is with your mouth that you confession and are saved. Romans 10:9-10 NIV)

And if Christ be not risen, then is our preaching vain, and your faith is also vain. Yea, and we are found false witnesses of God; because we have testified of God that he raised up Christ: whom he raised not up, if so be that the dead rise not. For if the dead rise not, then is not Christ raised: And if Christ be not raised, your faith is vain; ye are yet in your sins. (1 Corinthians 15:14-17 KJV)

In other words, according to St. Paul, there is nothing that Christianity can offer humankind other than the blood and gore of Jesus Christ (ﷺ). If Jesus (ﷺ) did not die and was not resurrected from the dead, then there could be no salvation in Christianity, for all your good deeds are like filthy rags (Isaiah 64:6), or so I was taught in the church.

This kind of dogma is a denial not only of the mercy of God, but also of His abundant mercy and love. To demand a price of blood in order to forgive the sins of humankind is to show a complete lack of love and mercy, and to punish an innocent person for the sins of others, whether the former is willing or not, is the height of injustice. Yet as a Christian, I believed in this for many years.

Going through the Gospels and the Qur'an, I found that it is not historically acceptable to say that Jesus Christ (ﷺ) willingly gave himself to die on the cross for the sins of humankind, for there are numerous passages in the Bible saying the contrary. In fact, when we read the Bible, we come to the conclusion that Jesus (ﷺ) was not ready to die for anybody's sins.

The following are just a few of those passages in the Bible indicating that Jesus (ﷺ) never at any time wanted to die:[11]

Jesus Christ (ﷺ) was reluctant to die

According to the Bible, when he came to know that his enemies were looking for and plotting to kill him, he worked out a strategy for defence to repel the Jews who wanted to eliminate him, because he wanted to stay alive.

Then Jesus asked them, "When I sent you without purse, bag, or sandals, did you lack anything?" "Nothing," they answered. He said to them, "But now if you have a purse, take it, and also a bag; and if you have no sword, sell your cloak and buy one." It is written: "and he was numbered with the transgressors; and I tell you that this must be fulfilled in me. Yes, what is written about me is reaching its fulfilment." The disciples said, "See Lord here are two swords." "That is enough," he replied. (Luke 22:35-38 NIV)

Jesus replied, "Friend do what you came for." Then the men stepped forward, seized Jesus and arrested him. With that, one of Jesus' companions reached for his sword, drew it out, and struck the servant of the high priest, cutting off his ear. (Matthew 26:50-51 NIV)

Jesus beseeched God for help

With strong cries and tears, Jesus Christ (ﷺ) prayed earnestly for God to keep him alive.

Then cometh Jesus with them unto a place called Gethsemane, and saith unto the disciples, Sit ye here, while I go and pray yonder. And he took with him Peter and the two sons of Zebedee, and began to be sorrowful and very heavy. Then saith he unto them, My soul is exceeding sorrowful, even unto death: tarry ye here, and watch with me. And he went a little further, and fell on his face, and prayed, saying, O my Father, if it be possible, let this cup pass from me: nevertheless not as I will, but as thou wilt. (Matthew 26:36-39 KJV)

Saying, Father, if thou be willing, remove this cup from me: nevertheless not my will, but thine, be done. And there appeared an angel unto him from heaven, strengthening him. And being in an agony he prayed more earnestly: and his sweat was as it were great drops of blood falling down to the ground. (Luke 22:42-44 KJV)

God heard the prayers of Jesus (ﷺ)

This means that God accepted his prayers and answered his prayers so as to keep him alive.

> During the day of Jesus' life on earth, he offered up prayers and petitions with loud cries and tears to the one who could save him from death, and he was heard because of reverent submission. (Hebrews 5:7 NIV)

> Ask, and it shall be given you; seek, and ye shall find; knock, and it shall be opened unto you: For every one that asketh receiveth; and he that seeketh findeth; and to him that knocketh it shall be opened. Or what man is there of you, whom if his son ask bread, will he give him a stone? Or if he asks a fish, will he give him a serpent? If ye then, being evil, know how to give good gifts unto your children, how much more shall your Father which is in heaven give good things to them that ask him? (Matthew 7:7-11 KJV)

An angel of God was sent to strengthen Jesus (ﷺ)

In the hope and belief that God would save him alive:

> The prayer of a righteous man is powerful and effective. (James 5:16 NIV)

> An angel from heaven appeared to him and strengthened him. (Luke 22:43 NIV)

Pilate found Jesus not guilty of the charges against him

When Pilate went through the charges against Jesus (﷽), he could not find any fault with the man. This was good reason to keep him alive.

> Pilate saith unto them, "What shall I do then with Jesus which is called Christ?" They all say unto him, "Let him be crucified." And the governor said, "Why, what evil hath he done?" But they cried out the more, saying, "Let him be crucified." When Pilate saw that he could prevail nothing, but that rather a tumult was made, he took water, and washed his hands before the multitude, saying, "I am innocent of the blood of this just person: see ye to it." Then answered all the people, and said, "His blood be on us, and on our children." (Matthew 27:22-25 KJV)

> Pilate called together the chief priests, the rulers and the people, and said to them, "You brought me this man as one who was inciting the people to rebellion. I have examined him in your presence and found no basis for your charges against him. Neither has Herod, for he sent him back to us; as you can, he has done nothing to deserve death." (Luke 23:13-15 NIV)

Jesus was supposedly on the cross only for three hours

According to the system used at the time to fasten a person on the cross for crucifixion, no person could die by crucifixion in such a short time, which means that even if Jesus (﷽) was fastened on the cross, he must still have been alive.

> From the sixth hour until the ninth hour darkness came over all the land. About the ninth hour Jesus cried out in a loud voice, "Eloi, Eloi, lama sabachtani?" — which means "My God, my God why have you forsaken me?" (Matthew 27:45-46)

Two men crucified with Jesus were alive

The two other people who were crucified were found to be alive on their respective crosses. So Jesus (﷽) too, for the same reason, having supposedly taken the same period of time on the cross, must have been alive.

> The soldiers therefore came and broke the legs of the first man who had been crucified with Jesus, and then those of the other. But when they came to Jesus and saw that he was dead already they did not break his legs. (John 19:32-33 NIV)

According to this Biblical story, there was a mistake in seeing Jesus (﷽) on the cross and judging that he was dead already, because they did not use a stethoscope, nor did the soldiers feel his pulse nor heartbeat. It is possible that he could have been in a coma, rather they only assumed by seeing, and judged that Jesus (﷽) was dead already.

Forthwith came out blood and water

When the soldiers assumed that Jesus (﷽) was dead, they pierced him in his side with a spear. Immediately, blood and water came out, which was a sure sign that he was alive.

> But when they came to Jesus, and saw that he was dead already, they brake not his legs: But one of the soldiers with a spear pierced his side, and forthwith came there out blood and water. And he that saw it bare record, and his record is true: and he knoweth that he saith true, that ye might believe. For these things were done, that the scripture should be fulfilled, A bone of him shall not be broken. And again another scripture saith, they shall look on him whom they pierced. And after this Joseph of Arimathaea, being a disciple of Jesus, but secretly for fear of the Jews, besought Pilate that he might take away the body of

Jesus: and Pilate gave him leave. He came therefore, and took the body of Jesus. (John 19:33-38 KJV)

Thunderstorm, earthquake, and darkening of the sun

It is taught in Christianity that when Jesus Christ (ﷺ) was put on the cross, there was a thunderstorm, an earthquake and darkening of the sun all within three hours, in order to disperse the sadistic mob and to enable his secret disciples to help keep him alive.

At that moment the curtain of the temple was torn in two from top to bottom. The earth shook and the rock split. (Matthew 27:51 NIV)

It was now about the sixth hour, and darkness came over the whole land until the ninth hour, for the sun stopped shining. And the curtain of the temple was torn in two. (Luke 23:44-45 NIV)

After the Sabbath, at dawn on the first day of the week Mary Magdalene and the other Mary went to look at the tomb. There was a violent earthquake for an angel of the Lord came down from heaven, and going to the tomb, rolled back the stone and sat on it. His appearance was like lightning, and his clothes were white as snow. The guards were so afraid of him that they shook and became like dead men. (Matthew 28: 1-4 NIV)

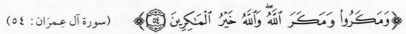

﴿وَمَكَرُواْ وَمَكَرَ ٱللَّهُ وَٱللَّهُ خَيْرُ ٱلْمَـٰكِرِينَ ٥٤﴾ (سورة آل عِمرَان: ٥٤)

﴿And they planned and plotted [to kill Jesus] and Allah also planned and plotted, and Allah is the best of planners.﴾   *(Qur'an 3: 54)*

The Jews doubted whether Jesus was dead

The Jews suspected that Jesus (﷽) had escaped death on the cross because he had only stayed on the cross for three hours, and because since his crossmates were alive, he must also for the same reason be alive. Moreover, it was his secret disciple Joseph of Arimathea who sought Pilate's permission to take the body, and put it in a spacious tomb, not a grave. All this made the Jews suspicious that Jesus (﷽) was alive.

> The next day, the one after Preparation Day, the chief priests and the Pharisees went to Pilate. "Sir" they said, "We remember that while he was still alive that deceiver said, 'After three days I will rise again'. So give the order for the tomb to be made secure until the third day. Otherwise, his disciples may come, steal the body, and tell the people that he has risen from the dead. This last deception will be worst than the first." (Matthew 27:62-64)

The questions are: what was the 'first' error that the Jews made in trying to eliminate Jesus (﷽) and what was the 'last' error that they were trying to avoid? Most probably, the first error was permitting Jesus (﷽) to be brought down from the cross without breaking his legs like the other two crossmates, under the false assumption that the soldiers had seen that he was dead already. The last error, which would be worse than the first, would be to allow the secret disciples of Jesus (﷽) to render help to the wounded man, by not sealing off the tomb. Yet, in their hurry to do away with Jesus (﷽), they made a third mistake of approaching Pilate the next day instead of that very day, and that was too late.

Pilate was surprised to hear that Jesus was dead

Pilate knew very well from experience that no one died so soon by crucifixion, so he also suspected that Jesus (﷽) must be alive.

Pilate was surprised to hear that he was already dead. Summoning the centurion, he asked him if Jesus had already died. And when he knew it from the centurion, he gave permission to Joseph of Arimathea to take the body. And he bought fine linen, and took him down, and wrapped him in the linen, and laid him in a sepulcher which was hewn out of a rock, and rolled a stone unto the door of the sepulcher. (Mark 15: 44-46 KJV)

Stone and winding sheets had to be removed

The stone covering the tomb, which was to secure and confine Jesus (ﷺ) inside, was found to have been removed from the mouth of the tomb, and the winding sheets that were used to wrap the body of Jesus (ﷺ) were found inside the tomb. This would only have been necessary if Jesus (ﷺ) was alive.

After the Sabbath, at dawn on the first day of the week Mary Magdalene and the other Mary went to look at the tomb. There was a violent earthquake for an angel of the Lord came down from heaven, and going to the tomb, rolled back the stone and sat on it. His appearance was like lightning, and his clothes were white as snow. The guards were so afraid of him that they shook and became like dead men. (Matthew 28: 1-4 NIV)

On the first day of the week, very early in the morning, the women took the spices they had prepared and went to the tomb. They found the stone rolled away from the tomb, but when they entered, they did not find the body of the lord Jesus. While they were wondering about this, suddenly two men in clothes that were gleaming like lightning stood besides them. In their fright the women bowed down with their faces to the ground, but the men said to them, "Why do you look for the living among the dead?" (Luke 24:1-5 NIV)

The first day of the week cometh Mary Magdalene early, when it was yet dark, unto the sepulcher, and seeth the stone taken away from the sepulcher. Then she runneth, and cometh to Simon Peter, and to the other disciple, whom Jesus loved, and saith unto them, They have taken away the Lord out of the sepulcher, and we know not where they have laid him. Peter therefore went forth, and that other disciple, and came to the sepulcher. So they ran both together: and the other disciple did outrun Peter, and came first to the sepulcher. And he stooping down, and looking in, saw the linen clothes lying; yet went he not in. Then cometh Simon Peter following him, and went into the sepulcher, and seeth the linen clothes lie, And the napkin, that was about his head, not lying with the linen clothes, but wrapped together in a place by itself. Then went in also that other disciple, which came first to the sepulcher, and he saw, and believed. (John 20:1-8 KJV)

If the angel came down from heaven and rolled the stone away from the tomb, as in the Biblical story, then it is clear that Jesus (ﷺ) was not resurrected from the dead. If he were, there would have been no need for the stone to be rolled away from the mouth of the tomb, because resurrected bodies are spiritualized; they can pass through the wall and would not even need a door.

The disciples were petrified on seeing Jesus alive

All the knowledge the disciples had about the whole ordeal of the crucifixion was from hearsay. They were not eyewitnesses to the happenings, because at the most critical juncture in Jesus' life, they all forsook him and fled; therefore, they could not believe that he was alive.

And he that betrayed him had given them a token, saying, Whomsoever I shall kiss, that same is he; take him, and lead him away safely. And as soon as he was come, he goeth straightway

to him, and saith, Master, master; and kissed him. And they laid
their hands on him, and took him. And one of them that stood by
drew a sword, smote a servant of the high priest, and cut off his
ear. And Jesus answered and said unto them, Are ye come out,
as against a thief, with swords and with staves to take me? I was
daily with you in the temple teaching, and ye took me not: but
the scriptures must be fulfilled. And they all forsook him, and
fled. (Mark 14:44-50 KJV)

And as they thus spoke, Jesus himself stood in the midst of
them, and saith unto them, "Peace be unto you". But they were
terrified and affrighted, and supposed that they had seen a spirit.
And he said unto them, "Why are ye troubled? And why do
thoughts arise in your hearts? Behold my hands and my feet, that
it is I myself: handle me, and see; for a spirit hath not flesh and
bones, as ye see me have." And when he had thus spoken, he
showed them his hands and his feet. And while they yet believed
not for joy, and wondered, he said unto them, "Have ye here any
meat?" And they gave him a piece of a broiled fish, and of an
honeycomb. And he took it, and did eat before them. (Luke
24:36-43 KJV)

The fact that Jesus (ﷺ) had a physical body, which had flesh and
bones, and moreover he ate earthly food in the very sight of his
disciples, all goes to prove the point that he was not what they
thought; they thought he had died and now was resurrected, and so
they were frightened to see him. However, his behaviour and
reactions all show that, to the contrary, he never died. He was the
very Jesus (ﷺ) alive, not resurrected.

The miracle of Jesus was like that of Jonah

According to the Bible, Jesus (ﷺ) had himself foretold that he
was not going to die at the hands of his enemies; instead, the miracle

of his remaining alive, when he was expected to die by crucifixion, was going to be like the miracle of Prophet Jonah (﷽). He was swallowed by the whale and was also expected to die but was vomited out of the whale's belly alive.

> Then certain of the scribes and of the Pharisees answered, saying, Master, we would see a sign from thee. But he answered and said unto them, An evil and adulterous generation seeketh after a sign; and there shall no sign be given to it, but the sign of the prophet Jonas: For as Jonas was three days and three nights in the whale's belly; so shall the Son of man be three days and three nights in the heart of the earth. The men of Nineveh shall rise in judgment with this generation, and shall condemn it: because they repented at the preaching of Jonas; and, behold, a greater than Jonas is here. (Matthew 12:38-41 KJV)

According to the Book of Jonah in the Bible, when he was thrown into the raging sea, logically he was expected to die. If he had died, there would have been no miracle, but since he was praying to God while in the whale's belly in order to remain alive, the All-Merciful God saved him by answering his supplication. After three days, he was vomited on the seashore alive. In a similar manner, according to the Bible, Jesus (﷽) was fastened to the cross, and therefore he was expected to die. If he had died, then there would have been no miracle, and Jesus (﷽) would not have referred to the miracle of Jonah (﷽) as being it would be similar to his miracle. Just as Prophet Jonah (﷽) prayed for help from God, Jesus (﷽) did the same, and the same God who saved Jonah (﷽) from the whale's belly saved Jesus (﷽) from the cross alive. Jesus (﷽) said:

> A wicked and adulterous generation asks for a miraculous sign! But none will be given it except the sign of prophet Jonah. For as Jonah was three days and three nights in the belly of the huge fish, so shall the Son of man be three days and three nights in the heart of the earth. (Matthew 12:39-40 NIV)

As I said before, what I found is that the dogma of atonement as a way of salvation is a complete denial of God's abundant love, mercy, and justice. To demand a price of blood in order to forgive sins is to show a complete lack of mercy. Moreover, to punish an innocent man for the sins of others sounds like the physician breaking his own head to cure the headache of his patients. I found that the idea of substitution or vicarious sacrifice is illogical, meaningless, and unjust.

Furthermore, the idea that shedding blood is necessary to appease the wrath of God came to Christianity from the primitive human's image of God as an all-powerful demon. There is absolutely no connection between sin and blood. What is necessary to wash away sins is not blood but sincere repentance, persistent struggle against evil inclinations, good character and behaviour towards fellow humankind, and upholding the will of Allah (ﷻ) in all our life, as taught by Jesus Christ (ﷺ) and other prophets in the Bible.

> For I desire mercy, not sacrifice, and acknowledgment of God rather than burnt offerings. Like Adam, they have broken the covenant — They were unfaithful to me. (Hosea 6:6-7 NIV)

> Now ye are clean through the word which I have spoken unto you. Abide in me, and I in you. As the branch cannot bear fruit of itself, except it abide in the vine; no more can ye, except ye abide in me. I am the vine, ye are the branches: He that abideth in me, and I in him, the same bringeth forth much fruit: for without me ye can do nothing. If a man abides not in me, he is cast forth as a branch, and is withered; and men gather them, and cast them into the fire, and they are burned. If ye abide in me, and my words abide in you, ye shall ask what ye will, and it shall be done unto you. Herein is my Father glorified, that ye bear much fruit; so shall ye be my disciples. As the Father hath loved me, so have I loved you: continue ye in my love. If ye keep my

commandments, ye shall abide in my love; even as I have kept my Father's commandments, and abide in his love. These things have I spoken unto you, that my joy might remain in you, and that your joy might be full. This is my commandment, That ye love one another, as I have loved you. Greater love hath no man than this that a man lay down his life for his friends. Ye are my friends, if ye do whatsoever I command you. (John 15:3-14 KJV)

From the above teachings, we can clearly see that Jesus (﷽) came to rescue men from sin, not by dying for them on the cross but by commanding them to follow his teachings and his example of righteousness. This is why when a young man came and asked about the way to salvation in the hereafter, he answered him as follows:

And, behold, one came and said unto him, Good Master, what good thing shall I do, that I may have eternal life? And he said unto him, Why callest thou me good? There is none good but one, that is, God: but if thou wilt enter into life, keep the commandments. (Matthew 19:16-17 KJV)

In his answer, Jesus (﷽) mentioned nothing about his atoning sacrifice or the redeeming power of his blood, as I was taught in the church. His answer to the young man was to keep the commandments. Accordingly, the way to salvation and eternal life is by sincerely believing in God, eschewing evil and doing good, and not by accepting Jesus (﷽) as a personal saviour through his redeeming blood atonement.

In my quest for Islam, I found that Islam completely and strongly rejects this dogma of blood atonement for salvation and declares that forgiveness of sins cannot be obtained by the suffering and sacrifice of any other person, human or divine, but by the grace of God and by our own sincere and persistent efforts to fight against evil and do good. Allah (﷽) says:

﴿أَلَّا نَزِرُ وَازِرَةٌ وِزْرَ أُخْرَىٰ ۝ وَأَن لَّيْسَ لِلْإِنسَـٰنِ إِلَّا مَا سَعَىٰ ۝ وَأَنَّ سَعْيَهُۥ سَوْفَ يُرَىٰ ۝﴾   (سورة النجم: ٣٨-٤٠)

❬That no bearer of burdens can bear the burden of another; That man can have nothing but what he strives for; That [the fruit of] his striving will soon come in sight.❭   *(Qur'an 53: 38-40)*

﴿مَّنِ ٱهْتَدَىٰ فَإِنَّمَا يَهْتَدِى لِنَفْسِهِۦ وَمَن ضَلَّ فَإِنَّمَا يَضِلُّ عَلَيْهَا وَلَا تَزِرُ وَازِرَةٌ وِزْرَ أُخْرَىٰ وَمَا كُنَّا مُعَذِّبِينَ حَتَّىٰ نَبْعَثَ رَسُولًا ۝﴾   (سورة الإسراء: ١٥)

❬Whoever is guided is only guided for [the benefit of] his soul. And whoever errs only errs against it. And no bearer of burdens will bear the burden of another. And never would We punish until We sent a messenger.❭   *(Qur'an 17: 15)*

Islam's scheme of salvation to be attained in the hereafter is based on:

1. The grace of God.
2. True and sincere faith in God, and not lip service.
3. Good works, which are the fruits of sincere true faith.
4. Repentance of sins committed, whether major or minor, before one dies.

In this respect, Allah (ﷺ) said in several verses of the glorious Qur'an:

﴿ثُمَّ نُنَجِّى ٱلَّذِينَ ٱتَّقَوا۟ وَّنَذَرُ ٱلظَّـٰلِمِينَ فِيهَا جِثِيًّا ۝﴾   (سورة مريم: ٧٢)

❬Then We will save those who feared Allah and leave the wrongdoers within it [Hellfire], on their knees.❭   *(Qur'an 19: 72)*

﴿يَـٰٓأَيُّهَا ٱلَّذِينَ ءَامَنُوا۟ لَا تَتَّبِعُوا۟ خُطُوَٰتِ ٱلشَّيْطَـٰنِ وَمَن يَتَّبِعْ خُطُوَٰتِ ٱلشَّيْطَـٰنِ فَإِنَّهُۥ يَأْمُرُ بِٱلْفَحْشَاءِ وَٱلْمُنكَرِ وَلَوْلَا فَضْلُ ٱللَّهِ عَلَيْكُمْ وَرَحْمَتُهُۥ مَا زَكَىٰ مِنكُم مِّنْ أَحَدٍ أَبَدًا وَلَـٰكِنَّ ٱللَّهَ يُزَكِّى مَن يَشَاءُ وَٱللَّهُ سَمِيعٌ عَلِيمٌ ۝﴾   (سورة النُّور: ٢١)

❨O you who believe! Follow not Satan's footsteps: if any will follow the footsteps of Satan, he will [but] command what is shameful and wrong: and were it not for the grace and mercy of Allah on you, not one of you would ever have been pure: but Allah purifies whom He pleases: and Allah is One Who hears and knows [all things].❩

(Qur'an 24: 21)

Prophet Muhammad (ﷺ) is also reported to have taught salvation based on the grace of God.

«Narrated 'Â'ishah (﵂): The Prophet (ﷺ) said: Do good deeds properly, sincerely and moderately, and receive good news because one's good deeds will not make him enter paradise. They asked: Even you, O Allah's Apostle? He said: Even I, unless and until Allah bestows His pardon and Mercy on me.» (Bukhari)

«Narrated Abu Hurayrah: Allah's Apostle (ﷺ) said: The deeds of anyone of you will not save you [from the (Hell) Fire]. They asked: Even you (will not be saved by your deeds), O Allah's Apostle? He said: No, even I (will not be saved) unless and until Allah bestows His mercy on me. Therefore, do good deeds properly, sincerely and moderately, and worship Allah in the forenoon and in the afternoon and during a part of the night, and always adopt a middle, moderate, regular course whereby you will reach your target (paradise).» (Bukhari)

This is the humility of all the messengers of Allah. Compare this with the humility of Jesus (ﷺ), as quoted before from the Bible; when a rich ruler came and called him good master, he declined to be called good master, and said, "None is good except one, that is God alone, but if you want eternal life keep to the commandments."

According to the verses of the Qur'an and the narrations of the Prophet Muhammad (ﷺ) quoted, we can see that there is a direct link between the divine grace of God, faith, and righteous deeds. God's mercy is not arbitrary, in that it could cause a disbelieving, evil, wretched person to enter paradise, while causing a noble, believing soul to go to hell.

Such a state of affairs would deny humankind's free will and make the Day of Judgement meaningless. Allah's wisdom and justice work along with His grace and mercy. There is, of course, an aspect of His infinite mercy that covers all creatures, both deserving and undeserving. However, the greater part of this infinite mercy of Allah (ﷻ) is reserved as grace for the righteous believers in the next life.

﴿وَلَا تُفْسِدُواْ فِي ٱلْأَرْضِ بَعْدَ إِصْلَٰحِهَا وَٱدْعُوهُ خَوْفًا وَطَمَعًا إِنَّ رَحْمَتَ ٱللَّهِ قَرِيبٌ مِّنَ ٱلْمُحْسِنِينَ ۝﴾ (سورة الأعراف : ٥٦)

❝Do no mischief on the earth, after it has been set in order, but call on Him with fear and longing. For the Mercy of Allah is near to those who do good.❞

(Qur'an 7: 56)

﴿ ۞ وَٱكْتُبْ لَنَا فِي هَٰذِهِ ٱلدُّنْيَا حَسَنَةً وَفِي ٱلْأَخِرَةِ إِنَّا هُدْنَآ إِلَيْكَ قَالَ عَذَابِي أُصِيبُ بِهِۦ مَنْ أَشَآءُ وَرَحْمَتِي وَسِعَتْ كُلَّ شَيْءٍ فَسَأَكْتُبُهَا لِلَّذِينَ يَتَّقُونَ وَيُؤْتُونَ ٱلزَّكَوٰةَ وَٱلَّذِينَ هُم بِـَٔايَٰتِنَا يُؤْمِنُونَ ۝ ﴾ (سورة الأعراف : ١٥٦)

❝And ordain for us that which is good, in this life and in the hereafter: for we have turned unto You. He said: With My punishment I afflict whom I will; but My Mercy extends to all things. That [Mercy] I shall ordain for those who fear Me, and practice regular charity, and those who believe in Our Signs.❞

(Qur'an 7: 156)

«Narrated Abu Hurayrah (ﷺ): I heard Allah's Apostle (ﷺ) saying: Verily Allah created mercy. The day He created it, He made it into one hundred parts. He withheld with Him ninety-nine parts, and sent its one part to all His creatures. Had the non-believer known of all the mercy which is in the Hands of Allah, he would not lose hope of entering paradise, and had the believer known of all the punishment which is present with Allah, he would not consider himself complaisant and safe from the hellfire.» (Bukhari)

Thus, I learned that in Islam, the keys of entry into paradise through Allah's grace and mercy are none other than what I have already mentioned. First and foremost is sincere faith in the one true God Who alone deserves our devotion and worship; secondly the performance of righteous deeds that are prescribed by Him; and lastly is the sincere and true consistent repentance. This has been neatly summed up by Allah (ﷻ) in the following verses:

﴿مَن كَفَرَ فَعَلَيْهِ كُفْرُهُ وَمَنْ عَمِلَ صَٰلِحًا فَلِأَنفُسِهِمْ يَمْهَدُونَ ۝ لِيَجْزِيَ ٱلَّذِينَ ءَامَنُوا۟ وَعَمِلُوا۟ ٱلصَّٰلِحَٰتِ مِن فَضْلِهِۦٓ إِنَّهُۥ لَا يُحِبُّ ٱلْكَٰفِرِينَ ۝﴾

(سورة الرُّوم: ٤٤-٤٥)

﴿Those who reject faith will suffer from that rejection: while those who work righteousness have prepared for themselves [places in paradise], in order that He may reward those who believe and work righteousness out of His Grace. For, surely He does not love those who reject faith.﴾ *(Qur'an 30: 44-45)*

﴿وَٱلَّذِينَ إِذَا فَعَلُوا۟ فَٰحِشَةً أَوْ ظَلَمُوٓا۟ أَنفُسَهُمْ ذَكَرُوا۟ ٱللَّهَ فَٱسْتَغْفَرُوا۟ لِذُنُوبِهِمْ وَمَن يَغْفِرُ ٱلذُّنُوبَ إِلَّا ٱللَّهُ وَلَمْ يُصِرُّوا۟ عَلَىٰ مَا فَعَلُوا۟ وَهُمْ يَعْلَمُونَ ۝ أُو۟لَٰٓئِكَ جَزَآؤُهُم مَّغْفِرَةٌ مِّن رَّبِّهِمْ وَجَنَّٰتٌ تَجْرِى مِن تَحْتِهَا ٱلْأَنْهَٰرُ خَٰلِدِينَ فِيهَا وَنِعْمَ أَجْرُ ٱلْعَٰمِلِينَ ۝ قَدْ خَلَتْ مِن قَبْلِكُمْ سُنَنٌ فَسِيرُوا۟ فِى ٱلْأَرْضِ فَٱنظُرُوا۟ كَيْفَ كَانَ عَٰقِبَةُ ٱلْمُكَذِّبِينَ ۝ هَٰذَا بَيَانٌ لِّلنَّاسِ وَهُدًى وَمَوْعِظَةٌ لِّلْمُتَّقِينَ ۝﴾

(سورة آل عِمْرَان: ١٣٥-١٣٨)

﴿And those who, when they commit an immorality or wrong themselves [by transgression], remember Allah and seek forgiveness for their sins — and who can forgive sins except Allah? — And [who] do not persist in what they have done while they know. Those

— their reward is forgiveness from their Lord and gardens beneath which rivers flow [in paradise], wherein they will abide eternally; and excellent is the reward of the [righteous] workers. Similar situations [as yours] have passed on before you, so proceed through out the earth and observe how was the end of those who denied. This [Qur'an] is a clear statement to [all] the people and a guidance and instruction for those conscious of Allah.⟩   *(Qur'an 3: 135-138)*

Thus, it is due to the grace of Allah (ﷻ) that His doors of repentance are wide open, as they were to our first parents who were deceived by the devil and, being forgetful of the commandment of Allah, sinned against Him. However, they were taught words of repentance, and they repented and asked forgiveness from Allah (ﷻ), Who graciously forgave them once and for all; thus began the concept of repentance as taught by the prophets John the Baptist (Yahya), Jesus, and Muhammad (peace be upon them). Therefore Allah (ﷻ) continuously reminds us to repent to Him and ask for His forgiveness for our sins.

﴿يَـٰٓأَيُّهَا ٱلَّذِينَ ءَامَنُوا۟ تُوبُوٓا۟ إِلَى ٱللَّهِ تَوْبَةً نَّصُوحًا عَسَىٰ رَبُّكُمْ أَن يُكَفِّرَ عَنكُمْ سَيِّـَٔاتِكُمْ وَيُدْخِلَكُمْ جَنَّـٰتٍ تَجْرِى مِن تَحْتِهَا ٱلْأَنْهَـٰرُ يَوْمَ لَا يُخْزِى ٱللَّهُ ٱلنَّبِىَّ وَٱلَّذِينَ ءَامَنُوا۟ مَعَهُۥ نُورُهُمْ يَسْعَىٰ بَيْنَ أَيْدِيهِمْ وَبِأَيْمَـٰنِهِمْ يَقُولُونَ رَبَّنَآ أَتْمِمْ لَنَا نُورَنَا وَٱغْفِرْ لَنَآ إِنَّكَ عَلَىٰ كُلِّ شَىْءٍ قَدِيرٌ ۝﴾   (سورة التحريم : ٨)

⟨O you who believe! Turn to Allah with sincere repentance: in the hope that your Lord will remove from you your ills [misdeeds] and admit you into gardens beneath which rivers flow; the Day that Allah will not permit to be humiliated the Prophet and those who believe with him. Their light will run forward before them and on their right, while they say, "Our Lord! Perfect our light for us, and grant us forgiveness: for You have power over all things."⟩ *(Qur'an 66: 8)*

﴾ ... وَتُوبُوٓاْ إِلَى ٱللَّهِ جَمِيعًا أَيُّهَ ٱلْمُؤْمِنُونَ لَعَلَّكُمْ تُفْلِحُونَ ﴿۳۱﴾ ﴿

(سورة النُّور: ۳۱)

﴾...And turn all of you in repentance to Allah, O believers so that you
may be successful.﴿   *(Qur'an 24: 31)*

According to this understanding, Allah (ﷻ) deliberately created
humankind with an inclination to do wrong, so that pardoning those
who turn to Him in repentance should be a channel through which
Allah's divine attributes of mercy, grace, and forgiveness would be
made manifest in His creation. Allah (ﷻ) says:

﴾ ... إِنَّ ٱللَّهَ يُحِبُّ ٱلتَّوَّٰبِينَ وَيُحِبُّ ٱلْمُتَطَهِّرِينَ ﴿۲۲۲﴾ ﴿   (سورة البَقَرَة: ۲۲۲)

﴾...Indeed, Allah loves those who are constantly repentant and loves
those who purify themselves.﴿   *(Qur'an 2: 222)*

The last messenger of Allah, Muhammad (ﷺ), not only complied
with these commands but also urged his Companions, and all those
who believe in Allah (ﷻ), to turn regularly to Allah in repentance.
«Abu Burdah narrated that he heard Al-Agharr al-Muzani, who was
from amongst the Companions of Allah's Apostle, reporting that Ibn
'Umar (ؓ) stated to him that Allah's Messenger (ﷺ) said: «O
people seek repentance from Allah. Verily, I seek repentance from
Him a hundred times a day.» (Muslim)

Islam: The religion of all the prophets

After embracing Islam, I realized that one of the most important
duties in Islam was to seek authentic Islamic knowledge. Knowledge
sets one free from many things such as biases and superstitious
beliefs. It liberates one from the enslavement of the mind. The more
books I read on Islam, the more I had the feeling that Islam was so

natural and close to my heart, as if it was something I had been yearning for and believed in, but had not been informed about by anybody. The more books I read, the more I wanted to read, and this has never stopped. The feeling that I do not know enough still lingers in my mind, and the reading continues.

I was taught in the church that Islam is Muhammadanism, the religion of Arabs who worship Muhammad. Through my reading, though, I discovered that Islam was not only the religion brought by Prophet Muhammad (ﷺ), but it was also the religion of all the prophets. For indeed, all the prophets submitted their will to the will of Allah (ﷻ). Prophets Abraham, Moses, Jesus, and Muhammad (peace be upon them) were all brothers in faith descending from their father Abraham (عليه السلام).

﴿ شَرَعَ لَكُم مِّنَ ٱلدِّينِ مَا وَصَّىٰ بِهِۦ نُوحًا وَٱلَّذِىٓ أَوْحَيْنَآ إِلَيْكَ وَمَا وَصَّيْنَا بِهِۦٓ إِبْرَٰهِيمَ وَمُوسَىٰ وَعِيسَىٰٓ أَنْ أَقِيمُوا ٱلدِّينَ وَلَا تَتَفَرَّقُوا فِيهِ ... ﴿١٣﴾ ﴾

(سورة الشُّورىٰ: ١٣)

﴾He has ordained for you of religion what He enjoined upon Noah and that which We have revealed to you, [O Muhammad], and what We enjoined upon Abraham and Moses and Jesus — to establish the religion and not be divided therein...﴾ *(Qur'an 42: 13)*

﴿ وَمَا كَانَ إِبْرَٰهِيمُ يَهُودِيًّا وَلَا نَصْرَانِيًّا وَلَٰكِن كَانَ حَنِيفًا مُّسْلِمًا وَمَا كَانَ مِنَ ٱلْمُشْرِكِينَ ﴿٦٧﴾ ﴾

(سورة آل عِمْرَان: ٦٧)

﴾Abraham was neither a Jew nor a Christian, but he was one inclining toward truth, a Muslim [submitting to Allah]. And he was not of the polytheists.﴾ *(Qur'an 3: 67)*

﴿ وَمَن يَرْغَبُ عَن مِّلَّةِ إِبْرَٰهِمَ إِلَّا مَن سَفِهَ نَفْسَهُۥ وَلَقَدِ ٱصْطَفَيْنَٰهُ فِى ٱلدُّنْيَا وَإِنَّهُۥ فِى ٱلْءَاخِرَةِ لَمِنَ ٱلصَّٰلِحِينَ ﴿١٣٠﴾ إِذْ قَالَ لَهُۥ رَبُّهُۥٓ أَسْلِمْ قَالَ أَسْلَمْتُ لِرَبِّ

ٱلْعَٰلَمِينَ ۞ وَوَصَّىٰ بِهَآ إِبْرَٰهِمُ بَنِيهِ وَيَعْقُوبُ إِنَّ ٱللَّهَ ٱصْطَفَىٰ لَكُمُ ٱلدِّينَ فَلَا تَمُوتُنَّ إِلَّا وَأَنتُم مُّسْلِمُونَ ۞ أَمْ كُنتُمْ شُهَدَآءَ إِذْ حَضَرَ يَعْقُوبَ ٱلْمَوْتُ إِذْ قَالَ لِبَنِيهِ مَا تَعْبُدُونَ مِنۢ بَعْدِى قَالُوا نَعْبُدُ إِلَٰهَكَ وَإِلَٰهَ ءَابَآئِكَ إِبْرَٰهِمَ وَإِسْمَٰعِيلَ وَإِسْحَٰقَ إِلَٰهًا وَٰحِدًا وَنَحْنُ لَهُۥ مُسْلِمُونَ ۞ تِلْكَ أُمَّةٌ قَدْ خَلَتْ لَهَا مَا كَسَبَتْ وَلَكُم مَّا كَسَبْتُمْ وَلَا تُسْئَلُونَ عَمَّا كَانُوا يَعْمَلُونَ ۞ وَقَالُوا كُونُوا هُودًا أَوْ نَصَٰرَىٰ تَهْتَدُوا قُلْ بَلْ مِلَّةَ إِبْرَٰهِمَ حَنِيفًا وَمَا كَانَ مِنَ ٱلْمُشْرِكِينَ ۞ قُولُوٓا ءَامَنَّا بِٱللَّهِ وَمَآ أُنزِلَ إِلَيْنَا وَمَآ أُنزِلَ إِلَىٰٓ إِبْرَٰهِمَ وَإِسْمَٰعِيلَ وَإِسْحَٰقَ وَيَعْقُوبَ وَٱلْأَسْبَاطِ وَمَآ أُوتِىَ مُوسَىٰ وَعِيسَىٰ وَمَآ أُوتِىَ ٱلنَّبِيُّونَ مِن رَّبِّهِمْ لَا نُفَرِّقُ بَيْنَ أَحَدٍ مِّنْهُمْ وَنَحْنُ لَهُۥ مُسْلِمُونَ ۞ فَإِنْ ءَامَنُوا بِمِثْلِ مَآ ءَامَنتُم بِهِۦ فَقَدِ ٱهْتَدَوا وَّإِن تَوَلَّوْا فَإِنَّمَا هُمْ فِى شِقَاقٍ فَسَيَكْفِيكَهُمُ ٱللَّهُ وَهُوَ ٱلسَّمِيعُ ٱلْعَلِيمُ ۞ صِبْغَةَ ٱللَّهِ وَمَنْ أَحْسَنُ مِنَ ٱللَّهِ صِبْغَةً وَنَحْنُ لَهُۥ عَٰبِدُونَ ۞ قُلْ أَتُحَآجُّونَنَا فِى ٱللَّهِ وَهُوَ رَبُّنَا وَرَبُّكُمْ وَلَنَآ أَعْمَٰلُنَا وَلَكُمْ أَعْمَٰلُكُمْ وَنَحْنُ لَهُۥ مُخْلِصُونَ ۞ أَمْ تَقُولُونَ إِنَّ إِبْرَٰهِمَ وَإِسْمَٰعِيلَ وَإِسْحَٰقَ وَيَعْقُوبَ وَٱلْأَسْبَاطَ كَانُوا هُودًا أَوْ نَصَٰرَىٰ قُلْ ءَأَنتُمْ أَعْلَمُ أَمِ ٱللَّهُ وَمَنْ أَظْلَمُ مِمَّن كَتَمَ شَهَٰدَةً عِندَهُۥ مِنَ ٱللَّهِ وَمَا ٱللَّهُ بِغَٰفِلٍ عَمَّا تَعْمَلُونَ ۞

(سورة البقرة: ١٣٠-١٤٠)

❋And who would turn away from the religion of Abraham except one who makes a fool of himself. And We had chosen him in this world, and indeed he, in the hereafter, will be among the righteous. When his Lord said to him, "Submit," he said, "I have submitted [in Islam] to the Lord of the worlds." And Abraham instructed his sons [to do the same] and [so did] Jacob, [saying], "O my sons, indeed Allah has chosen for you this religion, so do not die except while you are Muslims." Or were you witnesses when death approached Jacob, when he said to his sons, "What will you worship after me?" They said, "We will worship your God and the God of your fathers, Abraham and Ishmael and Isaac, one God. And we are Muslims [in submission] to Him." That was a nation that has passed on. It will have [the consequence of] what it earned and you will have what you have earned. And you will not be asked about what they used to do. They say, "Be Jews or Christians [so] you will be guided." Say, "Rather, [we follow] the religion of Abraham, inclining toward truth, and he was not of the polytheists." Say, [O believers], "We have believed in Allah and what has been revealed to us and what has been revealed to Abraham and Ishmael and Isaac and Jacob and the descendants and what was given to Moses and Jesus and what was given to the prophets from their Lord. We make no distinction between any of them, and we are Muslims [in submission] to Him." So if they believe in the same as you believe in, then they have been [rightly] guided; but if they turn away, they are only in dissension, and Allah will be sufficient for you against them. And He is the Hearing, the Knowing [And say, "Ours is] the religion of Allah. And who is better than Allah in [ordaining] religion? And we are worshippers of Him." Say, [O Muhammad], "Do you argue with us about Allah while He is our Lord and your Lord? For us are our deeds, and for you are your deeds. And we are sincere [in deed and intention] to Him." Or do you say that Abraham, Ishmael, Jacob, and the descendants were Jews or Christians? Say, "Are you more knowing or is Allah?" And who is more unjust than one who conceals a testimony he has from Allah? And Allah is not unaware of what you do.❯ *(Qur'an 2: 130-140)*

All praise be to Allah (﷾) Who not only guided me to Islam but also guided both my elderly parents, as well as all my brothers and sister and their families. Had it not been for His grace and mercy, we would not be Muslims. Our last words are in accordance with the words of the Most Merciful:

﴾ ... اَلْحَمْدُ لِلَّهِ ٱلَّذِى هَدَىٰنَا لِهَٰذَا وَمَا كُنَّا لِنَهْتَدِىَ لَوْلَا أَنْ هَدَىٰنَا ٱللَّهُ ... ﴿ ۝

(سورة الأعْرَاف: ٤٣)

﴾...Praise be to Allah, Who has guided us; never could we have found guidance, had it not been for the guidance of Allah...﴿ *(Qur'an 7: 43)*

﴾رَبَّنَا لَا تُزِغْ قُلُوبَنَا بَعْدَ إِذْ هَدَيْتَنَا وَهَبْ لَنَا مِن لَّدُنكَ رَحْمَةً إِنَّكَ أَنتَ ٱلْوَهَّابُ ۝﴿

(سورة آل عِمْرَان: ٨)

﴾Our Lord! Let not our hearts deviate [from the truth] now after You have guided us, but grant us mercy from Your own Presence; for You are the Grantor of bounties without measure.﴿ *(Qur'an 3: 8)*

﴾ ... رَبَّنَا لَا تُؤَاخِذْنَا إِن نَّسِينَا أَوْ أَخْطَأْنَا رَبَّنَا وَلَا تَحْمِلْ عَلَيْنَا إِصْرًا كَمَا حَمَلْتَهُ عَلَى ٱلَّذِينَ مِن قَبْلِنَا رَبَّنَا وَلَا تُحَمِّلْنَا مَا لَا طَاقَةَ لَنَا بِهِ وَٱعْفُ عَنَّا وَٱغْفِرْ لَنَا وَٱرْحَمْنَا أَنتَ مَوْلَىٰنَا فَٱنصُرْنَا عَلَى ٱلْقَوْمِ ٱلْكَٰفِرِينَ ۝﴿

(سورة البَقَرَة: ٢٨٦)

﴾...Our Lord! Condemn us not if we forget or fall into error; our Lord! Lay not on us a burden like that which You laid on those before us; our Lord! Lay not on us a burden greater than we have strength to bear. Blot out our sins, and grant us forgiveness. Have mercy on us. You are our Protector; help us against those who stand against faith.﴿

(Qur'an 2: 286)

Notes

Introduction

[1] The following translation of the meanings of the Qur'an have been adapted for use in this book: Ṣaḥeeḥ International, *The Quran: Arabic Text with Corresponding English Meanings*, Riyadh: Abul Qasim Publishing House, 1997; Abdullah Yusuf Ali, *Al Qur'an al-Karim Arabic Text and English translation*, revised edition by Muhammad Abdul Haleem Eliasi, Indianapolis: Islamic Book Service, 2004; and al-Hilali M. T. and Khan M. M., *The Noble Qur'an Arabic-English*, Madinah: King Fahd Complex for the Printing of the Holy Qur'an.

[2] The term 'prophethood' is not in the English dictionary, but is an invented term, formed along the pattern of 'childhood' and 'manhood', as a noun reflecting a particular state of being. It is meant to translate the meaning of the Arabic word *nubuwwah*, which has no one-word equivalent in English, but which could be translated as meaning 'the state of being a prophet', and is also used to refer to 'all things that have to do with being a prophet'. The term 'prophethood' has since become common in English-language Islamic discourse. (Editor)

[3] "For God so loved the world that He gave His only begotten son that whosoever believes in him should not perish but have everlasting life." (Author of the gospel according to St. John 3:16)

[4] Ulfat Aziz-Us-Samad, *Islam and Christianity*, (Cairo: El-Falah Foundation for Translation, Publishing & Distribution, 1997), 2.

Chapter 1

[1] *New Encyclopedia Britannica*, vol. 7, p. 897-898, and vol. 16; *The World Book Encyclopedia*, vol. 1, p. 509; vol. 11 p. 146; vol. 3, p. 417, quoted in Abu Ameenah Bilal Philips, *The True Message of Jesus Christ*, (Sharjah: Dar Al Fatah, 1996).

[2] "The false objects of worship, which you have called 'gods'"

[3] Suzanne Haneef, *What Everyone Should Know about Islam and Muslims,* (New Delhi: Adam Publishers and Distributors, 1994), pp. 15-16.

[4] For an excellent exposition on Muhammad as prophesied in the Bible, see the book by former right Reverend Benjamin Abdul Ahad Daud entitled, *Muhammad in the Bible.*

[5] The well of Zamzam, found in Mount Paran in Makkah.

[6] The Kaaba

[7] The hajj

[8] The well of Zamzam found in the valley of Makkah

[9] Ibn az-Zubayr (رضي الله عنه) said that Allah's Messenger (ﷺ) said: «A prayer in this mosque of mine (at Madinah) is better than a thousand prayers in other mosques, except for Al-Masjid al-Ḥarâm (courtyard of the Ka'bah in Makkah) and a prayer in Al-Masjid al-Ḥarâm is better by a hundred times than a prayer in this mosque of mine.» (a sound hsdith recorded by Aḥmad and Ibn Ḥibbân)

[10] See Matthew 11:11 and Matthew 7:15-18

[11] 'Aḥmad' and 'Muḥammad' are two forms of the same name. They share the same Arabic root and Arabic infinitive: *ḥamada.* They both mean 'the praised one'. (Editor)

[12] Haneef, *What Everyone Should Know about Islam and Muslims,* 28-29.

[13] *The Concise Collection on Creed & Tauhid,* (Riyadh: Darussalam, 2001), 259.

[14] Ibn Katheer, *Al-Bidâyah wan-Nihâyah,* quoted in Umar S. Al-Ashqar, *The World of the Noble Angels,* trans. Nasiruddin al-Khattab (Riyadh: International Islamic Publishing House, 2002), 112.

[15] Trent C. Butler, *Holman Bible Dictionary,* (Holman Bible Publishers, 1991)

[16] Haneef, *What Everyone Should Know about Islam and Muslims,* 39-40.

[17] M.G. Easton, *Easton's Bible Dictionary,* PC Study Bible (Biblesoft, 2003).

[18] Ibid.

[19] Ibid.

Chapter 2

[1] Samuel Huntington, *The Clash of Civilizations and the Remaking of World Order* (London: Simon and Schuster, 1997), 210-211.

[2] Haneef, *What Everyone Should Know about Islam and Muslims*, v-vi.

[3] Sulaiman Swaleh Ashaqsi, "Tolerance in Islam." (Unpublished paper presented at the University of Nairobi, Kenya). Shaykh Ashaqsi is a Muslim Scholar, translator and author who is fluent in Arabic, English and Kiswahili.

[4] R. Pierce Beaver, *The World's Religions*, (Herts, England: Lion Publishing, 1988), 349-350.

[5] Alija Izetbegovic, *Islam between East and West*, (Washington: American Trust Publications, 1989), 254-255.

[6] Maryam Jameelah, *Islam Versus Ahl-al-Kitab,* (Delhi: Taj Company, 1998), 199.

[7] Ibid., 200.

[8] Ibid., 201-203.

[9] Matthew 5:17-19 KJV.

[10] Also see Romans 2:17-26, 3:1, 10:4-12.

[11] Jameelah, *Islam Versus Ahl-al-Kitab*, 203-206.

[12] Ibid., 207.

Chapter 3

[1] Paul Findley, *Silent No More: Confronting America's False Images of Islam*, (Maryland: Amana Publications, 2001), 110.

[2] Ibid., 110.

[3] Ibid., 111.

[4] For the official text of the summons of Pope Eugene III, The Second Crusade, on December 1, 1145: See Jameelah, *Islam versus Ahl-al-Kitab*, 263.

[5] Haneef, *What Everyone Should Know about Islam and Muslims*, 30.

[6] Ibid., 31-32.

[7] A. Cleveland Coxe, *Ante-Nicene Fathers: The Writings of the Fathers down to A.D. 325*, vol. 1, ed. Alexander Roberts and James Donaldson (New York: Christian Literature Publishing Co., 1885), 154-155, quoted in Aziz-Us-Samad, *Islam and Christianity*, 7.

[8] C. J. Cadoux, *The Life of Jesus, (*Penguin Books), 13, quoted in Aziz-Us-Samad, *Islam and Christianity*, 8.

[9] C. J. Cadoux, *The Life of Jesus, (*Penguin Books), 14-15, quoted in Aziz-Us-Samad, *Islam and Christianity*, 9.

[10] C. J. Cadoux, *The Life of Jesus,* (Penguin Books), 16, quoted in Aziz-Us-Samad, *Islam and Christianity*, 11.

[11] T. G. Tuncker, *The History of the Christians in the Light of Modern Knowledge*, 320, quoted in Aziz-Us-Samad, *Islam and Christianity*, 12.

[12] J. R. Dummellow, *Commentary on the Holy Bible*, 16, quoted in Aziz-Us-Samad, *Islam and Christianity*, 12.

[13] C. J. Cadoux, *The Life of Jesus,* (Penguin Books), 16-17, quoted in Aziz-Us-Samad, *Islam and Christianity*, 14-15.

[14] Ahmed Deedat, *The Choice: Islam and Christianity,* 1997, vol. 2 (Delhi: Millat Book Centre, 1997), 73.

[15] M. Wahiduddin Khan, *Islam: Creator of the Modern Age,* (New Delhi: The Islamic Centre, 1999), 7.

[16] Peter Odhiambo, "Some Contents of Tobacco and their Effects on the Human Body" (paper presented at Jamia Masjid, Nairobi, December, 21, 2002).

[17] Abu Ammaar Yasir Qadhi, *An Introduction to the Sciences of the Qur'aan*, (Birmingham: Al-Hidaayah Publishing and Distribution, 1999), 80.

[18] For full details on these facts, see this author's forthcoming book, *Islam and Science: Conflicting or Conciliating?* (Riyadh: International Islamic Publishing House).

[19] The sensitive sensors on board the COBE space satellite which was launched by NASA in 1992 captured evidentiary remnants of the Big Bang. This discovery served as evidence for the Big Bang, which is the scientific explanation of the fact that the universe was created from nothing.

[20] Harun Yahya, *Miracles of the Qur'an,* (Canada: Al-Attique Publishers, 2001), 12.

[21] Raymond A. Serway and Jerry S. Faughn, *College Physics*, (Brooks Cole, 2003), 42.

[22] Hugh Ross, "Big Bang Refined by Fire," in Mere Creation, ed. by William A. Dembski (Downers Grove, Illinois: InterVarsity, 1998), chapter 15, quoted in Yahya, *Miracles of the Qur'ân,* 25.

[23] Carolyn Sheets, Robert Gardner, Samuel F. Howe; *General Science* (Newton, MA: Allyn and Bacon Inc.: 1985), 319-322, quoted in Yahya, *Miracles of the Qur'an,* 29.

[24] Sheets, Gardner and Howe, *General Science*, 305, quoted in Yahya, *Miracles of the Qur'an*, 33

[25] "SAR Interferometry and Surface Change Detection", last modified September 8, 1995,
http://southport.jpl.nasa.gov/scienceapps/dixon/report6.html

[26] Rod R. Seeley, Trent D. Stephens and Philip Tate, *Essentials of Anatomy & Physiology*, (St. Louis: Mosby-Year Book Inc., 1996), 211, quoted in Yahya, *Miracles of the Qur'an.*

[27] Seeley, Stephens and Tate, *Essentials of Anatomy & Physiology*, 211, quoted in Yahya, *Miracles of the Qur'an.*

[28] Haneef, *What Everyone Should Know about Islam and Muslims,* 34-35.

[29] Ibid., 37.

[30] Aziz-Us-Samad, *Islam and Christianity,* 19.

[31] Philips, *The True Message of Jesus Christ,* 7-8.

[32] John Hick, *The Myth of God Incarnate*, ix, quoted in Philips, *The True Message of Jesus Christ*, 8-9.

[33] Easton, *Easton's Bible Dictionary*, PC Study Bible.

[34] Jesus rejects being called 'Perfectly Good' because Perfection belongs to God alone. He was 'good' but, being the son of man (Matthew 19:29), as he always called himself, he was capable of error.

[35] Murad Hofmann, *Religion on the Rise: Islam in the Third Millennium,* (Maryland: Amana Publications, 2001), 139-140.

[36] Ahmed Deedat, *Christ in Islam,* (Al-Ain, UAE: Zayed Welfare Centre of New Muslims), 32.

[37] Hofmann, *Religion on the Rise: Islam in the Third Millennium*, 143. Also see Philips, *The True Message of Jesus Christ,* 66-69.

[38] Abu Ameenah Bilal Philips, *The Purpose of Creation,* (Sharjah: Dar Al Fatah, 1995), 42-43.

[39] Mark 14:32, Matthew 26:36-39, Luke 5:16 KJV.

[40] Philips, *The True Message Of Jesus Christ,* 76-77.

[41] Izetbegovic, *Islam between East and West,* 254-255.

[42] Full accounts of these incidents can be found in most well-known biographies of the Prophet (ﷺ), such as Mubarakpuri's *The Sealed Nectar.* (Editor)

[43] Lamartine, *Histoire de la Turquie*, vol. 2 (Paris, 1854), 276-277, quoted in Aziz-Us-Samad, *Islam & Christianity,* 34-37.

[44] Qur'an 3: 19; Qur'an 2: 111; Qur'an 2: 120; Qur'an 2: 135-136.

Chapter 4

1 For a full exposition see Jameelah, *Islam Versus Ahl-al-Kitab*, 250-252.

2 Jameelah, *Islam Versus Ahl-al-Kitab*, 252-253.

3 Ibid., 253-261.

4 The Prince of Wales, "A speech by HRH The Prince of Wales titled 'Islam and the West' at the Oxford Centre for Islamic Studies, The Sheldonian Theatre, Oxford", accessed November 12, 2010, http://www.princeofwales.gov.uk/speechesandarticles/a_speech_by_hrh_ the_prince_of_wales_titled_islam_and_the_wes_425873846.html.

5 Abu A'la Maududi, *Islamic Law of Constitution,* chapter 8, quoted in Ashaqsi, *Tolerance in Islam.*

6 Dr. 'Ali Muhammad aş-Şallâbi, *The Biography of 'Uthmân ibn 'Affân — Dhun-Noorayn,* (Riyadh, Darussalam, 2007), 213-214.

7 Maududi, *Islamic Law of Constitution*, 179, quoted in Ashaqsi, *Tolerance in Islam.*

8 Ashaqsi, who quoted *Tolerance in Islam.*

9 M. Zakaula, *Tarikh-I-Hind*, vol. 3, 341, quoted in Ashaqsi, *Tolerance in Islam.*

10 T.W. Arnold, *The Preaching of Islam: A History of the Propagation of the Muslim Faith* (India: Adam Publishers, 2002), 55

11 Dr. Ahmed Khurshid, *Fanaticism, Intolerance and Islam,* 44, quoted in Ashaqsi, *Tolerance in Islam.*

12 Dr. Abdul Karim, *Islam — A Universal Religion of Peace and Progress*, 41, quoted in Ashaqsi, *Tolerance in Islam.*

13 Safi-ur-Rahman Al-Mubarakpuri, *Ar-Raheeq al-Makhtum*: The Sealed Nectar (Riyadh: Darussalam, 1996), 197-198. Also see Muhammad Al-Ghazali, *Fiqh-us-Seerah*, (Riyadh: International Islamic Publishing House), 207-209.

14 Edward Gibbon, *The History of the Decline and Fall of the Roman Empire,* 309-310, quoted in Ashaqsi, *Tolerance in Islam.*

15 Syed Abdul Latif, *The Minds Al-Qur'ân Builds,* 75, quoted in Ashaqsi, *Tolerance in Islam.*

16 Arnold, *The Preaching of Islam*, 57.

17 Gibbon, *The History of the Decline and Fall of the Roman Empire*, 269-270, quoted in Ashaqsi, *Tolerance in Islam.*

[18] Robert Briffault, *The Making of Humanity*, 113, quoted in Ashaqsi, *Tolerance in Islam*.

[19] Sir William Muir, *The Caliphate: Its Rise, Decline and Fall*, 128, quoted in Ashaqsi, *Tolerance in Islam*.

[20] Ahmed, *Fanaticism, Intolerance and Islam*, 35-53, quoted in Ashaqsi, *Tolerance in Islam*.

[21] John L. Esposito, *Islam: The Straight Path*, (New York: Oxford University Press 1991), 58.

[22] Al-Aqṣâ mosque was originally built by Caliph 'Umar at the place where Muhammad (ﷺ) prayed in Jerusalem during his night journey. What is being referred to here most likely is the rebuilding of it later by the Umayyad Caliph Abdul-Mâlik.

[23] Esposito, *Islam: The Straight Path*, 59, who quoted Francis E. Peters, *The Early Muslim Empires: Umayyad, Abbasids, Fatimids in Islam: The Religious and Political Life of a World Community*, 85.

[24] Esposito, *Islam: The Straight Path*, 61, who quoted Roger Savory, "Christendom vs. Islam: Interaction and Co-existence" in *Introduction to Islamic Civilization*, 133.

[25] Esposito, *Islam: The Straight Path*, 61.

Chapter 5

[1] But in the third Gulf war, which was started on the pretext of searching for weapons of mass destruction, they decided to depose Saddam Hussein and later executed him after he had become a Frankenstein that they themselves created.

[2] Huntington, *The Clash of Civilizations and the Remaking of World Order*, 252.

[3] Ibid., 251.

[4] Ibid., 210.

[5] al-Roubaie, Amer, *Globalization and the Muslim World*, (Selangor Darul Ehsan: Malita Jaya Sdn, 2002), 92-93 who quotes *The Economist*, 26 January 1991, 31 and 33.

[6] For the meaning of an Islamic curriculum of education and how it works, see this author's forthcoming book, *Islam and Science: Conflicting or Conciliating?* (Riyadh: International Islamic Publishing House).

[7] Huntington, *The Clash of Civilizations and the Remaking of World Order,* 144.

[8] Haneef, *What Everyone Should Know about Islam and Muslims,* 129-130.

Chapter 6

[1] Huntington, *The Clash of Civilizations and the Remaking of World Order,* 213-214.

[2] Mumtaz Motiwala, *Studies in Islam GCE 'O' Level,* (Sharjah: Dar Al Fatah Printing, Publishing & Distribution Co., 1997), 183.

[3] Ibid., 204.

[4] Huntington, *The Clash of Civilizations and the Remaking of World Order,* 212.

[5] Hofmann, *Religion on the Rise: Islam in the Third Millennium,* 67-69.

[6] Esposito, *Islam: The Straight Path,* 36.

[7] The Byzantine Roman and Sassanid Persian empires.

[8] Esposito, *Islam: The Straight Path,* 36.

[9] Ibid., 37.

[10] Huntington, *The Clash of Civilizations and the Remaking of World Order,* 211.

[11] Findley, *Silent No More: Confronting America's False Images of Islam,* 275-277.

[12] Ibid., 277-278.

[13] Ibid., 278-283.

[14] Ibid., 284-288.

Epilogue

[1] That is why there have been several massacres in NEP, for instance, the Wajir massacre of 1966, Mandera, Elwak, and most recently, 2005 in Marsabit-Turbi that left a hundred people massacred, including women and children. The Kenyan government does absolutely nothing to help the people, only because they are Muslims, as if they do not deserve security like any other part of the country.

[2] Shahâdah means to accept with full conviction in your heart and bear witness with your tongue that there is no deity worthy of worship but Allah alone, Who has no associates and to accept Muhammad (ﷺ) as the last and final Prophet and Messenger. For a full exposition of the

meaning and conditions of shahâdah, refer to this author's forthcoming book entitled *The Seven Conditions of Shahâdah* (Riyadh: International Islamic Publishing House).

3 Aziz-Us-Samad, 43, who quoted Rev J. F. De Groot, *Catholic Teaching*, 101.

4 Aziz-Us-Samad, 45, who quoted *The New Catholic Encyclopaedia (1967)*, *art.* "The Holy Trinity" vol. 14, 295.

5 Aziz-Us-Samad, 46, who quoted *The New Catholic Encyclopaedia (1967)*, *art.* "The Holy Trinity" vol. 14, 299.

6 Aziz-Us-Samad, 50, who quoted Rev. J. F. De Groot, *Catholic Teaching*, 149.

7 Prophet Moses was referred to in Exodus 7:1 as 'god' when he was sent to Pharaoh.

8 Meaning that you cannot contradict me on the fact that prophets were called 'gods'.

9 Which scripture has Jesus broken by calling himself 'god' or 'son of God' when prophets of old like Moses are addressed in the same terms?

10 Aziz-Us-Samad, 65, who quoted Rev. W. Goldsack, *The Atonement,* 5.

11 For more comprehensive analysis of whether Jesus was crucified or not, see Ahmed Deedat, *Crucifixion or Crucifiction*, (Jeddah: Abul-Qasim Publications, 1984).

Bibliography

Abdulsalam Rukaiyah Hill. *Women's Ideal Liberation: Islamic versus Western Understanding.* Jeddah: Abul-Qasim Publishing House, 1998.

Ali, Abdullah Yusuf. *The Meaning of The Holy Qur'an.* Brentwood, MD, U.S.A.: Amana Corporation, 1993.

Arnold, TW. *The Preaching of Islam : A History of the Propagation of the Muslim Faith.* India: Adam Publishers, 2002.

Ashaqsi, Sulaiman Swaleh. *Tolerance in Islam.* Unpublished paper presented at the University of Nairobi, Kenya.

Atei, Yahya. *Essential Islamic Religious Education Text Book 2,* Nairobi: Unpublished, 2004.

al-Ashqar, Umar S. *The World of the Noble Angels.* Translated by Nasiruddin al-Khattab. Riyadh: International Islamic Publishing House, 2002.

al-'Awâyishah, Husayn. *The Prayer: Its Effect in Increasing Eeman and Purifying the Soul.* Birmingham: Al-Hidâyah, 1995.

Aziz-us-Samad, Ulfat. *Islam and Christianity.* Cairo: El-Falah Foundation for Translation, Publishing & Distribution, 1997.

Beaver, R. Pierce. *The World's Religions.* Herts, England: Lion Publishing, 1988.

Butler, Trent C. *Holman Bible Dictionary.* Holman Bible Publishers, 1991.

Cragg, Kenneth. *The Call of the Minaret.* Oxford: Oneworld Publications, 2000.

Darussalam. *The Concise Collection on Creed and Tauhid.* Riyadh: Darussalam, 2001.

Dawud, Abdul-Ahad. *Muhammad in the Bible.* Al-Kitab Publications.

Deedat, Ahmed. *Christ in Islam.* Al-Ain, U.A.E.: Zayed Welfare Centre For The New Muslims.

Deedat, Ahmed. *The Choice: Islam and Christianity.* Volumes 1 and 2. Delhi: Millat Book Centre, 1997.

Esposito, John L. *Islam: The Straight Path.* Expanded Edition. New York: Oxford University Press, 1991.

Easton, M.G. Easton's Bible Dictionary, PC Study Bible. Biblesoft, 2003.

Findley, Paul. *Silent No More: Confronting America's False Images of Islam.* Maryland: Amana Publications, 2001.

al-Ghazali, Muhammad. *Fiqh-us-Seerah.* Riyadh: International Islamic Publishing House.

Hamid, Abdulwahid. *Islam: The Natural Way.* London: MELS, 1989.

Haneef, Suzanne. *What Everyone Should Know about Islam and Muslims.* New Delhi: Adam Publishers and Distributors, 1994.

al-Hilali M. T. & Khan M. M. *The Noble Qur'an Arabic-English.* Madinah: King Fahd Complex for the Printing of the Holy Qur'an.

Hofmann, Murad H. *Religion on the Rise: Islam in the Third Millennium.* Maryland: Amana Publications, 2001.

Holy Bible. *King James Version.* Cambridge: Cambridge University Press, 1957.

Holy Bible. *The New King James Version.* Nashville: Thomas Nelson Publishers, 1987.

Holy Bible. *New International Version.* New Jersey: 1978.

Huntington, Samuel P. *The Clash of Civilizations and the Remaking of World Order.* London: Simon and Schuster, 1997.

Ibrahim, Ezzeddin & Johnson-Davies, Denys. *Forty Hadith*, United Arab Emirates: Dar El Shououk, 2003.

Izetbegovic, Alija. *Islam between East and West*. Washington: American Trust Publications, 1989.

Jameelah, Maryam. *Islam Versus Ahl-al-Kitab*. Delhi: Taj Company, 1998.

al-Jaza'iry, Abu Bakr Jabir. *Minhaj Al-Muslim*. Riyadh: Darussalam.

Khan, Muhsin M. *Sahih al-Bukhari, Arabic-English*. Riyadh: Darussalam Publishers & Distributors.

Khan, M Wahiduddin. *Islam: Creator of the Modern Age*. New Delhi: The Islamic Centre, 1999.

Malik, M.H. *The Mission of Jesus: Divine Principles of World Order*. Nairobi: Islamic Foundation, 1993.

Motiwala, Mumtaz. *Studies in Islam GCE 'O' Level*. Sharjah: Dar Al Fatah Printing, Publishing & Distribution Co., 1997.

al-Mubarakpuri, Safi-ur-Rahman. *Ar-Raheeq al-Makhtum (The Sealed Nectar)*. Riyadh, Darussalam Publishers & Distributors, 1996.

Odhiambo, Peter. "Some Contents of Tobacco and their Effects on the Human Body." Paper presented at Jamia Masjid, Nairobi, December, 21, 2002.

Philips, Abu Ameenah Bilal. *The Purpose Of Creation*. Sharjah: Dar Al Fatah, 1995.

Philips, Abu Ameenah Bilal. *The True Message Of Jesus Christ*. Sharjah: Dar Al Fatah, 1996.

Qadhi, Abu Ammaar Yasir. *An Introduction to the Sciences of the Qur'an*. Birmingham: Al-Hidâyah Publishing and Distribution, 1999.

Al-Roubale, Amer. *Globalization and the Muslim World*. First Edition. Selangor Darul Ehsan: Malita Jaya Sdn, 2002.

aṣ-Ṣallâbi, Dr. 'Ali Muhammad. *The Biography of 'Uthmân ibn 'Affân — Dhun-Noorayn*. Riyadh: Darussalam, 2007.

Scroggie, W. Graham. *Is the Bible the Word of God?* Chicago: Moody Press, 1950.

Serway, Raymond A. and Jerry S. Faughn. *College Physics*. Brooks Cole, 2003.

Siddiqi, A. *Sahih Muslim, English Translation*. Beirut: Dar Al-Arabia, 1972.

Saheeh International. *The Qur'an: Arabic Text with Corresponding English Meaning*. Jeddah: Abul-Qasim Publishing House, 1997.

Yahya, Harun. *Miracles of the Qur'an*. Canada: Al-Attique Publishers, 2001.

Glossary of Islamic terms[*]

abu (or abi)	أبو، أبي	father (of)
âmeen	آمين	O Allah, accept our invocation; amen
deen	الدين	religion
dhimmi	ذمّي	people covenanted or protected: non-Muslims who must pay the jizyah in lieu of zakât
Eid ('eed)	عيد	lit. festival; the two celebrations: one at the end of Ramadan and the other at the culmination of the Hajj
Hadith (ḥadeeth)	حديث	the collected statements and actions of Prophet Muhammad (ﷺ) that with the Qur'an form the basis of Islamic law
hadith (ḥadeeth)	حديث	a statement or action of Prophet Muhammad (ﷺ) that was remembered and recorded by his Companions and followers

---

[*] The Arabic words are transliterated according to the conventions of the Transliteration Chart found in this book. If a word has become part of the English language (i.e., is found in a dictionary of Standard English), that spelling is used in this book and appears first in this Glossary, with the transliterated form in brackets after it.

Hajj (ḥajj)	حج	the major pilgrimage to the Sacred Mosque, site of the Ka'bah at Makkah, to be undertaken by every able Muslim once in his/her lifetime
Iblees	إبليس	another name for Satan in Arabic
iḥsân	إحسان	goodness, perfection, excellence; to worship Allah as if you see Him, but even if you do not see Him you know that He sees you
jinn (plural of jinni)	جن	non-human, rational beings created by Allah from fire, often referred to as 'demons' or 'devils'; They have free will like humans: some are Muslims, others disbelievers; some are obedient to Allah, others disobedient. Satan is a jinni. Some people try to 'foretell' the future by contacting a jinni. Some disobedient jinn mislead people into thinking that they can tell them what will happen in the future, near or far, or that the jinn can provide people with riches or some sort of power
jizyah	جزية	a tax levied on the people of the Scriptures when they are under the protection of a Muslim government: it is in lieu of the alms tax paid by Muslims
Kaaba (Ka'bah)	الكعبة	the House of Allah in Makkah, originally built my prophets Ibrâheem and Ismâ'eel, and which Muslims face whenever they pray

al-Masjid al-Aqṣâ	المسجد الأقصى	the 'Farthest Mosque', mentioned in the Qur'an (17: 1)
al-Masjid al-Ḥarâm	المسجد الحرام	the Sacred Mosque in Makkah where the Kaaba is situated
Quraysh	قريش	the dominant tribe in Makkah at the time of the Prophet's mission; their society was based on polytheism
Ramadan (Ramaḍân)	رمضان	the ninth month in the Islamic calendar; the month of obligatory fasting; the month in which the first verses of the Qur'an were revealed
shahâdah	الشهادة	testimony, *usu.* the statement *lâ ilâha illâ Allâh, Muḥammadun rasoolullâh* [There is none worthy of worship other than God (Allah); Muhammad is the Messenger of God]
Sharia (shari'ah)	شرعة	Islamic law derived from the Qur'an and the Sunnah
shaykh	شيخ	teacher, mentor; scholar
soorat or soorah	سورة	chapter of the Qur'an
Sunnah	سنّة	the practice and collected sayings of Prophet Muhammad (ﷺ) that together with the Qur'an forms the basis of Islamic law
tawḥeed	التوحيد	the Oneness of Allah: that He alone deserves to be worshipped and that He has no partners
Zamzam	زمزم	the blessed spring of water that Allah caused to gush out at baby Ismâ'eel's feet; located near the Ka'bah

Notes

....

....

....

....

....

....

....

....

....

....